Assessing Students:

How shall we know them?

Derek Rowntree

Professor of Educational Development,
The Open University

 **NP**

Kogan Page, London
Nichols Publishing Company, New York

First published in hardback 1977
Paperback edition 1979
by Harper & Row Ltd
28 Tavistock Street, London WC2E 7PT

Revised edition published in Great Britain in 1987
by Kogan Page Ltd, 120 Pentonville Road, London N1 9JN
Reprinted 1988 (twice), 1989, 1991, 1992, 1994

British Library Cataloguing in Publication Data

Rowntree, Derek
Assessing students: how shall we know them.—2nd ed.
1. Grading and marking (Students)
I. Title
371.2'64   LB3051

ISBN 1-85091-300-5

Revised edition published in the United States of America
in 1987 by Nichols Publishing Company, Post Office Box 96,
New York, NY 10024
Reprinted 1988, 1989, 1991

Library of Congress Cataloging-in-Publication Data

Rowntree, Derek
  Assessing students.

  Bibliography: p.
  Includes index.
  1. Students—Great Britain—Rating of. 2. Students—
Rating of. I. Title.
LB3056.G7R68   1987   371.2'64   87-5489
ISBN 0-89397-271-1

Printed and bound in Great Britain by
Biddles Ltd, Guildford and King's Lynn

17/7/96   1114346O

A Death in the Desert

This is the doctrine he was wont to teach,
How divers persons witness in each man,
Three souls which make up one soul: first, to wit,
A soul of each and all the bodily parts,
Seated therein, which works, and is *What Does*,
And has the use of earth, and ends the man
Downward: but, tending upward for advice,
Grows into, and again is grown into
By the next soul, which, seated in the brain,
Useth the first with its collected use,
And feeleth, thinketh, willeth, - is *What Knows:*
Which, duly tending upward in its turn,
Grows into, and again is grown into
By the last soul, that uses both the first,
Subsisting whether they assist or no,
And, constituting man's self, is *What Is* –
And leans upon the former, makes it play,
As that played off the first: and, tending up,
Holds, is upheld by, God, and ends the man
Upward in that dread point of intercourse,
Nor needs a place, for it returns to Him.

What Does, what Knows, what Is; three souls, one man.

Robert Browning

Contents

INTRODUCTION

This book was first published ten years ago. On being asked to bring out a new edition, I did what any author would do. I got in touch with several teachers who had been using the book and asked them what they thought needed changing, and I read it again myself. The general consensus from users was 'leave it alone'. To be sure, each had his or her own favourite bits that they wouldn't mind seeing expanded — or neglected topics that they would quite like to see brought in. But there was no unanimity other than in urging me to maintain the flavour of what they agreed was a unique treatment of what one of them called 'the timeless, enduring issues underlying our changing assessment practices'.

When I re-read the book myself, I agreed with them. Unlike most things I have written, I find I still hold to my views of ten years ago. For once, I think I got it right — right for me, that is — first time. To be sure, if I were writing the book now rather than then, some of my references would be more recent. But that would not make them any more pertinent, only more recent. Even then, a great many of the authors I quoted were writing long before

I was born. This is no bad thing, either, for a book that is supposed to be dealing with the 'enduring issues' (rather than with the latest 'flavour of the month' in curriculum realpolitik).

I never intended the book to be a comprehensive 'survey of the literature'. It was (and is) a book about assessment, not a book about the literature of assessment. I have resisted the temptation to list all such writings produced since my own, not because I believe nothing of value has been produced, but because I know that if you have managed to track down this book, you should have little trouble finding plenty of other writings on the subject of assessment for yourself.

Despite abundant new activity in the field of assessment, there are no new fundamental issues involved — either in Britain (where new school-leaving examinations are being introduced) or in the USA where there are renewed calls for teacher accountability in the face of allegedly falling academic standards, and where the issue is in the forefront of education today.

England and Wales would appear to be embarking on a major revolution in assessment with the General Certificate of Secondary Education (GCSE) — an amalgamation of GCE and CSE for which the first pupils will be examined in Summer 1988. The trade press is thick with rhetoric about new assessment techniques and criterion-related grading, and about raising the attainment standards of the 10-20% of pupils who currently leave school with little more than a certified grade in woodwork or domestic science to show for their eleven years in the classroom. But all the conceptual tools you need to analyse the new venture are already explored in this book. Overlooking the muddle and haste with which the changeover is being implemented, will the new system be less confusing, divisive, bureaucratic, inflexible, inconsistent and educationally subversive than the old? You have the tools: I leave you to use them in making your own evaluation.

So too if you work in further education. What are the implications for assessment of the new emphasis on vocational and post-experience training? Here the current buzz words seem to be 'needs analysis', 'competence testing', 'workplace assessment' and 'testing for transfer'. But only the jargon changes: the ideas (and the ideologies) underlying it are all here in this book. And, as for higher education, what is left of the 1960s-inspired adventures in assessment (and curriculum development) that were thin on the ground but no less promising for all that when first this book was published? Have 'the Cuts' and the new bogey of 'graduate unemployment' sent our universities and polytechnics scuttling back to the traditional values and the unassailable bastion of the three-hour 'unseen' examination? Is 'course work' now the assessment that dare not speak its name? Have 'take away' papers and 'open book' exams returned to the closet? Of course not; though perhaps we are more reticent about them nowadays and innovators have to be mightily self-confident, especially since one of the latest buzz words in this area of education is 'performance indicators' (which is short for 'how to assess the teachers').

But, despite such pressures in all areas of education, teachers still seem open to looking at assessment in new ways. I have appreciated the many letters received from teachers who were influenced — either to re-appraise their existing systems or to develop new ones — by the first edition of this book. (You will find one example of such 'feedback' included at the end of this edition.) Even my reviewers have been moved to recount their favourite horror stories. Stuart Trickey, in the *British Journal of Teacher Education*, recalled that:

> A new colleague of mine who has just completed a 'taught' MA course remarked the other day that her tutor appended the comment of 'borderline' with a mark of 51% to one candidate's essay and 'excellent' with a mark of 59% to another. She wondered what had happened to the rest of the marking scale.

Professor Tony Becher, in *Studies in Higher Education*, mentioned that, in his university (where students' final, overall results depend on how the Exam Board chooses to combine their continuous assessment and examinations marks):

> Students submitting a piece of work for adjudication in the course of their second or third year naturally want to know how well they have done. It is forbidden to tell them, except indirectly (by some quaint formula as 'If I were allowed to say what you'd got, I might well be congratulating you on a B'). The reason is that if the students were given this information, they might work out their final entitlement, thus depriving the Exam Board of its discretion; or even — if the Board exercised it — embarking on a subsequent lawsuit.

Such comments, and the letters I've had from teachers at all levels of education, confirm that the book addresses issues of common concern. And I have needed, over the last ten years, to apply the ideas discussed in the book not just to my teaching activities but to a host of others — from salary reviews and staff promotions, through advising on industrial training, to jury service and the writing of job references. Anyway, if you have your own assessment stories to tell — whether of despair or optimism, or merely of puzzlement — I would be pleased to hear from you. Maybe I will be able to share them with new readers in the next edition.

One thing is certain. Assessment will remain with us from the cradle to beyond the grave. Scarcely have we taken our first breath before we have a label fastened to our wrists, giving weight at, and method of, birth; and, somewhere, our first file (medical) has already been opened. From then on, the assessments come thick and fast — from doctors, parents, siblings, peers, teachers, employers (and prospective employers), and practically everyone we have dealings with.

Some of these assessments we ignore or are scarcely conscious of. Others shape the way we assess ourselves and what we become. As Marx once said: 'I wouldn't want to be a member of a club that would have someone like me as a member.' (Groucho that was, of course, not Karl.) At the same time, we spend our lives assessing others, trying to know them and explain them to ourselves — and often influencing them by our consequent decisions. And even in death we cannot escape the assessors — obituary-writers for the famous; just family, workmates and friends for the rest of us. Indeed, years after we've become dust, our deeds on this earth may be re-assessed — and those that were earlier considered worthwhile may be vilified, and those that were once disregarded or abused may be hailed as 'ahead of their time'.

That is the background. But the foreground, as far as this book is concerned, is a special kind of assessment — *educational* assessment. For most of us, it is confined to a fairly small proportion of our life-span. But it often has a disproportionate effect on what happens in the rest of it. The 'truths' that emerge from it tell other people (and often ourselves) what to think and feel about us — and thus open or close to us life's opportunities and rewards. So the responsibility of teachers in trying to 'know' their pupils —

especially if that 'knowledge' is to be passed on to others — is a heavy one. As the late James Cameron, the journalist, once realized, reacting to a hostile, and as he thought, unfair review of one of his books: 'This Mr W. was of course not reviewing my fairly inconspicuous book; he was reviewing me.' And how often are we educational 'reviewers' unwittingly encouraging other people to form unjustified judgements about our students as people, rather than merely passing on our opinions about their individual bits of work — which may or may not be typical of what they could or might yet do, and which in any case might be evaluated quite differently by other assessors? That, in large measure, is what this book is about — though W. B. Yeats gave us the warning more succinctly:

I have spread my dreams under your feet;
Tread softly, because you tread on my dreams.

Derek Rowntree, January 1987

CHAPTER 1

WHAT IS ASSESSMENT ?

If we wish to discover the truth about an educational system, we must look into its assessment procedures. What student qualities and achievements are actively valued and rewarded by the system? How are its purposes and intentions realized? To what extent are the hopes and ideals, aims and objectives professed by the system ever truly perceived, valued and striven for by those who make their way within it? The answers to such questions are to be found in what the system requires students to *do* in order to survive and prosper. The spirit and style of student assessment defines the *de facto* curriculum.

A Cause for Concern

I was constantly reminded of the crucial nature of assessment during the writing of a previous book on curriculum development (Rowntree, 1974). There I found that in every chapter, whatever I was writing about — aims and objectives, the design of learning experiences, the sequencing and structuring of knowledge, the evaluation and improvement of teaching — questions of assessment kept rearing their heads and threatening to dominate the discussion.

If assessment is so crucial, one might expect the subject to have an extensive literature already. So why add to it? Indeed much has been written (see, e.g. Ebel, 1972; Gronlund, 1971; Hudson, 1973; Lewis, 1974; Pidgeon and Yates, 1969; Schofield, 1972; Terwilliger, 1971; Thorndike, 1972; Thyne, 1974; etc.) But, for the most part, the literature takes for granted the present nature of assessment and seeks improvement merely through increasing its efficiency. Thus, for example, it is easy to find writers concerned with how to produce better multiple-choice questions, how to handle test-results statistically, or how to compensate for the fact that different examiners respond differently to a given piece of student work. It is much less easy to find writers questioning the purposes of assessment, asking what qualities it does or should identify, examining its effects on the relationships between teachers and learners, or attempting to relate it to such concepts as truth, fairness, trust, humanity and social justice. Writers of the former preoccupation rarely give any indication of having considered questions of the latter kind. Insofar as they appear to regard assessment as non-problematic, their writings, though often extremely valuable in their way, gloss over more fundamental questions about whether what we are doing is the right thing and offer simply a technical prescription for doing it better. This James Thyne (1974) approvingly calls 'the goodness of examinations as technical instruments'. Even then, the implications of doing it 'better' are rarely pursued very far. In short, the literature addresses itself chiefly to the question 'How?' rather than the question 'Why?'. In this book I shall try to adjust the emphasis.

The discontinuity between technical and philosophical considerations in assessment is not new and has long been recognized. Here is Kandel (1936) saying of examinations what I would wish to say of all forms of assessment:

> . . . the problem of examinations is not primarily one of discovering more accurate scientific and technical methods of constructing and scoring examinations. The problem of examinations strikes at the very roots of the whole meaning and significance of education in society. . . . The essence of the problem is the validity of education. (p. 151)

My hope is that this book will encourage colleagues in education (by which I mean students as well as teachers) to bring together the technical and the philosophical, and to examine assessment anew from a broader perspective. Teachers tend to be trapped in a time-vortex that inhibits them from giving too much thought to assessment that has happened previously, or will happen later, to their students in institutions other than their own. Awareness is greatest near the gateways between two stages in a student's career, e.g. top juniors, or 6th-form, or first year at college. But, even then, attention tends to be restricted to the last or next gateway. My contention is that we can all learn much by considering how assessment operates in learning mileux other than the ones with which we are directly concerned. Thus the university teacher may gain substantial insights from thinking about assessment in the primary school, and so may the primary school teacher from thinking about assessment in higher education. Similarly, teachers in one country can learn from the practices of those in another country or another time. Hence I make no apology for including examples from all levels of education, and from other countries (especially the U.S.A.) and other times. Further, we should at least be aware that educational assessment has more than a family resemblance to many other forms of assessment prevalent in our society. To name but a few:

everyday conversational dialogue;
medical and psychiatric diagnosis;
the writing of biography;
forensic cross-examination;
job-interviews and promotion appraisals;
criticism of art and literature;
'refereeing' of books and of papers submitted for publication in scholarly journals.

Such forms of assessment will sometimes offer revealing parallels and contrasts with those common in education.

In recent years, writings and conferences debating basic aspects of student assessment have begun to occur more frequently. Extreme positions get taken up. People may be passionate apologists for the system as it is now held to exist. Or they may be equally passionate denouncers of assessment as a tyrannical means of persuasion, coercion and social control, enhancing the power of one group of people (the teachers, together perhaps with whatever others they may believe them-selves to be representing — 'the discipline' or profession, parents, employers, 'society') over another group (the students). Not surprisingly then, debates on assessment can raise strong feelings. The clash of ideologies — in the Marxian sense of ideas being used as weapons in a struggle for dominance between groups with conflicting interests — can be more in evidence than honest reflection and rational analysis. Consequently, assessment debate is awash with hidden assumptions, unstated values, partial truths, confusions of ideas, false distinctions, and irrelevant emphases. It is also flooded with specialist terminology — jargon, even — which we will have to find our way around in the following pages.

The Nature of Assessment

Some of the confusions and false distinctions will become apparent as we begin exploring a working definition of assessment. Dictionary definitions tend to agree that to assess is to put a value on something, usually in financial terms. Such definitions are clearly not centred on educational assessment, although it is true that certain outcomes of educational assessment, e.g. a student's degree class, may well determine the salary he can expect. Again, such valuational definitions do chime in with what many teachers think of (erroneously, I would say) as essential components of assessment, *viz* the assigning of numerical marks or letter grades, and the ranking of students in order of preference or relative achievement.

More basically, assessment in education can be thought of as occurring whenever one person, in some kind of interaction, direct or indirect, with another, is conscious of obtaining and interpreting information about the knowledge and understanding, or abilities and attitudes of that other person. To some extent or other it is an attempt to *know* that person. In this light, assessment can be seen as human encounter. In education we are mainly conscious of this 'encounter' in the shape of teachers finding out about their students. But we must not forget that students also assess one another, especially when working together as co-operative teams. They also assess their teachers (see Miller, 1972; Page, 1974). Mutual assessment is perhaps what Nell Keddie (1971) has in mind when she refers to 'the ways in which teachers and pupils scan each other's activities in the classroom and attribute meaning to them' (see also Downey, 1977). Nor should we hesitate to turn the definition in upon itself and think of the person (student or teacher) finding out about *himself* — self-assessment.

Despite one of the assumptions commonly made in the literature, assessment is not obtained only, or even necessarily mainly, through tests and examinations. Finding out about a student's abilities and so on may not involve testing him or measuring his performance in any formal way. We can imagine a spectrum of assessment situations ranging from the very informal, almost casual, to the highly formal, perhaps even ritualistic. At the informal end of the spectrum we have, for instance, the continuous but unself-conscious assessment that takes place between partners in an everyday conversation where each is constantly responding to what he takes to be the emerging attitudes and understandings of the other as he decides what to say next in consequence. Compare this with the monologue of a platform speaker or with the programmed patter of the kind of door-to-door evangelist who steadfastly ignores all responses that might suggest he should depart from his 'script'.

In a classroom conversation, however, where the intentions of the participants may be rather more directed to specific tasks and goals, the assessment may be slightly more formal, or at least more self-conscious. When assessment becomes the purpose, even if unstated, of initiating a conversation, e.g. in asking the student what he knows or feels about an issue, the formality becomes yet greater. So too, as far as the teacher at least is concerned, when he unobtrusively observes the student in action in order to assess. The ultimate in formality, for both teacher and student, is reached when the student is required to perform in what is patently a test-situation — quiz, interview, practical test, written examination, or whatever.

But it is worth noting here that, despite another common confusion, all these shades of assessment can be practised without any kind of measurement that implies absolute standards; it may be enough simply to observe whether, for each student, some personal, even idiosyncratic, trait or ability appears discernible to greater or lesser extent than hitherto. There need be no requirement to compare the findings for one student with those for another, let alone arrange students in some kind of order as a result of any such comparisons. Joan Tough (1976, p. 32) makes the point very well in distinguishing between testing and 'appraisal':

> How does the child walk and run? What is the quality of his movement? What kind of control does the child have of fine and intricate manipulation and of movement that needs concentration of strength and effort? What is the child's general coordination of movements like? Is he awkward and ungainly or does he move easily and smoothly without apparent effort? Many of these qualities would defy measurement, and many would defy comparison with other children. But all could be appraised, i.e. described in terms which build up a picture of what the child is like.

Again, despite many assumptions to the contrary, assessment is not the same thing as grading or marking. If you 'grade' or 'mark' a student (or his work — the distinction is often unclear both to students and teachers) you are attaching a letter or number that is meant somehow to symbolize the quality of the work and allow comparison with the work of other students. Such grading cannot take place without prior assessment — the nature and quality of the student's work must be determined before it can be labelled with a suitable symbol. But assessment can, and perhaps usually does, takes place without being followed by grading. Assessment can be *descriptive* (e.g. 'Bob knows all his number bonds up to 20') without becoming *judgemental* (e.g. 'Bob is good at number bonds'). It may be that in secondary and higher education the only assessments that count are those which are, in fact, followed by grading. But in infant schools and, to a large extent, in junior schools (with the exception of those still preparing children for the 11-plus exam) developing skills are constantly being assessed without any apparent compulsion to label them with letter grades or numerical marks. Odd, then, that a colleague of mine, admittedly in higher education, should rebuff a suggestion that we abandon the grading of essays by saying 'No, we can't claim to be teaching properly unless we know how our students are progressing.'

Just as tests and examinations are possible means of assessment, so grades and marks are possible outcomes. But they are not the only ones possible. Assessment is also a necessary pre-condition for *diagnostic appraisal* — ascertaining the student's strengths and weaknesses, and identifying his emerging needs and interests. In truth it is the practice of diagnostic appraisal (not grading) that enables us to claim we are teaching. Given that the student has reached such-and-such a state, what can he or should he aim for next? What implications does this have for the ensuing learning experiences? Diagnostic appraisal does not involve grading. Nor need it necessarily be based on formal tests and measurements. It is dependent on some kind of assessment having taken place, however, together with pedagogic judgements as to what new learning experiences are possible, and value-judgements (the student's perhaps, as well as the teacher's) as to which are desirable.

There is a further useful distinction we can make between two words which, in everyday parlance, and indeed in most dictionaries, seem virtual synonyms — assessment and evaluation. In education, though, it is common in Britain to use the two words to refer to two rather different, though closely-related activities. If assessment tries to discover what the student is becoming or has accomplished, then evaluation tries to do the same for a course or learning experience or episode of teaching. Evaluation is an attempt to identify and explain the effects (and effectiveness) of the teaching. In such an attempt, assessment is clearly a necessary component. Assessment, whether formal or informal, reveals to us the most important class of 'effects' — the changes brought about in the knowledge and understanding, abilities and attitudes of our students. If students have not changed or have somehow changed for the worse, e.g. they may have learned to solve simultaneous equations but also to detest algebra, we suspect something is wrong with the teaching. But student assessment is only part of evaluation. A full evaluation will also need, for example, to consider the effects of the course on people other than students — on the teachers participating, on other teachers who have contact with the students, on parents, on employers, on other people in the community, and so on. Thus, data additional to the assessment data — gained perhaps through participant observation, discussions, interviewing, reading of local newspapers, internal memoranda, etc. — will be needed. Incidentally, in the U.S.A. the word 'assessment' is rarely used in this context at all; instead, the word 'evaluation' usually has to do duty for both the concepts described above. In scanning the American literature, one must know whether one is looking for evaluation (of students) or evaluation (of courses).

The American literature (Scriven, 1967) has, however, developed a distinction between types of evaluation (of courses) that is equally useful in thinking about assessment. Thus, *formative* evaluation is intended to develop and improve a piece of teaching until it is as effective as it possibly can be — a well-tested programmed textbook would be a prime example. *Summative* evaluation, on the other hand, is intended to establish the effectiveness of the teaching once it is fully developed and in regular use. The distinction is, in fact, rather hard to preserve in considering the evaluation of most kinds of teaching; but it is very descriptive of what goes on in student assessment. Diagnostic appraisal, directed towards developing the student and contributing to his growth, can be thought of as formative assessment. Summative assessment, on the other hand, is clearly represented by terminal tests and examinations coming at the end of the student's course, or indeed by any attempt to reach an overall description or judgement of the student (e.g. in an end-of-term report or a grade or class-rank). Peter Vandome and his colleagues (1973) recognize this distinction and remind us that each is generally used (though it need not be) for a different purpose, by labelling the former 'pedagogic' and the latter 'classificatory'. In formative (pedagogic) assessment the emphasis is on potential, while in summative (classificatory) assessment it is on actual achievement.

The Dynamics of Assessment

In Rowntree (1974) I considered how the concepts we have been talking about flow together in a teaching situation. Figure 1.1 illustrates the dynamic relationships between formative assessment, formative evaluation and summative assessment. At each stage in his teaching (T) the teacher makes an assessment (A) of the student's learning which, together perhaps with non-assessment data on the effects of the teaching (N), enables him to evaluate how successfully he has taught so far (E). The assessment also helps him to diagnose (D) the new needs of the student, and diagnosis and evaluation together go to determine the purpose and nature of the next stage of the teaching (T). This 'teaching', which may be of a few seconds' or a few weeks' duration, continues until further assessment gives rise to more evaluation and diagnostic appraisal. If these essentially formative assessments are trans-

Figure 1.1
Assessment, Evaluation, Diagnosis, and Grading

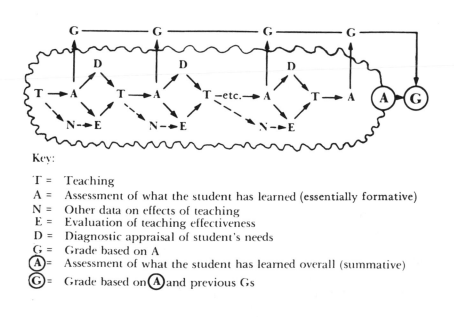

Key:

T =   Teaching
A =   Assessment of what the student has learned (**essentially formative**)
N =   Other data on effects of teaching
E =   Evaluation of teaching effectiveness
D =   Diagnostic appraisal of student's needs
G =   Grade based on A
(A)=   Assessment of what the student has learned overall (summative)
(G)=   Grade based on (A) and previous Gs

lated into grades (G) for the student and some or all of these grades are to count towards an overall summative assessment, the system may be called 'continuous assessment'. Strictly speaking it might better be described as 'continuous grading'. The student may, in addition, be given a final summative assessment (big A), perhaps taking account of some or all of the previous formative assessments as well as a special end-of-course examination assessing what he has learned over the course as a whole. He may also be given a final, overall grade (big G), made up out of some or all the grades awarded so far.

Clearly, then, the field of assessment is full of conceptual quagmires and terminological traps for the unwary or short-sighted. Further specimens will be identified later. But already we see the need for considerable circumspection when approaching the literature. We must keep asking ourselves, for instance, whether an author is talking about evaluation or assessment, informal assessment or formal, formative or summative, pedagogic or classificatory. And, if it is possible to tell which kind of assessment he is talking of, we must ask whether what he says really applies to that kind and to that kind only.

Questions of Responsibility

Nor should we overlook, at a practical level, the conflict and ambivalence of purpose that can arise in a teacher as he decides what to do about the result of an assessment. Especially, he may be troubled as to how sensible it is both to evaluate the effectiveness of his own teaching and to grade the students according to what they have learned from it. Who or what is on trial? Who deserves the grade — the teacher or the student? If, in an extreme case, the teacher 'fails' his student, has the course indeed failed him or has the student failed the course? (Note, as a grim parallel, that many a terminally ill patient feels that he has 'failed' his surgeon.) Of course, when a student has been openly uninterested and has made no effort to learn, then it may be only in a weak sense that the responsibility can be laid upon the teacher rather than the student. But suppose the student has shown great interest and worked conscientiously, perhaps even learned a great deal, though not entirely what the teacher wanted him to learn, and gained personal satisfaction from his progress? Then the teacher who sees fit to penalize the student for having failed to satisfy teacher's requirements may in quite a strong sense be asked to consider that he has failed his student.

Does it matter who is 'to blame' for ineffective learning? Not much when assessment is used privately for diagnostic appraisal or evaluation and therefore benefits the student. More so, however, when assessment is done with public grading in view; for this is often not so much for the student's benefit (through discovering his learning needs and improving the teaching) as for the benefit of other people who will use it (with no thought of shared 'blame') to determine what the student's life-chances are to be.

The most casual browse through the literature of assessment is enough to establish that the vast bulk is concerned with how to use assessment for purposes of grading and ranking. Only a minuscule proportion considers how to use it to enhance the student's educational growth. This bias in the literature faithfully reflects the priorities of the education industry. As Donald McIntyre (1970) forthrightly says:

> . . . although we spend an enormous amount of time and money on assessment, very little is obtained which helps teachers to teach. Instead, we give pupils marks or grades, that is, we concentrate on *judging* them, on saying how 'good' or 'bad' they are, on putting them in an 'order of merit'. Assessment of this . . . sort can make no contribution to effective teaching. Its function is to select pupils, gradually as they pass through our schools, for different positions in the socio-economic hierarchy of our society, positions for which we then proceed to train them.

Such ideological interpretations can easily be attached to the grading decisions that arise out of assessment, but not so easily to diagnostic and evaluational decisions. Assessment itself can be a reasonably objective gathering of information; though, of course, some kind of subjective preference will inevitably be directing the assessor's attention to some things rather than others. But the form assessment takes, and the uses to which the gathered information is put, may vary with the assumptions that are being made about the division of responsibility in teaching and learning. Thus, 'grading' assumes that the teaching is essentially beyond reproach, and that the student is to be rewarded according to how well he has discharged his responsibility to learn from it, and that this will be revealed objectively and reliably by assessment. 'Diagnostic appraisal' makes no assumptions about the responsibility for teaching and learning; and its value-judgements about the student's apparent strengths and weaknesses and needs are not published as objective truths about the student. 'Evaluation' does tend to make assumptions about responsibility, however, and they may be quite the opposite of those made by 'grading'. Evaluation assumes that weaknesses in the student's learning may well be explicable by weaknesses in the teaching and that it is the responsibility of the teaching to change in such a way as to optimize the student's learning.

In educational practice, of course, these three attitudes to assessment often operate together. Clearly, different teachers within a teaching team may take up different stances. But even the teacher who is assessing with a view to ranking his students according to how much they have learned may be shocked into an evaluational stance if he discovers that scarcely any of them have learned anything. And, of course, a given teacher may intentionally operate with different assumptions at different times. If he slips unwittingly from one set of assumptions to another, or if he needs to co-operate with people whose assumptions he fails to recognize as being different from his, then confusion can arise.

Five Dimensions of Assessment

To provide a framework for our exploration of assessment, I have chosen to identify within it five dimensions. These five dimensions refer to five different kinds of mental activity among people who undertake assessment. Each kind of mental activity results in decisions being made and actions being taken. Naturally, the five dimensions correspond to what seem to me to be the key activities in the process of assessment. The questions underlying these five dimensions are as follows:

Why assess?   Deciding why assessment is to be carried out; what effects or outcomes it is expected to produce.

What to assess?   Deciding, realizing, or otherwise coming to an awareness of what one is looking for, or remarking upon, in the people one is assessing.

How to assess?   Selecting, from among all the means we have at our disposal for learning about people, those we regard as being most truthful and fair for various sorts of valued knowledge.

How to interpret?   Making sense of the outcomes of whatever observations or measurements or impressions we gather through whatever means we employ; explaining, appreciating, and attaching meaning to the raw 'events' of assessment.

How to respond?   Finding appropriate ways of expressing our response to whatever has been assessed and of communicating it to the person concerned (and other people).

To put some flesh on that austere framework, let me give a couple of examples. An infants' teacher may wish to assess the developing self-confidence of a new child in her class with a view to helping him settle in; she may do this by observing the child in situations that he might see as threatening; she may interpret the behaviour she observes by comparing it with behaviour in similar situations in the past and considering what experiences have contributed to the child's growth; she may respond by encouraging the child, providing some 'growth-experiences' for him, and perhaps by writing some brief diary-comment. On the other hand, a secondary school mathematics teacher may wish to predict his students' chances in a public examination; he may therefore assess their ability to solve a range of problems under 'mock' examination conditions; he may interpret their performance by comparison with what he believes to be the standards of the examiners; he may respond by giving each student a grade for the examination as a whole and giving extra tuition to those students he feels are not yet ready to enter for the public examination. (He may also notice areas in which his previous teaching might have been improved.)

Some words of warning. I am not suggesting that the five dimensions will all be present in any given assessment situation — certainly not all consciously, or all in the mind of any one individual. Nor am I suggesting that those that do enter a person's mind will or should arrive in the sequence I followed in my list and examples. Nor, yet again, am I suggesting that the dimensions are clearly separable from one another or that any one of the mental activities can be carried out and 'completed' without either reference to one of the others or the need to return to it later with 'second thoughts'. In fact, as in most human information-processing, we start where our situation demands, putting the emphasis where we feel it is wanted and pursuing each activity as far as we need, returning if necessary more than once to re-cycle our earlier decisions. Thus, if a teacher is limited as to the assessment techniques he can choose among (as in the Open University where he cannot easily meet his students face-to-face), his decisions about what to assess will be highly dependent on prior decisions (and not necessarily his) about what techniques are available, rather than vice versa. But any teacher, once he has engaged with the problems of how to assess, how to interpret the outcomes and how to respond to them, is likely to see development in his views as to what should be assessed and why.

Interestingly, for the parallels between teaching and doctoring are always illuminating, the How to Assess / Interpret / Respond dimensions are very similar to what Michael Balint (1964, Preface) described as the successive phases of the *diagnostic* process in medicine — listening, understanding, and using the understanding so that it should have a therapeutic effect. That is, ' "listening" provides the material which is then ordered into "understanding" . . . "using the understanding so that it should have a therapeutic effect" is tantamout to a demand for a more exacting form of diagnosis; the therapist is expected to predict with a fair amount of accuracy what sort of effect his envisaged interventions will have.' So too is the teacher.

But before we consider further the dynamics of assessment, we must consider why it is done at all. In the next chapter we'll examine some functions and purposes commonly ascribed to assessment. And in the chapter after that we'll consider some outcomes that are not so generally ascribed, or even admitted.

CHAPTER 2

THE PURPOSES OF ASSESSMENT

Already we have seen that assessment has several purposes — diagnosis, evaluation, grading. But these are not ends in themselves, of course. They are means towards further ends. What are those over-arching purposes? In this chapter we shall consider why assessment is carried out at all. How is it justified? (Later we must ask what else is achieved that may not be explicitly claimed for it or even welcomed by the people involved.) More ominously, we can ask the question so often posed by the sleuth in old-fashioned crime-stories when considering whom to suspect of the murder: 'Who benefits?'

In general, the beneficiaries can be seen to be the student, his teacher and 'other people' (often referred to as 'society' — chiefly comprising parents, teachers and administrators in other educational institutions, and employers). Who benefits in particular instances depends on the nature and purpose of the assessment, e.g. formal or informal, formative or summative, pedagogic or classificatory, etc. Brian Klug (1974, p. 5), in what he says 'is undoubtedly an incomplete list', has gathered together thirty-two reasons for formal assessment. Here I shall concentrate on what I see as the six main reasons commonly advanced.

1. Selection by Assessment

One very common purpose of assessment is the *selection* of candidates for various kinds of educational opportunity or career. In some parts of Britain, children are still assessed at the age of '11-plus' to decide for them whether they should have a grammar school education aiming towards university and the professional life, or some other sort. Again, at 16-plus, another batch of examinations or other assessment devices acts effectively to select some students for 6th-form education, some for other less prestigious further education, and some for the world of work. The '18-plus' controls entry to university and the professions and, of course, the universities and professional bodies have their own tests to select those students who are to be awarded degrees or professional standing. Even when he is well into his working life, a person's progress is still dependent on assessment. Whether by formal interviews or less formal observation and reporting by his boss, or by the appraisal of his peers, he is selected for advancement or redundancy. Such assessment always involves some kind of grading and the putting of people into categories, even if 'Pass' and 'Fail' are the only two used.

Selection tests are probably what most people think of when they talk about assessment. Actually, it is often somewhat euphemistic to call them 'selection' tests. For the majority of candidates many such tests function rather as *rejection* tests. Thus, the 11-plus rarely selected more than 20% of the children in an area to attend the local grammar school, and thereby rejected 80%. In the U.S.A., where selection testing, especially for college entrance, is big business and heavily bureaucraticized, Hillell Black (1963) minced no words when he called his book on the subject *They Shall Not Pass*.

Selection (and rejection) is necessary because no country believes it can afford to give every citizen all he might desire in the way of education. A basic minimum may be available for everyone, e.g. ten years of normal schooling; but anyone who wants access to additional resources may have to prove that his need, or ability to benefit, is greater than that of others. We usually identify this competition for extra resources with the scramble for places in college and university. But, at the other end of the age-range, places in 'special schools' for children with learning difficulties are also limited: not every child whose parents and teachers believe he could profit from their more costly facilities will be selected. In many developing countries, places are in short supply even for secondary education and most children will fail to be selected.

One of the assumptions implicit in selection tests for advanced education is that only the brightest, most promising, and patently talented should be funded to continue. Now it is not logically obvious that extra educational resources should go to students who are already highly accomplished rather than to those with more ground to make up. However, advanced education is largely financed in the expectation that it will produce sufficient numbers of people capable of carrying out complex tasks in society — doctors, lawyers, engineers, etc. — and with the minimum investment of resources. To select students by lottery from among all interested candidates would clearly be egalitarian, and many students might gain entry and do well who would, at present, be considered too weak for selection. But such students might also make disproportionate demands on the teaching resources available, causing a reduction in the total number of 'capable persons' that could be produced.

Selection of 'students most likely to succeed' usually depends on public examinations. Since the Chinese invented them (before Europe had even evolved the feudal system) they have done something (though far less than as is usually assumed) to preserve some opportunities for talented children from poor families that might otherwise go to less promising children from richer homes. Essentially, selectors assume that the students who perform best in current examinations are those who would become most capable as a result of further educational investment. This is open to question, however: 'Correlation between GCE examinations and University examinations are, in general, low. . . . Whatever may be the value of the GCE 'A'-level examination as a school-leaving examination, as a basis for student selection for the University it has serious shortcomings' (Nicholson and Galambos, 1960). Comparisons of 'A'-level grades and degree class have rarely shown much of a correlation: see, for example, Petch (1961), Barnett and Lewis (1963), Nisbet and Welsh (1966), and UCCA (1969) which reports correlation coefficients between final degree and three 'A'-level results of between $r = 0.33$ (engineering) and $r = 0.17$ (social sciences). Such low correlations would suggest that less than 11% of the variation in university success can be 'explained' by variation in academic attainment at the time of entry. Perhaps such factors as personality and motivation may have as much or more influence on success in higher education (see Holland, 1960; Wankowski, 1970). For instance, medical students with poorer entry qualifications but with concern and empathy for ordinary people may emerge as better general practitioners than academic high-fliers who may feel they have failed if they do not get to be specialists or researchers. Of course every profession needs some reasonable level of academic performance from its would-be entrants. But there is little doubt that this level could, without detriment, be significantly lower than it is today if more serious attempts were made to assess interests and motivation and other personal qualities in applicants.

Assessment results are also used in selection for job and career opportunities. This is especially true of summative assessments at the end of a student's school or college career, or at the end of a period of professional training. In the absence of any thorough research, our knowledge of how employers actually use this assessment data is patchy and impressionistic (see Cox and Collins, 1975). Clearly, many use it as a screening device. That is, a candidate won't be looked at or even encouraged to apply unless he can offer a degree, or two 'A'-levels, or five 'O'-levels (including maths and English), or whatever is the going rate. This may be administratively convenient in cutting down the number of applicants. Again there may be a superstitious belief that the required qualifications betoken some kind of general quality of mind or spirit that will be useful to the employer. He may unconsciously be echoing the assumptions made by Lord Macaulay in defending the use of academic examinations to select administrators for the India Civil Service:

> Whatever be the languages — whatever be the sciences, which it is, in any age or country, the fashion to teach, those who become the greatest proficients in those languages and those sciences, will generally be the flower of youth — the most acute — the most industrious — the most ambitious of honourable distinctions. (quoted in Keith, 1961, pp. 252-3)

Admittedly, a reverse tendency may sometimes operate here among many employers, perhaps based on more than superstition, to view 'the flower of youth' as being *less* useful in that they may think they 'know it all' and so object to undergoing further training.

As a pamphlet produced jointly by Army personnel staff and British Airways Staff College points out, there is a tendency to use examination results, so conveniently and effortlessly available, 'without due regard to their relevance. It is a safe bet that most entry qualifications expressed in terms of exam performance are the result of armchair deliberations rather than empirical investigation' (Kilcross and Bates, 1975). Even within education itself the respect paid by employers to qualifications (and other previous experience) is arbitrary and often capricious. Thus English schoolteachers start higher up the salary scale and enjoy better promotion prospects if they have a degree, regardless of the subject studied and whether or not it has any bearing on their work with children.

Again, too, universities are sometimes accused of encouraging 'qualifications for qualifications' sake' — perhaps as a means of ensuring a continuing market for their 'product'. Here the critic might point at the 'academic inflation' that results when universities begin to encourage their graduates to take up work that was not formerly done by graduates, and then infiltrate more and more graduates into that area until it eventually becomes spoken of as a 'graduate profession' and a degree becomes an *essential* entry qualification. Business management and accountancy and law appear to be heading in this direction. Ronald Dore (1976) gives many further examples. Having examined numerous career guides published since the beginning of the century, he sees their emphasis 'slowly shifting from personal aptitudes to quantitatively measurable educational achievement' (p. 24). The 'institutionalizing' of professional education has resulted in fewer and fewer opportunities for young people to work their way up from artisan to professional status (e.g. as an engineer) by 'learning on the job'. Consequently, employers are having to put more and more faith in certificates and diplomas awarded on the basis of other people's assessments.

Clearly there is no way of comparing the success in a job of people with qualifications and people without them if, in fact, the latter group were rejected as candidates. However, there is little evidence of a close connection between high educational qualifications and success in later life. In the U.S.A., for example, Donald Hoyt (1965) reviewed 46 studies of the relationship between college grades and subsequent achievement, only to conclude that 'present evidence strongly suggests that college grades bear little or no relationship to any measures of adult achievement'. Even medical school grades appear not to predict future proficiency as a general practitioner (see Taylor *et al*, 1965). The statistical investigations of Ivar Berg (1973) confirm that the variety of academic achievement among people doing the same job and earning the same rewards is as great as it is between people doing different jobs; and in some cases, selling insurance for instance, people with least education but most experience perform best. Fewer such studies have been carried out in Britain, but Liam Hudson (1966a) examined the degree-class gained by each of a large sample of distinguished scientists, politicians and judges, concluding that 'there was evidence of some slight relation between eminence and degree-class, but it was far from clear-cut and there were many striking exceptions'. For instance, more than half of High Court judges, and a third of Fellows of the Royal Society, had gained only second-, third- or fourth-class degrees. Is it the case that a person's job experience and achievements *since* gaining his qualifications generally assume far more relevance and significance in selection for later career opportunities? The suggestion made in recent years that a degree should carry an expiry-date, with the warning that its validity is not guaranteed beyond that time, would then be almost superfluous.

Nevertheless, most people still do need the ritual assessment 'qualifications' if they are to get started at all. It is not their fault if selectors place more trust than is justified in such credentials and then ludicrously over-generalize in ascribing qualities and special status to the possessor. Although Dave and Hill (1974) are talking about effects of school-leaving examinations in a developing country, India, are things so different in the West?

> A person's standing in the examinations affects many aspects of his life. Not only is it a basis of his economic success, but it affects his prestige in his family and his (or her) value in the 'marriage market'. The examinations thus form the basis of a kind of educational caste system, superimposed on the traditional caste system of the country.

2. Maintaining Standards

Closely related to the selection-purpose is this second purpose, but it has a life of its own. Teachers would probably still feel obliged to assess for this purpose even if they thought it immoral or impolitic to disclose individual results to outsiders. The clientele is broadly the same – employers and the 'invisible college' of academics in other institutions who must be assured that some form of 'quality-control' is in operation and that the people being certified this year are of pretty much the same standard as those certified last year and five years ago, and so on. Standards-oriented assessment can also be of interest to any administrators who want to 'keep tabs' on teachers.

As with purpose 1, the student is a secondary beneficiary insofar as he wants to be assured of the acceptability, almost literally 'the value' of his certificate. As one science student put it, rather more extremely than most would, in a debate reported by Ellsworth-Jones (1974): 'What matters to me is the job I get when I leave here. When I get a degree I want to know that employers will think it's worth something.'

Many difficulties attend the attempt to maintain standards. It is difficult enough to get teachers to agree on what the standard is or should be — whether, for example, the criterion is to be content covered, skills acquired, original knowledge created, attitudes expressed, none of these, or some of these and others in variously contested proportions. Discussions of standards easily degenerate into cliches, stereotypes and confident half-truths like 'the first-class mind proclaims itself'. Certainly one cannot judge the standard of, say, an examination paper simply by looking at the questions. One also needs to know what the markers accept as a satisfactory response. (For example, the spoof question-paper printed on p. 136 may appear quite stiff; but for all we know the candidate has merely to write his name correctly on the answer-paper to score the 85% pass-mark). When the argument does come down to cases, in the analysis of a student's work, there is typically considerable disagreement (though surmountable by consent) among any group of assessors as to just what standard the student has attained.

The difficulties are compounded when the content of the curriculum is changing. This year's students may be assessed on areas of knowledge quite different from those of a year or so ago, even though the 'subject' is nominally the same. Inevitably then, it is quite impossible to establish the equivalence of standards between subjects and institutions. It makes no sense to ask whether the standard reached by physicists labelled 'second-class' in a given university or school is 'really' the same as that reached by 'second-class' historians, mathematicians and musicologists in the same institution in the same year, let alone in other institutions in other years. In fact, one simply has to take it as axiomatic that the 'quality-controllers' in various subject areas will be equally stringent in bestowing their approval on students. (Though one might still speculate as to what happens in universities to result in subjects like law and mathematics 'approving' (i.e. producing) a much smaller proportion of 'good' degrees than subjects like psychology and zoology, despite the fact that they start off with a far higher proportion of students entering with particularly high 'A'-level grades.) Whatever it means in terms of standards, the approval bestowed tends to operate, as Jonathan Warren (1971) has suggested, 'like a set of recommendations to an exclusive club written by long-term members who know the kind of people the other club-members prefer'.

Even within a subject, the standards being maintained are more probably standard assessment procedures rather than standard attainments. Indeed, there is a distinct possibility that standard procedures — especially if they include awarding a *fixed* proportion of As, Bs, etc. —

may fail to acknowledge changes in level of attainment. Stuart Miller (1967) quotes statistics showing that even though the quality of students entering the University of California at Berkeley increased considerably between 1947 and 1960 (as measured by three different pre-entry criteria) their grade-point-averages in university remained precisely the same. Nearer home, in a letter to *The Times* (October 9th, 1972), Professor I. H. Mills argues that 'what we demand for "A"-level examinations in many subjects today is the same standard that was expected for final degree examinations thirty years ago'. Nor have the higher standards required of entrants to British universities in recent years been reflected in a proportionate increase in the 'good degrees' awarded. The standard of 'output' is maintained *despite* an apparent improvement in the standard of 'input'.

3. Motivation of Students

After two assessment purposes whose benefits appear to be mainly administrative and go chiefly to people outside the immediate teacher-student relationship, this third purpose seems to be more educational and more related to the present needs of the student. With motivation we are talking of using assessment — e.g. homework assignments, weekly quizzes, classroom questioning, project reports, examinations, etc. — in order to encourage the student to learn. Many students would endorse this purpose. For instance, the male undergraduate quoted by Gerda Siann and Kate French (1975):

> The idea of Edinburgh University becoming a three-year holiday camp, all expenses paid, galls me, and I am reactionary enough to believe that the 'threat' of exams (i.e. the inherent threat of failure and becoming an outcast) is the only reason that the library doormats are cleaned.

Though it must be noted that for every student who confesses himself in need of a constant prod from assessment there will be another who claims to be distracted and enervated by it. Whether we believe that such students are to be confirmed in these attitudes — or whether the former should be 'educated' to get on by himself without such constant stimulus and the latter 'educated' to come to terms with the need to periodically review his progress through others' eyes — may affect how we classify the use of assessment in particular cases.

However, we must also recognize that 'motivational' assessment could be used to benefit the teacher rather than the student. In effect, by structuring the student's allocation of time and effort, by legitimizing certain kinds of activity and outlawing others, by indicating what is to count as knowledge worth having and what is not, 'motivational assessment' can define the reality of academic life for the student and give the teacher control over his perceptions and behaviour. To be blunt, assessment can be used as an instrument of coercion, as a means of getting students to do something they might not otherwise be inclined to do — especially if unfavourable assessments can have unpleasant consequences. Thus, R. L. Bowley (1967) gives teachers a tip for a practice that sounds alarmingly like extortion:

> Occasionally it may be desirable to ask a class to make an especially hard effort when tackling a set piece of work. A simple but useful device to encourage this is to raise the total out of which the work is to be marked and inform the class accordingly beforehand. For example, if it is customary to mark out of a total of twenty, the raising of this figure to thirty will often have the desired effect. (p. 116)

Some teachers consider it as much a necessary part of their duties to supply students with motivation as it is to supply them with objectives and structured lessons. Even though they may believe it to be in the students' long-term interest to achieve the objectives, they believe the students cannot be expected to recognize this and so provide self-motivation. Thus, assessment (in the form of quizzes, exams, etc.) may be used as one side of a carrot-stick inducement-system (the other side being represented by 'trying to make it as interesting as possible', audio-visual 'treats', etc.). The fervour with which this particular stick is waved can perhaps be seen as gradually increasing after the student's infant school years and reaching its a peak in his later secondary school and college years.

But the line between coercion and encouragement is hard to draw. Much must depend on the intentions and perceptions of teacher and student and the relationship between them. Consider the teacher whose aim is for the student to become autonomous enough to develop his *own* goals and learning strategies. Even he may feel that the student's motivation will be all the better for some external stimulus from assessment. After all, many such a teacher, while valuing his own freedom to decide how he spends his time, will admit how the occasional deadline or external stimulus, like the imminent need to deliver a lecture, or prepare a report for a committee, or finish the next chapter of a book he is writing with a colleague, can concentrate and energize his activities. So too he is likely to encourage his students to work towards targets and deadlines, and public commitments — preferably ones they have identified and thought through themselves before agreeing them in discussion with him.

4. Feedback to Students

It is necessary to distinguish between the motivating effect of knowing that you are to be assessed and the quite different sort of motivation resulting from knowing how you performed on the assessment exercise. The latter is much more clearly perceivable by students as being meant to help them learn. The student stands to benefit educationally from his tutor's response to what he has produced. In his study of the reactions of San Francisco teenage gang members to assessment, Carl Werthman (1963) quotes a student describing how he worked at getting more helpful feedback than is contained in a grade:

> After we got our compositions back I went up to him you know. I asked him about my composition. I got a D over F and I ask him what I did wrong. He told me that he could tell by the way I write that I could do better than what I did. And he explained it to me, and he showed me what I need to improve. And he showed me, if I correct my paper, I would get a D, a straight D instead of that F. O.K. And I got the D for half the work. But any way he showed me how I could get a regular D and pass his class. I mean I feel like that teacher was helping me

Feedback, or 'knowledge of results', is the life-blood of learning. Having said or done something of significance — whether a physical action, a comment in conversation, or an essay in an examination — the student wants to know how it is received. He wishes to know whether he communicated what he intended to communicate, whether what he said seemed right or wrong, appropriate or inappropriate, useful or irrelevant to his audience. And he may need a response fairly rapidly if it is to confirm or modify his present understanding or approach. Effective feedback enables the student to identify his strengths and weaknesses and shows him how to improve where weak or build upon what he does best.

Feedback from assessment comes in many forms, of varying degrees of usefulness (see Sassenrath and Garverick, 1965). In its least useful form it comes as a mark or grade. The student may be told his work has earned a C or 55% or 6 out of 10. This may give him some hint as to whether or not his teacher thinks he is making progress. That is, he may be able to compare this grade or mark with those he has earned on similar assessment previously. But, of course, it is very non-specific. It tells him neither what he has done to merit such a mark nor what he could do to earn a better one. Such non-specific feedback becomes increasingly useless to the student as the size and diversity of the performance being assessed increases. Thus a grade for a single essay gives little enough information, but to be given merely an overall grade for, say, an examination in which several essays were written leaves the student uncertain even whether he did equally well on all essays or whether some were thought atrocious and some brilliant.

Institutions often find it administratively convenient not to give students feedback about individual answers in an examination. Very often the marked papers are not even returned to students. Only a few years ago, Hilda Himmelweit (1967) reported that 'In the University of London, the teacher is even *forbidden* to inform the student of his performance in the different subjects in Part I, at the very time when he has to select his major subjects for Part II.' This may save a lot of arguments about the fairness or otherwise of the marking, but it is also to neglect a valuable educational opportunity. Even in continuous assessment, feedback on answers may be withheld, as sometimes happens in the Open University, so as to economize on question-writing by using the same questions again on subsequent students. Inadequate feedback can indicate that the assessment is serving the interests of people other than the students.

Another kind of feedback the student may obtain, sometimes instead of a grade or mark, is knowledge of whether he has passed or failed. Or, more widely, whether or not he has reached some standard. If he has some conception of what knowledge or skill is required to meet this standard, then a pass will tell him that he has achieved them. It will not tell him how or in what way he may have over-achieved, of course. Similarly, to be told he has failed will not tell him what particular aspects of the required performance he is deficient in. Interestingly enough, people who fail a driving test are given more information about their faults and where improvement is needed than are students who do poorly in the educational examinations (CSE or GCE) at the end of their school careers.

Again, whether instead of marks or grades or as well as, a student may be given a rank. He may be told that his performance puts him third from top of the class or into the bottom 10% of his age group. The student can gain little from this sort of feedback: unless he knows what sort of performance the reference group has put up, he won't be able to judge his own either. Is he third-best of a bad bunch or is he in the bottom 10% of an excelling group? More generally, merely to be told he is better or worse than certain others tells him nothing at all about whether he is better or worse than he himself has been or would wish to be, let alone in which particulars.

Feedback from assessment only begins to be useful when it includes *verbal comments*. The teacher who has made the assessment needs to verbalize his reactions to the student's performance, saying which aspects strike him as strong, weak, or simply interesting. Ideally, he should give whatever suggestions he can to help the student improve. This kind of feedback flows out from diagnostic appraisal. Even the briefest of comments, e.g. 'A well-argued essay in the main, but what evidence are your third and fourth conclusions based on?', can be more helpful to the student than a C or a 65% if we want him to learn from considering his performance again in the light of our reaction. Research has confirmed (see Page, 1958) that students who are given individualized verbal comments on their work, incorporating suggestions for improvement, do tend to 'improve' significantly more than students who are given standard comments (e.g. 'poor', 'average', 'good', 'excellent') or grades.

Robert Birney (1964) found that college students were agreeable to frequent assessment — so long as it was 'in language they understand'. That is, not in grades or marks, which told them nothing specific about their strengths and weaknesses, but in detailed verbal commentary. If the information fed back is really intended to contribute to the student's growth it must tell him either that he has already achieved what he was trying to achieve or else must enable him to take some further action towards achieving it. Even in the former case it may be able to indicate possible *new* objectives and ways of approaching them. Useful feedback then is more to be expected from formative assessment than from summative. However, apart from the demands of common courtesy, any examiners who subscribe to the ideal of 'continuing education' should ponder the waste of not giving the student a detailed analysis of how he has performed at the climax of his formal education. They might consider also the ethics of involving the student in what may be a nerve-racking assessment experience that yet leaves him no wiser as to who he is and what he can do. It is in such a milieu that the student can be asked, 'What did you get out of this course?', and reply in all seriousness, 'I got a B' (see Kirchenbaum *et al.*, 1971).

Of course, feedback need not be supplied directly by a teacher. For many students, their first experience of sustained feedback has come from pro-grammed texts. In such texts, the author can weave into his line of argument occasional questions requiring the student to use the ideas that have been introduced so far. Having come up with his own answer to these self-assessment questions, the student reads on to compare it with the answer given and explained by the author. Thus the student is constantly informed as to how well he is learning and the assessment comes frequently enough for him to correct any significant misunder-standings as soon as they occur.

But nor does feedback have to be verbal. The teacher's smiles or scowls, the colleague's mirth or laudatory silences can have a shaping influence on the student's behaviour. Sometimes the student will get his feedback from pictures, e.g. when drawing graphs or envisaging the landscape depicted by a map. Sometimes real events will provide the feedback, e.g. when the screaming of his car's gears tells the driver that he has not got the feel of the clutch or when the smell from the test-tube indicates that the student has applied too much heat.

Such indirect kinds of assessment can be seen as steps towards *self-*assessment. Increasingly, if the student is to become capable of learning to work for his own satisfaction rather than for the approval of his teacher, he must assume responsibility for providing his own feedback. He must be weaned of dependence on others for knowledge of how well he is doing. This demands that he be encouraged to recognize and internalize rules and standards and strategies whereby he may test the validity of his own responses.

5. Feedback to the Teacher

Just as assessment may give the student feedback as to how well he has learned, so too it may give the teacher feedback as to how well he has taught. This is how assessment contributes to course evaluation. Insofar as the assessment data reveal strengths and weaknesses in the student's learning, the teacher may be able to identify where he has failed to explain a new concept, confused an issue, given insufficient practice, and so on. Knowing where and how his students have had difficulty may enable him now to teach so as to remedy the situation.

At times, however, e.g. in end-of-course examinations, the teacher may get this feedback too late for him to be able to use it for the educational benefit of the students who provided it. He may use it, instead, to report on their achievements. He may also use it to modify his teaching for the benefit of *subsequent* students. Thus, some assessment can have as its purpose feedback to the teacher but without feedback to the student also being intended.

One of the great weaknesses of externally marked examinations like GCE is that the teacher normally gets no feedback as to the strengths and weaknesses demonstrated by his students. He thus has no means of knowing which of his prior teaching interventions have borne fruit and which have not. Were this evidence available, it might enable him to improve as a teacher.

6. Preparation for Life

Some teachers would wish to justify assessment on the grounds that it reflects, and therefore prepares students for, 'real life'. Let us note, in passing, how odd it is to imply a distinction between the student's educational career and his real life. Education is *part* of his life, and an increasingly large part. Unavoidably, it may also in some sense prepare him for that part of real life which it is not. But this does not imply that education, or, to be exact, the people who control aims and objectives in education, should take the predicted real life for granted and merely train the student to 'cope'. Educationally, it would be equally valid, perhaps more so, to provide a counter-curriculum that might enable the student to challenge or ignore the pressures of 'real life'. Such an argument can be heard, for example, from teachers concerned about the power of commercial pop-culture.

How far is educational assessment a preparation? Certainly much of the *informal* assessment that goes on in school and college is related to the mainly informal assessment that goes on in the rest of life. Approbation and criticism (verbal or non-verbal) from teachers and fellow-students are not dissimilar to what the student will meet from parents, workmates and friends. But it is probably not this informal kind of assessment that teachers see as the life-preparer. Those who do see assessment as a preparation are most likely thinking of the competitive system of public examination, grading, and ranking. Such experience is thought to prepare students for the life-struggle in general and career-advancement in particular. The thoughts of Luther Evans (1942, p. 59) are representative: 'A student who completes a programme of higher education without facing the rigorous evaluations of a grading system has missed one great chance to learn the helpful lesson that life is full of tests and trials.' An even more emphatic statement has been made by the 'Black Papers' author, Brian Cox (1971): 'All life depends on passing exams. . . . To create an education system without examinations is to fail to prepare children and students for the realities of adult life.' Let's hope they are not thinking of the 'rigorous evaluations' and 'realities' evoked by Norman Russell's poem:

End of a Semester

This is the week of tests the season of fear
everywhere the running the typing the scritch scratch
shuffling of papers the door and the people
coming going looking for the symbols
looking for the little symbols written on the papers
stuck with tape to doors and walls
this is the week of the fearhope swallowed in the stomach
a time of livingdying a time of cominggoing
a time of inbetween the things one cannot grasp
too fast too fast we never sleep
we only keep ongoing.

and somewhere someone in a great office
pushing buttons marking papers calling telephones
we think a devil who we cannot see is laughing

and all the things we knew were true
will never do will never do
we all are weak we all are strong
the days are long the days are long

this is the week of tests the season of fear
somewhere we think a devil who we cannot see is laughing.

Norman Russell (1966)

Fortunately, life outside education is not really like that. With the exception perhaps of the civil service and the armed forces, most people seldom ever again meet the experience of being tested or examined on prescribed syllabuses for the purpose of being graded and ranked and chosen. Assessment in industry and the professions is generally informal, diffuse, *ad hoc* and continuous. It is based largely on the person's 'track record' over a *period* of time and in fulfilling his duties rather than on what he can write about something at a given *point* in time. Nor is such assessment quantitative in any simple way. The candidate for, say, a high academic post may be chagrined to find that his thirty published papers do not win him preferment over another candidate whose output is thought more significant even though his papers number only three!

As things are now, competitive public assessment does prepare for future job-competition — in the sense that success in previous competitions is normally demanded as an entry qualification for further competition. But this is an artefact of the system and, even if such competition were regarded as reasonable (e.g. on the grounds of greater efficiency, maximization of output, etc.), we have no means of knowing whether people excluded at earlier stages might not have proved 'winners' if allowed to 'work their way up' through the lower reaches of their chosen profession (see Dore, 1976). There is, of course, enough evidence of 'late developers', and of people unexpectedly 'finding themselves' in a situation where they were called upon to draw on unsuspected powers and grow into the job, to make us suspect the efficiency as well as the ethics of competitive elimination from further competition. But even if such people are held to be exceptions, there is still reason to doubt whether any but the winners benefit from preparation. The losers, through loss of self-respect and reduced optimism may be *less* prepared to face up confidently to subsequent life-struggles. Even with dogs, as Scott (1972) observes: 'In a test set up so that one dog can do it and another can barely succeed, the initial difference in hereditary ability may not be great. However, the dog which fails soon stops trying, while the one which succeeds becomes more highly motivated with each success. It keeps on trying and succeeding at more and more complicated problems so that in the end the hereditary difference has been immensely magnified' (p. 132).

There is a growing feeling among teachers that education should no longer meekly accept that society must necessarily be competitive. Many recognize the emerging need for people to share and collaborate rather than seek maximum personal and material advantage. They would not see eliminative assessment as a preparation for this kind of co-operative living. Nevertheless, it might still be argued that people will always be competing, if not with somebody then with some*thing* — the soil, the weather, disease, poor housing — and so on. Some such competition, together with the attendant storm and stress, might widely be agreed to be an inescapable component of 'real life'. But one could accept that education could reasonably be expected to help students prepare for it, without accepting that the appropriate means must be to promote interpersonal competition in school.

Naturally, teachers who see the student's future in terms of his being externally assessed in competition with others rarely extol the preparatory virtues of *self*-assessment. Insofar as schooling does give the student opportunities to develop criteria for assessing himself and encourages him to take decisions based on his assessments, it will be 'preparing' him for a life in which he expects to have some control over his own destiny. There is considerable lip-service paid to the ideal of self-assessment, but the practice very often belies or trivializes the intent. Students may, for example, be 'trusted' to mark their own work — but using teacher's criteria as to what counts as 'good' work. They may be asked to assess their own progress during a term or over a course, using whatever criteria seem appropriate to them — but their assessments are not allowed to influence the overall report that is given them. They are asked to choose which subjects to specialize in (e.g. Arts vs. Sciences) at an early age, without ever having been helped to develop relevant criteria for assessing their own strengths and weakness in relation to the various courses of action open to them. Obviously, self-assessment cannot be a preparation for anything, not even for further self-assessment, unless it is supported by open access to relevant information, unless the results of the assessment are regarded as significant and actionable, and unless the person assessing himself is to be allowed responsibility for the outcomes of his own judgements and decisions.

Balancing the Purposes

I have outlined six broad categories of purpose in educational assessment. They are not entirely without overlap and we might possibly need a seventh 'miscellaneous' category to catch a few more purposes that are less commonly spoken of. Even so, we have seen more than enough to suggest that the teacher who pauses to ask why he is assessing has plenty to think about. How does he, in fact, thread his way through the various potentially conflicting purposes and what determines his personal intentions?

The teacher's use of assessment will be heavily influenced by the expectations of the teaching system within which he is working. But his attitudes to assessment will largely depend on his ideas as to what teaching and learning and knowledge and education are all about. That is, on his professional world-view, or what some sociologists (see Esland, 1972) call his *pedagogic paradigm*. Different teachers can be seen, for instance, as taking up different positions along a continuum whose opposite extremes are labelled by writers using such terms as closed vs. open (Bernstein, 1971); manipulative vs. facilitative (Rowntree, 1975); or transmission vs. interpretation (Barnes, 1976).

To put it crudely, one end of the continuum tends to attract the teacher whose first loyalty is to a public corpus of pre-existing knowledge or expertise (which he knows everyone ought to acquire) and the need to 'get it across' to a succession of students who learn, as far as their limited capacity and motivation will allow, by absorbing and reproducing the products of other people's experience. The other end of the continuum attracts the teacher who distrusts generalizations about what everyone ought to know, and who, believing people to have unlimited potential for growth unless 'discouraged', gives his first loyalty to individual students and encourages them to exercise their own developing motivation and sense of purpose in mastering cognitive and affective capacities, making their own meaning and creating new knowledge out of their own ideas and experiences. The paradigm with which a particular teacher operates will rarely be so extreme, of course. Although most of his or her paradigm may consist of beliefs and assumptions from one end of the continuum, it is likely to be tempered with more moderate beliefs. Of the two extreme paradigms indicated, the former is more likely to be found in secondary schools, the latter in infant schools; perhaps also the latter paradigm is more typical of arts-based subjects than science-based subjects, and more typical of women than men.

In the paragraph above, I mentioned only a few of the kinds of belief and assumption that go to make up a teacher's pedagogic paradigm. What if we go on to consider beliefs relevant to student assessment? We may decide that teachers attracted towards one end of the continuum may be more inclined to see assessment as an objective and accurate means of determining a student's present achievement and future potential, thus legitimizing selection and special treatment; and, insofar as students are aware that many are called but few are chosen, as a powerful device for reinforcing teacher's control over the wayward and idle. Conversely, teachers attracted to the other end of the conti-nuum may tend to see assessment primarily as a means of developing the relationship between the student, themselves and the subject matter, by giving both the student and themselves more information about the present state of the student's understandings; but as incapable of providing valid information about the student to outside parties or about his long-term potential to anyone at all. Various belief-systems and attitudes will emerge as we push deep into the undergrowth of assessment. As I have indicated, we can look for them to tie in and be consistent with other aspects of the way the teacher sees education — his pedagogic paradigm.

Looking back over this chapter, it would appear that the 'purposes' I have discussed are those ascribed to assessment by the actions of *teachers*. Perhaps this is not surprising. It is, after all, teachers rather than students who develop the rules of the game and tell us what it is supposed to be achieving. Maybe in the next chapter, where we look at some of the *unintended* effects of assessment, we shall catch a glimpse of the purposes that *students* ascribe to assessment by the ways they use it.

CHAPTER 3

THE SIDE-EFFECTS OF ASSESSMENT

One way of evaluating any human activity is to ask whether it is achieving what it was meant to achieve. A rather more sophisticated way is to ask what it is achieving (see Rowntree and Harden, 1976). This second approach recognizes a truth that has become routinized in the clinical trial of new drugs — that the most well-intentioned acts often produce results other than were intended. We fail to comprehend the phenomenon being studied if we concern ourselves merely with a narrow range of pre-identified or publicly proclaimed effects and overlook its side-effects.

Now the assessment of students is much criticized on account of its allegedly malign side-effects. Teachers, students, parents, employers and all can be heard voicing disquiet. As always, however, in educational matters of real significance, reliable information is thin on the ground. Instead we have a wealth of impressions, opinions, personal experiences, and cries from the heart. Some may be soundly based, some not. Either way, they are liable to influence the reality of the situation, and so deserve attention.

I am going to examine eight aspects of assessment each of which, it seems to me, can be held to account for certain specific side-effects. The eight are:

1. The prejudicial aspects of assessment.
2. Students' knowledge of the assessment.
3. The extrinsic rewards of assessment.
4. The competitive aspects of assessment.
5. The bureaucratic aspects of assessment.
6. The nature of specific assessment techniques.
7. The giving of grades.
8. The reporting of assessment results.

1. The Prejudicial Aspects of Assessment

Students are affected by assessment even before they themselves are assessed. Knowledge of assessments made on other students (by himself or others) influences the teacher not just in how he appraises his present students' learning, but also in what he thinks it appropriate to teach them in the first place. Just as the nursery teacher may have in mind certain 'normal' stages of child development when assessing the progress of a three-year-old child, so the university teacher will plan a second-year course with the belief that it must be seen to make different demands than those that would be associated with work of first-year or third-year standard. In both cases, the teacher's expectations are based on previous assessment of other children or other undergraduates.

Deciding how to teach present students in the light of assessments of previous students may, of course, be of direct benefit to the student, e.g. when knowledge of what children of his age are 'typically' capable of restrains us from making unfair demands on a child or, conversely, when such knowledge enables us to expect more of him. Yet the knowledge of such 'other' assessment can have the side-effect of individuals being treated unfairly. A child may be different from the 'typical' child of his age in so many crucial respects that the demands we make of him should also be quite different. The danger of harmful side-effects arises only when such general assessments derived from other children are pursued in the face of contradictory evidence from the particular children we are working with.

This brings us to one ever-imminent side-effect of assessment — the prejudicial use of *stereotypes*. Just as teachers may come to the learning-situation with a more-or-less flexible idea (derived from their own or other people's previous assessment) as to what children of a certain age can do, so they may have similar ideas relating to the potentialities of children of a certain sex, social class, or race. Thus, when faced with a particular working-class black girl, they may tend to look for different qualities (at least at first) than they would from her white middle-class male classmate (see Leacock, 1969, and Coard, 1971). Some teachers operate with minimal stereotypes which they are rapidly able to modify or abandon altogether in making new relationships with individual students. Others work with very well-defended stereotypes that are impervious to contradictory messages beamed at them by individual students. Clearly, the more rigid the stereotype, that is, the more the teacher treats his pupil like a reach-me-down 'type' derived from the assessment of *other* pupils rather than seeking out what makes him unique, the less likely is the teaching to touch upon that pupil's needs. Instead, the pupil may get whatever standard 'treatment' is generally assumed appropriate to children carrying his label — 'culturally deprived child', 'professional family background', 'West Indian immigrant', or whatever.

Nell Keddie (1971) illustrates how secondary school teachers' generalized conceptions of 'A-stream' and 'C-stream' pupils result in quite different expectations for the children in those classes. This is revealed not only in the form of the teaching (C-stream pupils being allowed to make much more noise and achieve a great deal less work than A-pupils) but also in its *content*, and in how seriously the teacher responds to pupils' questions:

> C-pupils are not expected to progress in terms of mastering the nature of a subject, and so their questions are less likely to be seen as making a leap into the reality of the subject. The expectations seem to be implied in the remarks of teachers who said they could get away with not preparing work for C-pupils but would not risk that with A-pupils. The questions of the latter will require the knowledge of the teacher as 'expert'.

Some teachers are painfully aware of the danger of being prejudiced by judgements prefabricated for them by other teachers whose viewpoints may have been quite different from their own. As we can see from Herbert Kohl (1967):

> I was handed a roll book with thirty-six names and thirty-six record cards, years of judgements already passed upon the

children, their official personalities. I read through the names, twenty girls and sixteen boys. . . . Then I locked the record cards away in the closet. The children would tell me who they were. Each child, each new school year, is potentially many things, only one of which the cumulative record card documents. It is amazing how 'emotional' problems can disappear, how the dullest child can be transformed into the keenest, and the brightest into the most ordinary when the prefabricated judgements of other teachers are forgotten. (p. 10)

But the extent to which a teacher's impressions and expectations are based on other people's observations or his own is not the key factor in determining whether they work for good or ill. Their potential for helping or hindering appropriate teaching depends partly on their initial accuracy, but much more than that on their *flexibility* – on the degree to which the teacher holds them as being simply initial, working hypotheses about the student which are to be modified, perhaps even abandoned, in response to new knowledge of the student (see Hargreaves, 1972).

Like anyone else entering a social relationship, the teacher is in a position to learn about the people he will be involved with and modify his expectations of them as individuals. That is, he should be able to move away from prior categorizations and learn from his own experience. He should be discovering how a particular student differs from the stereotype rather than how he conforms. And he should be using these discoveries in individualizing his dealings with the unique person concerned. Hilda Taba (1962) discusses the process among a group of teachers who:

. . . complained that their classes contained large numbers of children who were slow in learning to read and that this slowness retarded them in all their work. The descriptions these teachers gave suggested that they viewed all slow learners as being alike, that slowness to them was a monolithic quality shared by all retarded children in a like manner. For this reason they treated all slow learners alike: they either intensified drill, gave individual help, or emphasized punishments and rewards. The thought that the slowness might have been caused by different factors in different individuals and hence also be correctible in different ways was both strange and unacceptable. (p. 240)

With Hilda Taba's help, those teachers were able to abandon their monolithic concept of 'slow learners'. They were encouraged to diagnose the specific nature and causes of the 'slowness' in individuals and develop *individualized* teaching strategies to overcome them.

But teachers are not all so susceptible to experience. Some will operate through what psychologists call 'selective perception'. They will tend to notice most, and respond most to, only those features of the student's behaviour that conform to their original diagnosis. Theodor Adorno and colleagues (1950) identified as one of the characteristics of the 'authoritarian' personality his tenacity in holding on to stereotyped views of others, remaining insensitive to evidence that they do not belong in the category he slotted them into. Contradictory evidence is 'screened out'. It is either not observed or else is interpreted in non-contradictory ways. 'Some teachers seem unable to respond to success when they are expecting failure,' say Brophy and Good (1974, p. 312). Thus, unusually good work from a 'weak' student might be explained away as 'cheating' or 'a flash in the pan'. This gives rise to a common source of unreliability in assessment — the so-called 'halo-effect'.

Popular wisdom recognizes the halo effect in phrases like 'That poor devil can't do a thing right for you, can he?', or 'Oh, you think the sun shines out of her eyes, don't you?'. That is, an early impression (favourable or unfavourable) relating to just one aspect of a student's work will often be *over-generalized*: the assessor will respond in the same sort of way (favourable or unfavourable) to other, or subsequent aspects of the student's work which impartial observers would see as deserving a different kind of response. The 'halo' round the head of the assessed person 'blinds' the assessor to real qualities (positive and negative) that might threaten the validity of that halo. Studies like that of Jenkins (1972) reveal that teachers asked to rate a student on a number of different traits and characteristics will tend to colour all their ratings according to their overall attitudes to the student. These attitudes or 'general impressions' may be based on just a few key criteria like frequency of hand-raising, frequency of correct answers and frequency of time-wasting. Even within an assessment task like the marking of an essay, the halo effect can be demonstrated. The marker's impression on one aspect of essay-writing he considers important may influence his judgements on other aspects of the same essay. Thus, if an essay is neatly written or typed, it is likely to be awarded a higher mark than if exactly the same content is presented in untidy handwriting (see Shepherd, 1929; Briggs, 1970).

But inaccurate or inflexible assessments of a student do not affect merely the teacher's impression of the student. They may also affect what the student actually becomes. If the teacher, for example, categorizes a certain child as 'unmotivated' or 'backward' he may, as Len Sperry (1972) points out, be using this label to imply a basically *unchangeable* feature of the child; and thus feel justified in making little progress with him. He may therefore take less notice of him, make fewer demands on him, be less patient with him when he finds difficulty in coping with a demand, take fewer pains in ensuring his understanding and be less concerned about it when he fails than he would with other children. Thus the child is likely to fall even further behind his classmates because he is getting less teaching. And the further behind he gets, the more he confirms the teacher's assessment (and behaviour). In fact, the teacher's assessment is acting as a 'self-fulfilling prophecy'. We'll discuss this phenomenon further in the next section because it becomes even more potent when the student is aware of the teacher's expectations.

2. Students' Knowledge of Assessment

What side-effects begin to occur when assessments are not only made but are *seen*—by the student—to be made? Once the student knows his behaviour is being observed and assessed he may change that behaviour (for good or ill). This may remind us of Heisenberg's 'Uncertainty Principle' which points out the uncertainty attached to observations or measurements of something when the very act of observing or measuring may alter the thing being observed or measured. Even a thermometer placed in a cup of tea will not tell you what the temperature of the tea was but only what it is after being altered, however slightly, by the immersion of the thermometer. Likewise, human beings can observe you observing them and change their behaviour accordingly. They can speculate about why you are observing them and about what expectations you may have of them or what conclusions you are coming to. They can then, according to temperament, either ignore you, or else act either to reinforce or to contest your expectations and conclusions. Among social scientists, this phenomenon has become known as the Hawthorne Effect (see Roethlisberger and Dickson, 1969).

In many instances, the side-effects of knowing that assessment is taking place may be benign. If students feel that a teacher is genuinely concerned about how they think and feel and is interested in learning how they progress over a period of time, they may well feel stimulated to maintain a high level of effort. (Insofar as teachers are relying on this 'motivational' effect, perhaps it should be classed as one of the main purposes rather than a side-effect.) But the side-effects are not necessarily benign. Thus, an adolescent who is gradually abandoning his previously hostile attitudes to children of another race may well assume them again, for fear of 'loss of face', if he becomes aware that the change is being remarked upon.

In any event, his awareness of being assessed is enough to remind a child of how he stands in relation to the assessor and others — his social situation. If we do not allow for the way he perceives this — what Erving Goffman (1966) called 'the neglected situation' — we are liable to misinterpret his performance and ability. Courtney Cazden (1970), for example, quotes research illustrating that children's verbal expressiveness is diminished in encounters with an unfamiliar 'authority figure'. Labov (1972) also has shown how student articulacy is dependent on the test situation, by comparing, for example, the effect of a formal, middle-class tester with an informal working-class tester. Several studies have shown that the performance of black children can be lower when tested by a white person than when tested by someone of their own race.

Sometimes children may perform poorly not because they cannot but because they do not *care* to do well. Herbert Kohl (1967) recalls his astonishment when a black 6th-grade pupil, Alice, who had achieved a very low reading score with other teachers, showed him that she could read all the printed material on his desk, including the novel he was reading on the way to school. He asked her how this was possible since she had such a low reading score:

> 'I wouldn't read for those teachers. Listen. . . .' Alice picked up a book and stumbled through several paragraphs. She paused, stuttered, committed omissions and reversals, i.e. read on a low third-grade level. Then she looked at my astonished face and burst out laughing. (p. 190)

So much for the student's knowledge that assessment is taking place. Usually, however, he knows more than this. He knows the *nature* of the assessment and what kinds of opinion his teacher has formed about him. Herbert Kohl mentions that Alice 'was hyper-sensitive and incapable of tolerating insult or prejudice'. Once the student knows what his teacher thinks of him, the door is open to one of the most potent side-effects of assessment — the *self-fulfilling prophecy* (see Insel and Jacobson, 1975).

In the self-fulfilling prophecy we have a new label for a phenomenon long-recognized in folk-wisdom: 'Give a dog a bad name and you may as well hang him' or 'Trust a man and he will prove true'. That is, if we constantly and powerfully express to a person our image of what he is (lazy, stupid, brave or dependable) he will often gradually adjust his behaviour so as to become more like our image than he was before. If our image was accurate, the person will have become more what he was. But if it was inaccurate he will have become something he was not. Nigel Dennis's hilarious novel *Cards of Identity* (1955) pursued the process to its wildest limits.

The self-fulfilling prophecy was first discussed by Robert Merton (1948) as a false belief, the expression of which starts off a chain of events that makes the initial belief come true. Believing something to be true will often make it so — especially if many people act on that belief. Our interpretations of experience are especially liable to be altered by our conversations with 'significant others' — parents, teachers, spouses, close friends and workmates — those with whom we identify and whose opinions seem important to us. Thus, we may come to see ourselves, and act, as those others seem to see us. As Berger and Luckman (1966) put it:

> the self is a reflected entity, reflecting the attitudes first taken by significant others towards it; the individual becomes what he is addressed as. (p. 152)

The most famous demonstration of the self-fulfulling prophecy in education was that reported by Rosenthal and Jacobson (1968) in *Pygmalion in the Classroom*. Teachers in a California elementary school were led to believe that tests indicated that some of their children (actually chosen at random) were 'late bloomers' who could be expected to make unusually high gains in achievement during the coming year. By the end of the year, the so-called bloomers (especially the younger ones) had indeed made bigger gains than their classmates — in reading and on a test of general intellectual abilities. An imaginary difference had become real. The prophecy appeared to have fulfilled itself. In fact, the Pygmalion experiment has been hotly contested ever since and, despite many follow-up studies, such striking results have never been replicated, not even by Rosenthal. (See Brophy and Good, 1974, for a commentary on more than sixty studies.) However, there seems little doubt that teacher-expectations can affect pupil attitudes and achievements, especially when they result from the teacher's own assessments and especially when pupils are aware of their nature (see Nash, 1976).

That such naturally-arising expectations do have their self-fulfilling effect is inferred from studies of children misplaced in classes that are streamed, or 'tracked' (to use the U.S. term). Consider Douglas (1964), for example, reporting on a three-year follow-up of children who were streamed 'by ability' at the age of eight. It was found that many children of higher social class or more pleasing personality were placed in higher streams than their measured ability would seem to warrant; while many children of lower social class or less pleasing personality were misplaced downwards — into lower streams than children of comparable ability. After three years in those streams, by which time the children were eleven, Douglas discovered that those misplaced upwards had improved, while those who had been misplaced downwards had deteriorated. Of course it is possible that such effects are partly due to the original placing being wiser and more prescient than would appear or to the stimulating or depressing influence of the stream-mates the child finds himself among. But it seems very probable that teacher expectation plays the major part in helping 'highs' to become higher and 'lows' to become lower.

The translation of teacher expectations into reality can be explained behaviouristically in terms of mutual conditioning and reinforcement. If a teacher has made an overall negative assessment of a particular student, for example, he may be less likely to ask him to contribute in a class discussion and may be less patient and supportive if he does try to contribute; being unrewarded, the student may then be even less likely to volunteer an opinion on another occasion; the teacher too being unrewarded may be even less likely to call for a contribution. However, it seems likely that the effect is all the stronger when students are *aware* of the nature of the assessment — and there is plenty of evidence that they generally are. Ray Rist (1970) quotes from teachers making their expectations horribly explicit. Again Gabriel Chanan and Linda Gilchrist (1974, p. 54) remind us of the kind of labelling language that is only too prevalent in the classroom — especially in secondary schools:

'Now listen, thickies!'

'You lot wouldn't be any good at this'

'Why do they always give me the worst classes?'

'Those are my bright ones over there. The dull ones are over here.'

(Said to a visitor in the hearing of the class.)

'They didn't teach you much out there, did they?'

'When are you going to learn to fit in with our way of life?' [To coloured immigrant children]; or, as one head said in an assembly: 'Now, I'm going to say this simply, so that everyone can understand it, even IX.' (IX being a bottom-stream form.)

Assessment-talk so richly offensive as this drives us beyond behaviourist explanation and into the mind and spirit of the child. It reminds us that when students are aware of how they are being assessed they may (let's put it no stronger) be affected in their self-esteem, receptiveness, and level of aspiration. For better or for worse.

3. The Extrinsic Rewards of Assessment

Learning, like virtue, might reasonably be expected to be its own reward. For some it is; for others not. Consider how we might describe what we got out of any episode of learning, say a research project, in which we have lately been engaged. We might talk of feeling intrigued, facing up to a challenge, puzzling out an approach, wrestling with frustrations and obstacles, overcoming the temptation to settle for the apparently reasonable compromise which we knew in our heart of hearts was not quite right; we might mention our absorption in the task, how fulfilling and enjoyable was our search for satisfying meanings, how we were able to express ourselves in our growing mastery of our topic; and we might recall flashes of insight and illumination, the 'ah ha! experience', and the exciting moments when 'everything began to fall into place'; we might further comment on how the knowledge and understanding we gained has enabled us to relate differently to the world and, in some way, has made us feel more alive and human, or simply more useful, than we were before.

On the other hand, we might say that what we got out of it was: B+, or a GCE 'pass', or a place in college, or a certificate, or a better job with a company car. That is, the rewards lay not in the learning nor even in the knowledge and skill that resulted — but outside of it.

Perhaps we can follow the distinction made by sociologist Talcott Parsons and ask whether the student regards his learning as *expressive* (valuing it as an opportunity to express and enlarge his capabilities) or as *instrumental* (valuing it as a means towards the satisfaction of goals external to itself). The burden of my argument in this section will be that too many students (especially once beyond primary school) are encouraged to regard learning and education instrumentally rather than expressively; and that this can be seen as a side-effect of assessment, and in particular of the extrinsic rewards so often emphasized by it. Too often, in brief, students come to want 'the certificate' more than (and, if necessary, instead of) the learning supposedly signified by that certificate.

It was not accidental that my example of a learning episode providing its own 'expressive' rewards was a personal research project. Personally directed learning, the kind we *choose* to engage in, or are unconsciously drawn to, is often undertaken either for its own sake, because we expect the activity itself to be rewarding, or else because we wish to use the knowledge and capabilities expected to result from it. However, as soon as we look to another person (e.g. a teacher) for assessments, we open up a potential for rewards that are not intrinsic to the learning experience or to our desired growth in capability. We may, for example, find ourselves learning in order to please the assessor or in order to win some prize or privilege to which he holds the key. We may be expected to gain satisfaction from the extent to which we meet someone else's criteria (as represented to us by the assessor) rather than our own. However, and here is an important qualification, this need not be our *only* expected source of satisfaction. We may still be expected to meet criteria of our own and gain rewards from the actual process of learning and the resulting knowledge.

Now, desiring the approval of others is not necessarily detrimental to learning. For most of us, one of the pleasures of learning lies in knowing that 'significant others' will share our enthusiasms and reward our further endeavours (as we will theirs), treating our contributions with respect. The pioneering chemist Sir Humphrey Davy once wrote of 'the love of praise that never, never dies'. When our learning endeavours could take us in a variety of different but (for us) equally valid directions, we lose nothing by choosing those that give us something in common, a vehicle for encounter, with people whom we admire and whose approval or respect we desire. .

But the case is altered when gaining the approval of others is our main reason for learning whatever it is we are learning. Such an instrumental tendency is common among students in the years immediately prior to their leaving school or college or university. Students may be constrained to regard the teacher's approval as indicative of approval by *other* powerful groups in society on which they are dependent for improvement in status and the earning capacity that goes with it. Here the student sees the teacher's (or the tester's or examiner's or society's) approval given a physical existence as a tangible reality — *reified* as the philosophers might say. Approval is reified as gold stars, marks, scores, grades, positions in class, passes, credits, certificates, testimonials, acceptances, entry to college, permission to continue and so on. Ray Hiner (1973) suggests that this labelling system has the cultural function of conditioning children 'to accept level of achievement as the primary criterion for the distribution of rewards'.

Howard Becker *et al* (1968) suggest that getting adequate approval (good enough grades) can become the ruling purpose in a college student's academic life. They see grades on campus serving the same function as money in the wider society. The student, they suggest, defines his situation as a 'workplace in which grades, the money of the college community, are exchanged for academic performance'. He sees himself as having a kind of implied contract with his tutors which regulates the rate of pay — the level of performance required for a given grade.

There would be less concern, of course, if it were widely felt that teacher-approval, as expressed in grades and such-like, truly goes only to students enjoying scholarship and growth of capability. A successful ⁓udent quoted by Becker *et al* seems eloquently aware that students can achieve one without the other:

> There's an awful lot of work being done up here for the wrong reason. I don't know exactly how to put it, but people are going through here and not learning anything at all. . . . There's a terrific pressure on everybody here to get good grades. It's very important. . . . And yet there are a lot of courses where you can learn what's necessary tó get the grade and when you come out of the class you don't know anything at all. You haven't learned a damn thing really. (p. 59)

This experience is reflected in the remarks of Robert Birney (1964) on research into student learning habits in the graduating class of a prestigious American university:

> Students displaying little effort at study, no faculty contact on academic matters, and no reputation with their peers for their scholarly interests or their realization of the benefits to be derived from college experience, nevertheless kept their grades at a

reasonable level by strategies of course selection, bursts of cramming, and adroit use of test-taking ability . . . . These results suggest that both aptitude scores and grades are distressingly unrelated to important student behaviours.

In such institutions, the student who values what he is learning because it intrigues him or because he wants to use it in a profession or some other aspect of living may be at a disadvantage. The rewards may accrue most easily to the student who is not primarily interested in the learning itself but to him for whom *any* learning will do, regardless of how absorbing or useful or permanent it is, provided it gets him a marketable ticket of approval.

We are unavoidably struck by the *alienated* nature of much of the learning activity that goes on in our universities and schools (see Holly, 1971). How closely such activity often resembles what Karl Marx (1844) described as alienated labour — to be recognized:

. . . in the fact that labour is *external* to the worker, i.e. it does not belong to his essential being; that in his work therefore he does not affirm himself, does not feel content but unhappy, does not develop freely his body and ruins his mind. The worker therefore only feels himself outside his work, and in his work feels outside himself . . . . It is therefore not the satisfaction of a need, it is merely a means to satisfy needs external to it. Its alien character emerges clearly in the fact that as soon as no physical or other compulsion exists, labour is shunned like the plague. (p. 69)

Alienation and instrumentality perhaps reach their apotheosis in the assessment technology associated with 'behaviour modification' and the 'token economy' (see Ayllon and Azrin, 1968). Such technology, based on Skinnerian principles of reinforcement, is already in use in schools for 'difficult' children and in mental hospitals. The child or patient is rewarded for approved behaviour, e.g. keeping quiet in class or making his bed, by tokens which can be saved up and eventually traded for some valued privilege like the opportunity to play or to see a film. The focus is not on valuing the activity that more powerful people approve of but on valuing the approval. It is difficult to see how the latter can lead to the former. One of Schulz's 'Peanuts' cartoons hits the nail on the head when young Schroeder tells Lucy that he is learning to play all of the Beethoven sonatas; Lucy, obviously impressed, asks him what he will *win* if he does learn to play them all; on being told that he won't win anything, she asks 'What's the sense in doing something if you don't win a prize?'.

To survive, the student often needs to 'play the system' and 'psych out' his teachers. He must find his way round what Benson Snyder (1970) called 'the hidden curriculum'. That is, the range of implicit demands that often runs counter to the explicit aims of the official curriculum. Thus the student will be at pains to discover which parts of the curriculum he can 'selectively neglect', and how to minimize risk and maximize his returns to effort. For example, he may find that rote-learning sometimes pays better dividends than striving after under-standing. Again, he may feel it prudent to side-step challenging courses or assignments, even though they might seem to offer him help in his weak areas, in favour of exercises relying more on capacities he knows he already possesses. Not unreasonably, this will annoy teachers who honestly want students to explore ideas of their own and take risks intellectually (see Torbert and Hackman, 1969).

Students may also reckon on the teacher or examiner having prejudices or idiosyncracies that they should cater to, or at least avoid falling foul of. Crudely, does he reward students for sharing his opinions as well as for a good grasp of facts and methods? That students are not being unduly cynical may be inferred from the chilling matter-of-factness of a footnote (referring especially to fields such as sociology and history) in an article on university examinations (Ager and Weltman, 1967):

> . . . there is a tendency for teaching faculties to build up a staff of fairly compatible academic or political viewpoints who may dis-criminate against students that apply themselves to the literature of a school they despise or are not familiar with. Under continuous assessment the student could not afford to write term time essays of which his tutors would disapprove. [This would imply] a policy in which continuous assessment could be used to move the examination marks up but not down (it being assumed that the student will write 'orthodox' answers in examinations to maximize his marks).

From here it is but a step for the instrumental student to decide that a carefully cultivated personal relationship with his tutor can be made to work to his advantage in times of assessment. Quite apart from the quality of his learning, the student may believe he can win approval (or at least avoid disfavour) by proper attention to personal appearance, punctuality, class attendance, style of speech, respectful manner and generally 'buttering up to' the assessor in the most subtle way he can. Howard Becker quotes a practitioner of this art of ingratiating oneself with teachers:

> What I do is apple-polishing, but it's not so obvious as that. . . . I might figure out a good question to ask them. That'll show them that I'm really thinking about the course. And sometimes I just go up and say hello and we sit down and start talking about things. . . . Now my English teacher last year, he was a tough one to figure out. . . . Finally, I figured it out, I praised him, that's what he liked. It paid off too. I got my mark raised a whole grade. (p. 99)

Students who are less aggressively instrumental may simply *worry* about the impression they are making on their teachers. Peter Vandome *et al* (1973) speak of students 'who feel that informal conversation with the staff will reveal them as "shallow thinkers" or who do not seek advice on troublesome problems in case they are thought "dense"'. Regardless of whether they are instrumentally inclined or not, some students find it difficult to open themselves as they might to their tutor's help if they know that he is also to be their judge.

Carolyn Miller and Malcolm Parlett (1973), in their field study of university students, identified three broad types of student attitude to 'playing the system'. They were particularly interested in the extent to which students were concerned about 'cues' given them by staff as to likely examination topics and how to create a good impression in class. Almost half the students they met appeared to be 'cue-deaf'. In general, they believed that revising everything was the best recipe for exam success, and that the impression they made in class would not affect the marking. A second group, not quite as large. were labelled 'cue-conscious'. These students tended to believe the cues were very important and should be looked out for and to hope that they were making a good impression on their tutors. The third category, however, a much smaller one, was labelled 'cue-seekers' because they actively sought out cues by button-holing staff and they deliberately attempted to create a good impression. Cue-seekers tended to get the best degrees and cue-deaf students the poorest.

Across all categories, however, the students were resolutely instrumental, the one exception being a cue-conscious student who confessed:

> I tend to spend a lot of time on things I am really interested in, so I won't get a good degree. If I swotted away diligently, I would get a better degree but I wouldn't be so intellectually broadened. (p. 56)

Even the cue-seekers, said to study extremely hard and have strong interest in certain of their subjects, were forced to sacrifice intrinsic interest for extrinsic reward when faced with what they regarded as 'artificial' assessment, e.g.:

> What is the purpose of the examination game? . . . . You know you want to get a certain class of degree within the system, but as far as assimilating knowledge properly is concerned, it just doesn't work, because if you play the game properly you're choosing all the time, and not getting an overview because you know there will be a certain question you have to answer. (p. 53)

Up to a point, 'playing the system' is condoned, even encouraged, by teachers. After all, many of them may attribute their own success to their adaptive intelligence in the academic 'game'. Beyond a certain point, however, adaptive strategies may be deemed illegitimate. Students practising them may be castigated as 'cheats'.

The gravity of offence might be judged by the student's intentions and the negotiable value of the extrinsic rewards so obtained from assessment. We can posit a few points along a scale of increasing 'criminality'. At the 'petty' end, the student may habitually cultivate an 'interested' expression for the benefit of the teacher even when his mind is on other things. He may go further by actively voicing a keenness and interest which he does not feel. Rather more serious, since it implies both greater deliberation and more recordable rewards, is the strategy of 'copying' another student's work — perhaps on the basis of 'You do my maths homework and I'll do your French'. Passing off another person's work as one's own becomes even more serious when the intention is to obtain a better 'certificate' or 'qualification' than one otherwise would, e.g. by having someone else impersonate one in the examination room. Beyond this one could only skip the educational experience altogether and *buy* the diploma or degree of one's fancy from one of the many bogus colleges and universities still advertising in the U.S.A. and in Britain, or simply claim qualifications one does not possess and rely on the prospective employer not bothering to verify their existence! Thankfully, few students travel far along this scale. Nevertheless, Philip Jackson (1968) concludes, rather bleakly, that: 'Learning how to make it in school involves in part learning how to falsify our behaviour' (p. 27).

What side-effects does extrinsically-rewarding assessment have on the mental health and self-imaging of the young? It can hardly produce attitudes consistent with the liberalizing aims officially professed by

education. The need to bend one's creativity to the conquest of
'artificial' demands may lead to intellectual growth of a kind, but at the
cost of what sort of ethical and emotional surrender? 'We're only faking
it; we're not really making it,' lament Simon and Garfunkel.

4. The Competitive Aspects of Assessment

The side-effects of learning for the sake of extrinsic rewards are bad
enough. But what when these extrinsic rewards are in short supply?
When there are not enough to go round? The side-effects are then
worsened by competition. In one sense, of course, there is more than
enough knowledge available for everyone to have a sufficiency. As
Robert Paul Wolff (1969, p. 66) points out: 'The Pythagorean theorem
does not flicker and grow dim as more and more minds embrace it.'
Learning is a 'free commodity'. But only so long as we are thinking of
knowledge as a source of intrinsic, expressive rewards. Think instead of
'approved' knowledge, legitimated and reified as GCE 'passes',
admissions to college, university degrees, and the like. No longer is the
supply unlimited. For one person to get more, another must make do
with less. A great many assessment systems are competitive in that the
extrinsic rewards they offer are in short supply and each student who
wants them is asked to demonstrate that he is more deserving than
others, or others less deserving than he is.

Contesting with others over the extrinsic spoils of learning is one aspect
of competitive assessment. Another, upon which it depends and which
usually arises early in a child's educational career, before the extrinsic
rewards have become so tangible and external, is his teacher's
public comparison of one student with another. A child will not have
been in school many days before he is made aware of individual
differences among his classmates. Roy Nash (1973, p. 17) discovered
that pupils as young as eight years were able to say which children in the
class were better than them at reading, writing and number; and their
self-perceived class rank correlated highly with the rankings made by
the teacher at the researcher's request (and therefore not explicitly
available hitherto for communication to the children).

Such awareness can encourage learning that is motivated (extrinsically)
by what John Holt called 'the ignoble satisfaction of feeling that one is
better than someone else'. Jules Henry (1969) describes how a classroom
atmosphere of competitive assessment fosters such a tendency. Eleven-
year-old Boris is out at the blackboard publicly trying to simplify a

fraction while his teacher is being excruciatingly patient and restraining the rest of the class who are bursting to put Boris right. Boris is mentally paralyzed by the situation, however. So teacher finally asks Peggy, who can be relied on to know the correct answer:

> Thus Boris' failure has made it possible for Peggy to succeed; his depression is the price of her exhilaration, his misery is the occasion of her rejoicing. This is the standard condition of the American elementary school. . . . To a Zuni, Hopi, or Dakota Indian, Peggy's performance would seem cruel beyond belief, for competition, the wringing of success from somebody's failure, is a form of torture foreign to those noncompetitive Indians. . . . (p. 83)

But why should it be that Peggy gets a lift from knowing that she has 'beaten' Boris? To say that she has been publicly compared with him and proved superior in fraction-simplification is insufficiently explanatory. No doubt the teacher too is superior but she would hardly be expected to feel joyful on that account. Why, for instance, does Peggy not get satisfaction instead from trying to eradicate the difference between herself and Boris, e.g. by helping him reach the answer himself rather than telling him? And if she has already enjoyed the satisfaction of having climbed to a new standard of proficiency, higher than she has been before, why should she care one way or another to know that others have not yet reached this standard? Perhaps the reason is that she has been persuaded that teacher-approval, and whatever other more tangible extrinsic rewards may follow, are in short supply and to gain what she needs she must not simply (or even necessarily) improve but also get (or merely stay) ahead of others.

Students generally have been led to believe that they cannot all achieve a worthwhile level of learning. They, and for the most part their teachers, often assume that only a few can do very well, the majority doing moderately only, and a few doing poorly or even failing. This expectation is seen institutionalized among teachers who 'grade on the curve'. (The practice is to be found in education everywhere, although the terminology is American — see Terwilliger, 1971, pp. 74-100 for a discussion of this and related techniques.) Such teachers, marking students' work with, say, the grades A, B, C, D, F, will set out with a predetermined grade-distribution in mind. (E is often skipped over because by 'happy' coincidence, the next letter is the initial letter of failure!) Among 100 students, for example, they may expect to award about 10 As, 20 Bs, 40 Cs, 20 Ds and 10 Fs. (Figure 3.1 shows this expected distribution graphically — and also the underlying 'normal distribution curve' from which the method gets its name, and which we'll meet again later.) The teacher who is 'grading on the curve' may, on marking a given set of students, allow himself to vary the proportions slightly. But he would likely feel uneasy if, say, twice as many students as expected appeared to deserve an A or a B. He might also fear being reproached by colleagues for lowering standards. Some teachers guard against this by making it a principle *never* to award an A. According to a French adage quoted by Remi Clignet (1974, p. 349), the maximum '20 is given only to God, 19 to his saints, 18 to the professor's professor, 17 to the professor himself' — so the student of French composition can't be expected to score more than 16!

Figure 3.1
Grading on the Curve

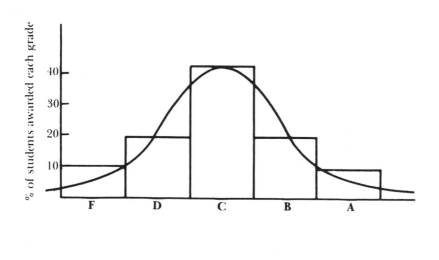

The expectation that students with A or B (or their equivalents in other systems for dispensing approval) will be in the minority has a strong hold in classrooms. Too easily it becomes a self-fulfilling prophecy: 'We can't expect the majority of students to do very well — so don't blame us for the failures.' When year after year the General Nursing Council failed one-third of candidates taking S.R.N. examinations after three years of preparation, few questioned the proportion (NT, 1972). Fear of passing too many students is still preventing the Esperanto Teachers' Association from getting Esperanto examined as a GCE 'O'-level subject. They are told the language is 'too easy'. Too many students would get top grades.

The competitive nature of public examinations was brutally brought home to me a few years ago when I was first impressed by the instructional potential of programmed learning. In an excess of enthusiasm I suggested to a GCE examiner that with the help of well-written programmes, we'd soon enable nearly all students to pass 'O'-level mathematics. 'Oh no you won't,' he said, 'we'll just raise the standard.' Conversely, the Black Paper pessimist (see Pollard, 1971) can accuse this same self-fulfilling mechanism of disguising the fact that standards are falling as the quality of candidates declines!

Such viewpoints I have since found elaborated in Brereton (1944) who records, almost as an educational 'law', that: 'the standard of an examination adjusts itself to the standard of those taking it' (p. 43). While suggesting the possibility that, as a result of the war, children may become more aware of and more knowledgeable about geography, he considers it obvious that School Certificate examinations should continue to give credit only to about half the candidates. He justifies this implicit raising of the required standard partly in order to encourage pupils to continue caring about geography lessons (as opposed to reading the newspapers) and partly because it would be unfair to give pupils taking geography a better chance of reaching university than pupils taking, say, physics under the war-time difficulties caused by shortage of laboratories and physics teachers.

In such situations — where the best X% of students are to get the As, the next best nX% the Bs, and so on — the grade awarded to a student depends not on the absolute level of performance he attains but on how he performs *relative to* other students. That is, he may improve his performance by 100%, but if everyone else improves similarly his grade will be no higher than before. To get a better grade he must take it from one of the students above him by out-performing him.

What are the side-effects of an assessment system believed by students (whether rightly or wrongly) to be competitive? For most students they are centred in the need to come to terms with failure. The psychiatrist Ronald Laing suggested once that 'to be a success in our society one has to learn to dream of failure'. And Bergman's film *Wild Strawberries* shows us an elderly professor at the peak of his career, about to receive the highest academic honour in the land, who dreams the night before of failing an examination.

For a few to emerge as outstandingly successful the majority must fail — to varying degrees. The failure may be only partial. Indeed, had the student been in a different (e.g. less selective) school or college, his performance might well have made him a success. But, by comparison with those he has been led to emulate, he has fallen short. Of course, it should be possible for a student who has 'failed' at one learning task to compensate by his success on another task. Unfortunately, the ethos of competitive assessment often leads the student who has failed on a few tasks (e.g. learned more slowly than other people) to feel that he has failed *as a person*. As a 'failure' himself he may (like Scott's dogs, p. 30) then become less capable of succeeding in subsequent tasks. His only consolation may be that most of his friends will soon be those who are failing at about the same level as he is. Between them they may be able to construct mutually defensive attitudes to those above them and those (if any) below them in the hierarchy.

These defensive attitudes, based on fear, envy, resentment and self-hatred, may be of various kinds. The least active response is what Philip Jackson (1968, p. 27) describes as 'devaluing the evaluations to the point where they no longer matter very much'. Perhaps this attitude of 'cooling it', 'turning off', 'keeping his head down', 'disengaging' on the part of the failing student is a special case of what Roy Cox (1967) had in mind when he said: 'It is clear that where students are assessed in a way which is not seen to be relevant to what they are aiming at they will tend to distort and degrade the assessment so that it does not become a source of esteem.'

More actively, students who cannot 'adjust' equally to being labelled 'failures' may seek alternative sources of esteem. Perhaps through their attempts to pull school (or society) apart out of hours. As Dr. Samuel Johnson pointed out: 'By exciting emulation and comparisons of superiority, you lay the foundation of lasting mischief; you make brothers and sisters hate each other.' A U.S. Senate subcommittee survey of 1975 reports the case of a seventeen-year-old Detroit schoolgirl who was awarded massive damages after being beaten up and stabbed with pencils by thirty girl classmates who apparently resented that she was more attractive than they and received better grades. This case may be an example, more physical than usual, of what Arnold Wesker calls 'Lilliputianism — the poisonous need to cut other people down to size'.

Who knows how much of the physical damage done to property and people arises out of the resentment and frustration smouldering on from school-days? (See Hargreaves, 1967, and Lacey, 1970, for accounts of the 'D-stream sub-culture' in secondary schools).

Peter Vandome and his colleagues (1972) neatly sum up some of the pernicious side-effects of competitive assessment at college level:

> Students feel they will gain through the poor performance of others and suffer by imparting their own knowledge to fellow students. In this way, a potentially rich source of knowledge — communication of ideas among students — tends to be stifled. To the extent that it does take place, any exchange is biased by the way in which a student's 'self-image' and his image of his fellows is affected by their grades. A 50% student for instance will think twice before putting forward one of his ideas for discussion with a group of 60% students. This is relevant not only to informal interchange between students but also to tutorial discussion. Competitive rather than co-operative behaviour may be manifested in other ways such as the 'illegal borrowing' of library books.

Sadly, teachers too are sometimes caught up in a competitive assessment system – perhaps even as beneficiaries. While the students compete for honours within their class, the teacher may be looking to the class as a whole, competing with other teachers' classes, to bring *him* esteem and promotion. The following quotation from Norman Conway, a grammar school chemistry teacher interviewed by Brian Jackson and Dennis Marsden (1962), shows how the competition for scarce university places (and ultimately for a better job for teacher), especially in the context of bureaucratic mass-assessment which is what we are going on to look at in the next section, can allow the instrumental pursuit of extrinsic rewards to drive out the expressive 'educational side':

> I reckon I can do 'A' level chem. in four terms. Four terms flat out mind. We have to go really fast. We have tests twice a week, but we get the results. For instance, last year I got an open at Pembroke, Cambridge, and an exhibition at Trinity Hall, Cambridge, and then I got half-a-dozen places. I've got fourteen places in the last two years and then these opens. I do pretty well; my results are all right. The way we teach, we teach for results. I want the passes, the schols and all those things. Tests all the time, and scrub the teaching methods, forget about the educational side . . . . What I want now is a head of department in a really good school, and then I'd do what our head of department has done. I'd put on the

pressure, really hard. Really work those children, tests, tests, tests, and get the results. Get them the results they should have, and that would establish me, wouldn't it? It would give me a reputation. People would know that I could do the job. I might slacken off when I got established — perhaps after ten years or so. I might start looking round and thinking more about the educational side. But you've got to establish yourself first, haven't you? (pp. 36-7)

5. The Bureaucratic Aspects of Assessment

When is assessment bureaucratic? Consider an extreme scenario: You have been summonsed to appear in court, some months in the future, to be tried on a number of offences which you may or may not have committed prior to your trial. In due course, you arrive in court only to find it empty of judge, jury and counsel. Nothing but a tape-recorder and a set of instructions await you. You are instructed to defend yourself as best you can on a number of standard charges within a strictly limited time-period. You are not told the precise nature of the evidence against you. Nor do you know sufficient about the alleged nature of the offences to be quite sure what evidence would count best in your defence. Judgement is to be made on the basis of the tape-recorded defences you leave behind. You have no idea who laid the charges against you in the first place; nor, when the verdict of the court is mailed to you some weeks later, do you know who made the judgement and decided the various restrictions that are to be imposed on your future movements. There is no means of appeal. Your only consolation is that thousands of others are being judged by identical process.

I do not need to point out all the parallels between this Kafkaesque experience and that of the candidate in a public examination. The feature I am interested in at present is its *impersonality*. It is impersonal in two senses. Firstly, in that you cannot identify the persons who are assessing you. Secondly, in that they, whoever they are, choose not to regard you as an individual or meet you personally to hear your case.

Norman Morris (1969) neatly exposes the bureaucratic approach: '. . . as likely as not the examiner has no interest in us as individuals. He is merely assessing us in order to maintain the efficiency of something else. In this sense the examination is an instrument of policy, designed to preserve a preconceived standard elsewhere.' Bureaucracies deal in huge numbers, following laws, formulating policies, seeking objectivity, preferring standardized routines, disliking exceptions and special cases, venerating, above all, administrative convenience. They are not normally staffed — whether in government, the health service, big business, the armed services, the trade union movement, education, or whatever — by people who take pleasure in celebrating the quirky individualities of other persons.

In their study of assessment in a university, Carolyn Miller and Malcolm Parlett (1973) explicitly distinguish between the 'bureaucratic' and the 'personalized' style. They see the predominant style as reflecting the extent to which the teaching-learning setting is impersonal or personal:

> In the first setting, for instance, the tutor (who was the only individual to know a student's work in any detail) neither set nor marked the exam papers of his students. The student did not know who his examiner was. And the tutors, though they got to know their students 'quite well' were still often surprised by results that struck them as 'odd'. In the contrasting setting . . . , the lecturer was also internal examiner, setting and marking student's papers while having a clear idea of the abilities, interests and previous performances of the students. Moreover, the student knew who the examiner was, (and in some cases also the name of the external examiner). (p. 15)

The Open University operates a highly bureaucratic assessment system, combining both continuous assessment and examinations. At intervals during his course, the student sends in his assignments to the University's headquarters. These assignments may be objective tests for marking by the computer, or they may be essays for marking by a human tutor. The student may or may not be in occasional face-to-face, or telephonic, contact with the tutor who marks his assignments. Thousands of students, up and down the nation, may all have been faced by the same assignment questions at the same time, though they may have been offered some limited choice. Examinations are compulsory even for a course that is the equivalent of less than a term in a 'conventional' university. Students produce answer-papers under normal test conditions and their papers are sent off to a set of markers who do not know the student's previous work and who give him no feedback at all, though it is usually possible for him to work out his overall grade on the exam. The bureaucracy generated by the need to cope centrally with tens of thousands of 'remote' students is tempered with considerable humanity by the tutorial and counselling staff spread around the Open University's thirteen regions. As one senior counsellor, David Kennedy (1973), cautions: 'this University, with its complex academic and administrative processes, will grow in moral stature only to the degree it indulges in self-questioning and heart-searching over the fall of even one sparrow' (p. 1).

But, by and large, bureaucratic assessment is less the rule in a student's university years than in those examination-dominated years immediately preceding them. (See Montgomery, 1965, for a history of English examinations as 'administrative devices'.) In Britain nowadays, the student is first likely to become aware of bureaucratic assessment as he approaches the age of '16-plus'. Here, if he is considered a likely candidate, he will prepare for the examinations leading to a Certificate of Secondary Education or General Certificate of Education (ordinary level) — one 'certificate' for each subject he 'passes'. This 16-plus assessment is big business. In the summer of 1974 more than 800,000 GCE candidates were taking more than 2¼ million subject papers between them. (In the same year, rather fewer CSE candidates generated almost as many subject entries.) All the GCE students' scripts (and most of the CSE scripts) have, of course, to be routed around Britain to the 'out-workers' who do the marking, and eventually results have to be returned to the students. The postal bill must be enormous for the annually growing traffic of items, and it is scarcely surprising that one GCE examining board alone (and there are eight) has an annual expenditure well over £2½ million. Naturally figures like this would pale into insignificance beside those current in the United States where mass testing supports a multi-million dollar test-publishing industry. One non-profit organization alone — Educational Testing Service, whose battery of tests and examinations helps control entry to the U.S. meritocracy — has an annual income of $50 million (see Rein, 1974). Yet size in itself is not a feature that damns the system. Giants can be benign. And large numbers of sixteen-year-olds could be satisfactorily assessed, for all reasonable purposes, without suffering the baleful effects of this particular giant system. No, these side-effects spring not so much from size as from *standardization*. In its zeal to claim comparability between large numbers of candidates (though the need would still arise, if less painfully, were there only two candidates), the examining authority imposes uniform conditions on candidates. (We won't examine you in Esperanto because it doesn't reach the same standard of difficulty as other languages. We won't examine you in anything except on our standard syllabus. We won't examine you at all if you have left school and are studying the syllabus under non-standard conditions.) The underlying assumptions are laid bare by Oppenheim *et al* (1967) who, although explicitly referring to university examinations, might well be analysing the 16-plus:

> Behind this lies the ideology of 'equality of opportunity', so that all students have an equal chance to fail, to pass or to distinguish between themselves. This uniformity is somewhat mitigated by allowing students a *choice* of questions. This practice makes very little allowance for the individual patterns of growth and interests of candidates. (In some cases we *do* set individual examinations for *higher* degrees.)

> The ideology of 'equality of opportunity' is itself part of broader ideas about fair play — all students must receive equal tuition, and sit for the same examinations, with no favours. This attitude is reinforced by the power of universities to bestow social mobility. The question is always: is this examination practice fair to other students? and not: is this practice fair to this particular student?

The reality of this last dilemma is well-caught in the example posed by Brereton (p. 54) who seems to settle for unfairly devaluing the knowledge of geography students in order not to be unfair to physics students. The 'fairness to whom' criterion is an important one when we consider the main bastion of standardized, bureaucratic assessment — the uniform syllabus.

To treat people eqully is not necessarily to treat them fairly. Indeed, people being so different, equal treatment probably means injustice for most. If I wish to offer myself as a candidate for an 'O'-level GCE in law, I must demonstrate my ability on the same set of syllabus topics as everyone else. Are these the only topics that could be considered to constitute 'law'? *No, there are many viable ways of construing the subject.* Then why can't I (and all others who care to) choose a set of viable topics to suit my own interests? *Because this might give you an advantage over others who tackle the set syllabus and would anyway make you difficult to compare with others, especially if everyone did it.* So we must all forgo the chance of being assessed on what most interests us and what we are most likely to be best at? *Yes, but it's the same for everybody.* It doesn't seem fair. *Perhaps it's not fair to individuals, but it's fair to students as a whole.*

Of course, the standard examination syllabus has long been accused of providing a mechanism whereby the ruling interests in society can define what is to count as knowledge — and determine what is learned.

Thorstein Veblen (1918) cannot have been the first to identify industrial leaders as the real clients of the university and claim that the pressure for examinations and grading arises out of their need for a bureaucratically efficient estimate of graduates' usability. Similarly, the universities, who control most of the GCE exam boards, have traditionally been chided for imposing criteria appropriate to university selection not only on likely applicants, but also, through syllabus uniformity, on students who have no intention of ever going near a university. 'Why should the curriculum of the rest be determined so largely by that required for the university students?' asked C. W. Valentine (1938) at a time when only about 5% of secondary school pupils went on to university. (Even within universities it is sometimes claimed that a syllabus is geared not to the needs of the majority of students but to those of the precious few who will go on to become researchers.)

Nowadays the same examinations are used, as Harry Judge (1974) points out: 'to assist everybody to select everybody else for everything' (p. 47). The lure of a prestigious standard examination syllabus is strong. William Taylor (1963) shows how it helped subvert the new ideas for a 'secondary modern' curriculum as, in all fairness, schools began entering their pupils, who had failed the 11-plus, for GCE. The need for external recognition fed upon itself, more and more examination work was demanded, traditional subjects and teaching methods regained dominance, streaming and segregation fostered success-rates, and thus secondary modern schools largely failed to develop an identity separate from the grammar schools whose assessment procedures they were aping.

There is little doubt that, just as trade follows the flag, so curriculum follows the examination. This is quite contrary to the intentions of the Board of Education of 1912 who, in initiating a national examination system out of the hitherto diverse activities of numerous local examining bodies, posited as a 'cardinal principle' that 'the examination should follow the curriculum and not determine it'. The Board had in mind that schools should not be dependent on some national curriculum but should have 'the right to submit their own syllabus for examination'. This right had been available with some of the boards examining for the School Leaving Certificate that preceded the Board's initiative and it continued to be available in the School Certificate Examinations that followed. Few schools exercised that right under either system. Nor have they done so more recently, despite the widely-acclaimed upsurge in 'curriculum innovation', when given the opportunity since 1964 under Modes 2 and 3 of CSE (and similarly with GCE in theory) to propose their own syllabus. Under Mode 3, schools also do their own assessing, subject to their grades being 'moderated' by external assessors. By 1974, Modes 2 and 3 together still accounted for less than a quarter of subject entries in CSE.

Perhaps teachers lack confidence to design their own curricula and assessment procedures. Perhaps they are wary of the enormous amount of extra work involved. Perhaps they fear that 'home-made' systems may put their pupils at some subsequent selection disadvantage compared with others who have taken the 'standard' syllabus, or spoil the chances of any who have to move to another school. Perhaps they find all the flexibility they can cope with under Mode 1. But certainly they cannot claim to be powerless to break away from the standard syllabus. They cannot so easily justify seeing the examinations almost superstitiously, like their pupils so often do as 'something that happens to them' rather than something they can influence or even control. CSE offers an alternative to the fatalistic acceptance implied in the comments of Charles Blount (1973), senior history teacher in a grammar school:

> When you move on to the upper part of the school, then you're tied to a rigid syllabus which . . . is always too long for the time available, and you've always got the feeling — and it's not only a feeling, it's a fact — that you've got to keep moving along. The result is that you've got to stick fairly closely to the imposed [sic] syllabus or you won't cover it. So I would say that nobody should take O-level history if they can possibly avoid it, because that merely has the result of the door of the prison house closing at the beginning of the fifth form instead of the beginning of the sixth form.

However, few schools reject the 'imposed' syllabuses in order to construct an assessable curriculum relevant to the interests of their particular staff and 'children as a whole'. Fewer still venture to develop multiple curricula appropriate to the diverse needs of *individual* students. The ruling maxim still is 'horses for courses' rather than 'courses for horses'. The student seems to be offered several kinds of freedom — to aim for GCE or CSE, to choose this subject or that, to answer questions, 3, 4, 7 and 10 rather than, say, questions 1, 5, 8 and 9 — but eventually his autonomy must deposit him in a box where he can be compared with others who have performed the same standard tasks. The revelatory optimism of William S. Learned (1935) turns out to have been at least forty years ahead of its time:

> The important question in an individual's education has shifted

entirely. Instead of asking solely, 'Have you at some time learned this or that?' specified by the institution as of old, the question which it now seems most profitable to hold before each student is 'What do you know?' — meaning by that 'What knowledge, skills and appreciations from the many sources available to you, have you, by virtue of your own evolving interests and abilities, gathered, organized and matured within you to the point of effective mastery and use? You are an artist; your materials are all about you; what sort of educated man do you have in mind to seek to become?' (p. 60)

Indeed the current examination ideology is such that 40% of British sixteen-year-olds will not even be asked if they've 'learned this or that'. It is still taken for granted by the GCE / CSE system that some horses will be too lame for any course. At present, the 'top' 20% of children are expected to take GCE, while the next 20% take a 'good' CSE and the next 20% take some CSE subjects. The remaining 40% are to be cooled out as 'unexaminable'. Admittedly, this is just half of the 80% who were previously cooled out by the 11-plus tests, but we are still talking of upwards of a hundred thousand young people a year leaving school with 'nothing to show for it' in terms of the national currency of creditation. However much some may wish to see the whole system dismantled, so long as it *is* running it should not run to the disadvantage of some of its would-be clientele.

In effect, two out of every five school-leavers are failed by the system. But failed, perhaps, before they even realize they have been judged and deemed wanting. Their situation recalls a dialogue, an exchange between Andy Capp and his wife, Florrie, in one of Smythe's *Daily Mirror* cartoons:

Florrie: Y'know what *you* are, don't yer? A *failure*!

Andy: A failure? 'ow can I be? I've never even TRIED!

This automatic manufacture of failure for 40% of the children compelled to stay in school led one headmaster (quoted by Joan Simon, 1973) to claim that the compulsory raising of the school-leaving age to 16 implies 'a civic right to have one's work nationally assessed'. Interestingly enough, in the first examination year since the raising of the school-leaving age in Britain (1975), the stayers-on were taking and passing examinations that they would not previously have had a try at — to such effect that only about 21% of school-leavers had no examination passes at all. Some 150,000 extra children had at least some work 'nationally assessed'. We must wait to see whether this becomes the new norm.

But the bureaucracy has its arrangements; they are highly efficient; and they are not lightly to be interfered with. Nor are radically new clienteles easily contemplated. Examinations Bulletin Number 23, issued by the Schools Council (1971) and discussing the need for a new combined examination to replace both GCE and CSE, argues the case for continuing to exclude the lower 40% (without apparent awareness that it sounds faintly contradictory in a document entitled A *Common System of Examining at 16+*) chiefly on the breathtakingly timid grounds that to extend the range 'would require the exploration of a considerable new area of assessment in which experience is at present very limited, and in which some largely novel methods of assessment might well need to be devised' (p. 9).

This last is, of course, the real rub. Current assessment methods work well enough with the students for whom they work well. But examiners are aware that not all students express themselves best through their written work. Whether they value qualities that cannot be so expressed is another question. Edgar Friedenberg (1970) points out that: 'Educational measurement . . . cannot usually muster either the imagination or the sponsorship needed to search out and legitimate new conceptions of excellence which might threaten the hegemony of existing elites.' There are more ways of coming to know a person than through poring over his recorded products — words on paper, drawings, models, etc. Many people best reveal their powers — for example of creativity, fluency, imagination, reasoning, drive, persistence, empathy — only in *interpersonal* situations; that is, not when faced with a blank piece of paper or the mental image of a remote identi-kit examiner, but only when involved in the cut-and-thrust of debate with a respected opponent, or the mutually supportive milieu of a small group with a purpose to achieve, or the quiet reflective conversation with a probing but sympathetic partner. As Robert Zoellner (1969) suggests, in dealing with a student who 'knows more than he can say (in writing)':

> The solution, of course, may be to exploit other available channels. Indeed, the most compelling and suggestive office-interview 'happening' occurs when I read the student's utterly opaque and impenetrable sentence or paragraph aloud to him. 'Mr Phillips,' I say, 'I simply can't make head nor tail out of this paragraph; what in the world were you trying to say?' When I pose

this question in this situation, large numbers of students, certainly a majority, respond with a bit of behaviour which I suggest may be of immense significance for the teaching of composition. They open their mouths, and *they say the thing they were unable to write.* 'Well, Dr. Zoellner,' they usually begin, 'all I meant to say in that paragraph was that . . .,' and out it comes, a sustained, articulated, rapid-fire segment of 'sound-stream', usually from five to fifteen seconds' duration, which communicates to me effectively and quickly what they 'had in mind' when they produced the impenetrable paragraph I hold in my hand.

We have scarcely yet begun to search for ways of coming to know what the student can do (let alone what he is) rather than whether he can do certain standardized tasks. Elliott Eisner, (1972, p. 211) reminds us that 'It's one thing to ask, "Did the student learn what (he or I) intended?" It is another to ask, "What did the student learn?"' One thing we can be sure of is that such enlightened assessing is likely to cost a great deal more than the current methods. It may well not even be possible in principle, if the bureaucratic ideals of uniform procedures and impersonal 'objective' standards are to be adhered to.

6.   The Nature of Specific Assessment Techniques

There are many different ways of coming to know the student — through conversation, observation, multiple-choice tests, essays, examinations, and so on. We can run into side-effects if we rely too much on any one such method of assessment, overlooking the fact that each has distinctive features of its own. Take, for instance, a teaching-learning system that relied entirely on, say, multiple-choice testing. Because of students' expectations of such tests, it might suffer the side-effect of students learning to scan the learning experience for factual, testable items, gobbets of detail or technical terms, rather than looking for the larger, encompassing insights that might be demanded of them in essays. Many critics would suggest that U.S. education suffers from undue emphasis on multiple-choice tests — from standardized testing of various kinds of achievement in elementary school through to the vital college entrance examinations and beyond. Jacques Barzun, in his foreword to Banesh Hoffman's book *The Tyranny of Testing* (1962) reminds U.S. educators that:

A pupil does not really know what he has learned till he has organized it and explained it to someone else. The mere recognition of what is right in someone else's wording is only the beginning of the awareness of truth. As for the writing of essays — and the art of correcting them — excellence can of course not be achieved without steady practice, which, once again, the fatal ease of mechanical testing tends to discourage. But if the tendency of such tests is to denature or misrepresent knowledge, to discourage the right habits of the true student, and to discriminate against the original in favour of the routine mind, of what use are such tests to a nation that has from its beginnings set a high value on instruction and the search for truth?

But multiple-choice testing is not the only assessment technique that might run into side-effects. Any technique may do so, if over-applied or expected to provide knowledge of student characteristics for which it is inappropriate. Take the celebrated case of the imperial Chinese government and the essay assessment which dominated its civil service selection procedure for about fifteen centuries (see Morris, 1969; Hyam, 1974; Miyazaki, 1976). In early times, Chinese assessment had been very practical and directly related to the skills required in leaders. Would-be governors, as potential leaders both in battle and in peaceful social life, had been assessed on their ability to ride fast, shoot arrows at targets, and sing songs of their own composition to their own guitar accompaniment. Gradually, perhaps as it became less necessary for the governor actually to be the best horseman, archer or minstrel himself, candidates were more and more expected to write essays about classical archery and horsemanship and music, rather than perform themselves. Eventually, as it became clear that such assessment was not really relevant, further essays were required of them on such subjects as civil law, military affairs, agriculture, geography of the empire, and so on. Also, students were examined on the theory and philosophy of what makes a good judge and governor. But, Norman Morris (1969) tells us: 'All these subjects came to be taught and examined on the basis of what the old classics said about them. . . . The emphasis shifted from the subjects to what the classics said about them, then to the classics themselves, until fossilization set in.' The ultimate symbol of this was the so-called 'eight-legged essay' on a Confucian theme; it had to contain a specified number of calligraphic characters and eight paragraphs arranged as follows: analysis of the theme; amplification of theme; explanation; post-explanation; argument 1; reassertion of theme; argument 2; argument 3. Eventually, as Ronald Hyam (1974) says: 'this form of writing put such a premium on stereotyped techniques of antithetical structure at the expense of knowledge and content that it became a notorious symbol of all that was rigid and stylized in old imperial China, and its abolition was decreed in 1901.' Remi Clignet (1974, p. 335) sees a direct parallel between ancient China and modern France where 'Access to the top echelons of the elite depends upon the demonstration of literary skills whose relevance to strictly administrative tasks remains problematic', specifically that essay writers should adhere to the Hegelian formula of a thesis, followed by an anti-thesis, reconciled in a synthesis.

There are many who would argue that, like nineteenth-century China (and modern France?), twentieth-century Britain is too essay-ridden (and especially too examination-essay-ridden). Many would feel the writing of an essay to be an unnatural act of communication. Not least in its dodging of the issue as to whom it should be addressed. Someone more knowledgeable than the writer? If so, what's the point of telling him what he already knows? Someone less knowledgeable? If so, what pre-requisite understandings can one assume of him? Does every detail have to be explained?'Write as if you were addressing the general reader' said one examination paper quoted approvingly by Stephen Wiseman (1969, p. 181). But would that be the 'general reader' of, say, *The Daily Mirror,* or of *The Times* — as if we need ask, but why shouldn't we? In 'real life', if we are moved to communicate our joy or indignation, sparkling new insights or painstaking reflections on something that moves us or intrigues us, we are unlikely to do so through any medium resembling the essay. More likely we'll button-hole whichever of our family, friends or colleagues we feel to be sufficiently 'on our wavelength' in such matters, and engage them in conversation. If no such confidants are immediately to hand, we may telephone them or write them a letter. True, some few of us may feel moved to express ourselves in the form of a poem, a letter to the editor of our favourite newspaper, a report to an appropriate committee, or even a book like this one. But none of these spoken or written communications would have much in common, either in form or intent, with the essays pupils write for assessment purposes in school. Most differently of all, perhaps, we would hope to be telling people things they didn't already know.

Doubtless our preoccupation with essays and other 'assessable *products*' is symptomatic and supportive of the bureaucratic tendencies in assessment we discussed in the previous section. Essays and other written offerings do lend themselves to being pored over and quantified by examiners with an ease that on-going *processes* (e.g. conversation, acting, debating, team-work, etc.) do not. Thus we may devalue many invaluable skills and humane gifts that children have, simply because they are not assessable in written form. We risk committing McNamara's Fallacy (named after the ex-U.S. Secretary of Defence) by making the measurable important when we would be better employed attempting to make the important measurable (or at least discernible).

7. The Giving of Grades

Much of the criticism of assessment is aimed at 'the grading system'. Thus we might expect to find that the giving of grades has a crop of side-effects peculiarly its own. This, however, is not the case. The side-effects usually blamed on grades are, in fact, those we have already seen associated with other aspects of assessment systems — emphasis on the easily-measured, unfairness, standardization, competition, extrinsic rewards. The giving of grades no doubt aggravates and facilitates such effects but mostly they could survive in its absence. So are grades an empty symbol, guilty by association but harmless in themselves? Not quite. Their special 'sin' is simply less obvious, being one of omission. (Remember Sherlock Holmes's clue of the dog that *didn't* bark in the night?) Grades are more to be blamed for what they don't do than for what they do do.

And what grades don't do is tell all that is known about the student's performance or abilities. Information is lost. Consider the assessment process. Someone — teacher, examiner, 'assessor' — observes the student at work, or perhaps interacts with him in some way, or more commonly analyses products of the student's work. The assessor forms impressions of the qualities and attainments discernible in the student's work — his interests and aversions, hang-ups and hobby-horses, strengths and weaknesses. These impressions he could perhaps spell out, verbalizing them for the benefit of the student and anyone else who has a legitimate interest in knowing how the student is seen by people close to him. Sometimes he will do this for an individual assessment event (e.g. in commenting on an essay):

> You have shown a general understanding of the assignment, but could have improved your answers by closer attention to detail. In the first section (music) you failed to answer the part of the question that asked why the particular form used was appropriate, rather than the other forms available. In the second section, although you noted some of the imagery and discussed it intelligently, you often moved too far away from the imagery itself and relied on an 'outside' view of the poem (what you thought it must be about) to interpret it. In the final section you did pay close

attention to detail, but it remained only observation of detail. You failed to connect the various elements together or to move *through* the detail to the larger issues of the painting. See the introductory section in the Unit and its explanation of the movement from meaning to form. It is a matter of working-at, responding to the detail, exploring the 'resonances' of the detail and moving from this to a full appreciation of the total effect. (Tutor's comments on an Open University student's assignment, quoted in Kennedy, 1974)

Such comments are more illuminating, particularly for the student, but also for anyone else concerned, than is a mark or grade or percentage label. (That student's essay, by the way, was graded C.) But when the assessor is expected merely to grade the product he will keep such insights to himself. Worse still, he perhaps never articulates them at all unless he expects to have to spell them out. And the tutor's impressions of one student are unlikely to remain vivid after he has looked at the work of a few more students. Thus his students will probably receive from him no feedback of a kind that might help them learn from his response to their work. Donald McIntyre (1970) illustrates what is missing when he suggests that the 'result' of a pupil's mathematics exam, *instead of* 40%, might be recorded as a 'diagnostic profile' thus:

> Has mastered ideas of variable and one-to-one correspondence; not yet clear about functions; gets confused with problems of proportions; still has difficulty in structuring verbal problems (lack of grammatical understanding?); geometry generally competent, but has not learned terminology adequately; considerable skill in analysing visual problems. ·

Important qualities and features differentiating one student from another are obliterated by the baldness of grades. Thus several students who've all got the same grade may have tackled quite different problems and in quite different ways. As a trivial example, one student may have scored five out of ten on his arithmetic test by answering the five additions correctly and the five subtractions incorrectly while his friend is given the same score for precisely the converse performance! Frances Stevens (1970) in reviewing the marking of examiners in 'A'-level English literature, compares the gradings given to two particular scripts and reveals how much information has been lost in labelling the girl C and the boy D:

> Is the more optimistic forecast to be made of the dutiful immature girl who has some mildly appreciative responses, knows her books and has paid careful attention to what she has been told to think,

but who has few independent ideas and writes with neither firmness nor joy; or of the mature and independent boy, who may not have studied his notes or perhaps his texts so thoroughly, but who has a sense of relevance, whose judgements are valid, who writes with assurance and betrays in his style . . . that he has made a genuine engagement with the literature he has encountered? (p. 130)

Whether or not the assessor's criteria were exactly the same as Frances Stevens's is neither here nor there. They are unlikely to have been less subjective — or contestable. Translating them into a grade is an act of reification, erecting a pseudo-objective façade on what is a very delicate personal judgement. One effect of this façade is to repel debate. The grade seems god-given and immutable whereas the grounds on which it was decided might seem only too human and open to dispute. If an assessor were to respond to the girl mentioned above in the terms of Frances Stevens's assessment, he might well find her anxious to draw his attention to other qualities of her work which had been overlooked and which might revise his overall assessment. Certainly it could lead to a valuable teacher-learner dialogue. In the context of bureaucratic assessment, however, it could only be regarded as 'noise in the system'.

Whether or not we're always aware of the fact, grades act like *averages*. They smooth out and conceal irregularities and variability. One essay may have both first-class and abysmal features and yet be graded neither A nor F; instead it may get a C which fails altogether in letting us know that it differs from another essay graded C which is consistently of that quality in all its parts. Similarly, of two 60% examination scripts, one may contain answers both of failure quality and distinction quality while the other is 60%-ish throughout. And of course, the same variability may lie behind the all-concealing degree class of 'lower second' or a diploma class of 'satisfactory' — for all we know. In short, numbers and labels do not allow us to discriminate even between stable performers and those not infrequently found (see Stevens, 1970, p. 125) 'in whose papers near-brilliance alternates with near-nonsense'.

Grades, percentages and category labels are hopelessly inadequate to convey the load of meaning that we sometimes believe we are putting into them and which other people desperately try to get out from them again. How could a single letter or number possibly tell as much, for example, as is contained in descriptive reports or profiles like those on page 69 or 235? There is a well-known Peanuts cartoon by Charles Schulz in which a girl is sitting at her school desk querying the C-grade she's been given for her 'sculpture' made from a coat-hanger. She wants to know whether she was judged on the piece of sculpture itself; and if so is it not true that time alone can judge a work of art? Or was she judged on her talent; if so, is it right that she should be judged on a part of life over which she has no control? If she was judged on her effort, then she regards the judgement as unfair since she tried as hard as she could. Was she being judged on what she had learned about the project; and if so, wasn't the teacher being judged on how well he had transmitted knowledge and therefore should he not share the C-grade? And finally, was she perhaps being judged by the inherent quality of the coat-hanger itself out of which her creation was made; and if so why should she be judged by the quality of the coat-hangers on which garments are returned by the laundry her parents patronize — since that's their responsibility shouldn't they share her grade? Her teacher's reply is not recorded.

I cannot applaud the rosy vision of a senior colleague whose spirited defence of grading (and rejection of profiles) climaxed as follows:

> Grading is a method of achieving a shorthand synthesis of every possible quality that one might wish to be included in a profile, consolidated into a symbol which examiners understand pragmatically with reference to a platonic point of reference existing in the minds of a group of examiners who have worked together, while a profile, however detailed, can never be more than an attempt to put down all those qualities.

To which perhaps the only reply is St. Augustine's lament:

> For so it is, O Lord my God, I measure it;
> But what it is that I measure I do not know.

8. The Reporting of Assessment Results

In Britain, assessment results are often reported in the press. Every summer, local newspapers will carry long lists naming school-children and the GCEs and CSEs they have gained. This is an interesting phenomenon, not to be taken for granted: what, for instance, would be our reactions if we opened the local newspaper to find it contained a list of all the people who had visited doctors during the previous week, together with the medical assessment of each patient's condition?

But in this section I am using the word 'report' more widely, to cover the publication of assessment results, by whatever means, and thereby encouraging others to believe that they share in the assessor's knowledge of the student. The assessor may, for example, report his assessment to the student concerned, to other teachers, to other students, to the student's parents, to his 'sponsor', to potential employers, and so on.

The Social Situation

Let us first establish the general social context for this passing on of information. Whenever we enter into a social relationship, whenever we do anything at all with other people, we open ourselves to their assessment. They form opinions of us, have an image of us, even judge us. If they did not, in some such sense and to some degree, get to know us, then we would be essentially unpredictable to them: they would not know what to expect of us or how to behave towards us. In informal relationships we expect people to make such assessments in the light of their own direct experience of us. Even here, however, some reporting occurs. People do share with others their impressions of mutual friends: 'What do you think of old X?' and 'How do you get on with Y?' and 'Have you heard the latest about Z?'. Gossip, of course: sometimes generous, sometimes malicious, but functional always as a means of establishing group norms, testing out one's own perceptions, re-asserting the mutual bonds of the group, and so on. An individual may in general claim a 'right to privacy' — to save his thoughts and feelings and actions from being known to others. But in order to open himself to particular relationships or apply for certain benefits, he partly waives this right and grants to his significant others the 'right to know'.

Sometimes the assessed individual may concede that the people from whom he is seeking benefit have a 'right to know' whatever truly relates to whether he most deserves that benefit, yet still be uneasy about his loss of privacy. He may, for one thing, question the accuracy or relevance of whatever information about him has been passed on. For another, he may doubt whether the recipients, even of true information, can interpret it correctly. Even more disturbingly, he may not know what information about him has been reported or, indeed, whether any has been at all. Now how is all this reflected in an educational context? What side-effects accrue from the passing on of assessment information?

Telling the Student

The first person to whom assessment results are reported is likely to be the student himself. His teacher may say what he thinks of him — either by means of a grade or a comment or by some line of action clearly implying a judgement on the teacher's part. For example, the teacher may tell the student what he sees as the strengths and weaknesses or dubious points in a particular piece of work, e.g. 'although you noted some of the imagery and discussed it intelligently, you often moved too far away from the imagery itself and relied on an "outside" view of the poem to interpret it.' To provide such illuminative feedback is, of course, a large part of what we mean by teaching — as opposed to telling. Formative assessment is intended to help the student grow. It may, therefore, be fruitful for him to know directly of the results

Summative assessment, however, is less obviously helpful and might, on its own, be harmful. The 'results' that are reported to the student may be too non-specific (e.g. 'very weak' or '48%') or too all-embracing, seeming to relate not just to specific pieces of work but also to himself as a person (which he doesn't see any obvious way of modifying), e.g. 'a careful, moderately intelligent reader with some feeling for style. She is docile, impressionable and not very confident or dynamic.' Such *ad hominem* assessment appears to offer the student no clues as to what he might do to overcome the negative judgements being made of him. It may even suggest to him that he is beyond redemption — irrevocably a C-student or 50-percenter. Knowledge of such assessment can therefore feed the self-fulfilling prophecy. It can help confirm the student in the identity that is being reflected back to him. It can inhibit learning and growth.

And Other Students

Now what happens when the results of assessment are communicated to people other than the student? To begin with, other students may be made aware of one another's results, perhaps through oral assessments being transmitted in their presence (e.g. 'Hasn't Helen got a lot of good ideas?'). This seems unavoidable where many students are in close proximity. And it can be valuable if done in such a way that a student is encouraged to believe that he can either learn to reach the successful performance or else achieve comparable success in some alternative activity of his own. In other words, assessments relating to one student *can* be used as formative influences in the development of others. But such assessments are often reported in such a manner as to threaten the psychological well-being of the less successful student (e.g. Boris vs. Peggy on p. 52) and unleash all the side-effects of competition we considered in Section 4. Peter Mitchell (1975) describes a particularly flagrant example from a school he attended in the 1950s:

> Every student in the school was listed on a large billboard. Here
> every week each student's average performance was represented by
> various coloured pins ranging from gold, for excellent, right
> down to black, for dreadful. Never was there any incentive for me
> to obtain a gold pin, but I always worried about receiving a black
> pin. In other words, my academic work was completed for the sake
> of not receiving a black pin.

There seems little excuse for this kind of publication, which is still to be
found today   even in some British primary schools. Successful
students should gain enough satisfaction from their learning without
the need to see it publicly contrasted with that of their less successful
colleagues; and the less successful students are unlikely to gain in confidence as learners by seeing their weaknesses publicly proclaimed. There
is no way in which one student can claim that his 'right to know'
another student's academic standing should override that other
student's 'right to privacy'.

Parents and Sponsors

The effects of informing parents of assessment results is one of the
numerous unexplored areas of education. Many schools still produce
quite perfunctory end-of-term 'reports' on a student's progress in each
subject, e.g. a grade or percentage or class-rank and some such classic
phrase as 'could try harder' or 'improvement expected next term' or
'satisfactory work'. It is difficult to believe that such reporting can have
any beneficial effects and, being essentially enigmatic, it may cause misunderstandings. For instance, take the phrase 'could try harder': what
evidence is there that he could; does 'could' mean 'should'; if so, why;
how can he be helped to try harder; but what might be lost in other
aspects of his life if persuaded to spend more time and energy on this
one? And so on. Again, should the second phrase quoted above delight
the parent because the teacher is predicting that his child is about to
make a spurt or depress him because the teacher is not satisfied with his
work so far? And 'satisfactory work' is just infuriatingly uninformative.
Such ambiguity is no substitute for face-to-face discussions between
teacher and parent, though admittedly it may sometimes give rise to
them.

Anyway, whatever the response, it seems unlikely that many school-
students would dispute the right of parents to know how teachers see

them — despite the long tradition of jokes about reports being tactfully lost, mutilated or otherwise rendered harmless on the way home from school. At college and university level, however, students have reached the age of majority and are deemed responsible for their own destinies. Unfortunately, they may not be able to afford such responsibility and must accept grants or loans to finance their studies. As providers of funds, therefore, various institutions (like local education authorities, large firms, and research councils) may expect reports about the students' progress. The side-effect of this kind of reporting, or even the *unfounded* fear that it may be taking place, is the generation of the kind of an atmosphere of 'them-us' suspicion and lack of trust that encouraged students to break open the university files at Warwick and other universities (Thompson, 1970).

Yet, how far can students claim a right to privacy here? If sponsors are financing students, have they not a right to make the funds conditional upon academic progress, and perhaps even upon whatever social or political activities they consider acceptable? Have they not, in other words, a 'right to know' about 'their' students? If it is decided they have not, then they may feel that they cannot properly claim to be guarding the interests of whichever public provides the funds. They may feel that they can no longer ensure that funds go to students their public would regard as the most worthwhile and deserving — a need that would presumably be as dear to a Maoist-Leninist sponsor as to ICI or a local education authority.

Other Teachers

Teachers also report assessment results to other teachers. Some of this is done casually, often orally. For instance, a teacher is marking some exercise books in a staffroom and suddenly lets out a cry of rage or pleasure. Someone asks him why. He mentions the name of the student and whatever is notable about the piece of work he is assessing. Several other teachers know that student: a discussion ensues comparing his performance in their various subjects. Such reporting of assessment results may, on occasion, be prejudicial — by reinforcing stereotyped perceptions of the student or creating biased expectations (good or ill) in teachers who have not yet met him. But it may, on other occasions, serve to dissipate prejudice by revealing and exploring the diversity among a group of teachers who have conflicting views of the same student. Either way, such reporting seems natural and unavoidable. Any group of professionals (e.g. doctors, lawyers, management consultants) would be likely to discuss shared clients in similar fashion.

The reporting of assessment findings to other teachers becomes slightly more risky, however, when it takes written form. Such 'records' are often passed from one teacher to another within a school, for instance when the student moves from one year-group to another. They are passed from one school to another. They are passed from teachers in school (through the media of examination results and references) to teachers in colleges and universities. (Very often these assessments are not disclosed either to students or their parents.) Where the assessments are personal opinions or judgements about the student they become less and less easy for the recipient to interpret the further removed he is from the teacher who made them. For instance, colleagues of the teacher know how to weigh up his comments, what allowances to make for his biases. In any case, they can always talk out any ambiguities with him over a cup of coffee. The teacher in another school, however, has only the written word to rely on. He may suspect that some teachers' assessments say more about *them* than about their students; but how is he to tell without access either to that teacher or to independent assessments of the students? And, if he is inexperienced, and the assessments sound weighty and plausible, he may not even suspect. Thus he becomes prey to the kind of prefabricated expectations that teachers like Herbert Kohl (see p. 37) are so anxious to avoid. Yet if the reports avoid judgement and concentrate instead on 'objective' facts (e.g. scores on tests, examinations passed, etc.) are they any less prejudicial? Without interpretation by someone (or several people) who knows the student as a person, how much sense do such facts make: e.g. why does the student have low scores here and high scores there; why does he concentrate on this area and avoid that; what is he like to work with? Unless we teachers publish assessment results in a form that yields rich and relevant yet reliable information to other teachers, there is a danger that our students will be mis-selected and mis-taught.

Potential Employers

And unless we can do likewise for *employers*, there is a danger that our students will be mis-employed or not employed at all. Potential employers are the recipients of much published information about students, usually in the form of grades, labels, and general-purpose references. On account of these credentials, which may tell little about the individuality of the holder, many people are barred from the life-chances they seek — whether more challenging jobs, further education, or whatever. And many are barred not because they are not qualified but simply because they are not *certified*. Or what they can offer 'doesn't add up right' for the opportunity they seek. Yet employers would often be quite incapable of explaining why the job could be done only by someone with the educational qualifications they are demanding.

Charles Dailey (1971) argues that the credentials assessment system is 'inherently prejudicial' — with the side-effect that some groups of people have their privileges and liberties unfairly restricted. This occurs because credentials absolve the assessment judges, or 'gate-keepers', who control access to desired status, of the need to consider people rather than dossiers 'about' them:

> A credentials judge fails in three ways: (1) He does not collect enough humanistic data to arrive at an understanding of the person; (2) he does not collect enough data to learn that the standards do not work very well [poor predictive validity]; a person lacking certain prescribed qualifications may have some personal qualities that would more than compensate, but the judge never learns about them; and (3) the judge acquires a negative point of view that strengthens the credential system's efforts. (p. 123)

That last point relates to what Dailey calls the 'prevailing negativism' of the credentials assessment system. Let one 'knock-out factor' (like 'insufficient' 'O'-levels) appear in an application and the 'gatekeeper' spends no time trying to get to know the applicant and discover whether he has personal (perhaps unrecorded) qualities that make the lack of 'O'-levels seem neither here nor there. Cost-effectiveness raises its head once more, the judge has many applicants to get through, and anything that can reduce the field, apparently with fairness and scientific objectivity, is all right with him.

Some people argue that schools should refuse to provide information to help employers and further education. Solving other people's selection problems is none of their business. Let the business world and further education devise their own ways of sorting out who is acceptable to them. This is an attractive idea, especially in view of the enormous amount of school time that goes into grooming children for terminal examinations. However, once the other institutions had devised their selection tests, I wonder how long schools could resist the pressures to start preparing students for them?

Besides, people who have known a student for a number of years, like teachers, should in theory be able to help other people come to know him too. And, again in theory, they should be able to do so in a way that protects both the aspirations and talents of their student *and* the general public that might suffer, e.g. from being operated on by ham-fisted brain surgeons. Most students probably accept at present that employers should be told their examination results. Even if schools were willing to withhold them at the student's request, employers would no doubt look askance, or not at all, at any student who refused to divulge. What probably causes more anxiety among students is the less-public knowledge about them that is transmitted by schools. The disquieting paradox is that much of the assessment data that is made *public* is actually kept *secret* (as far as the student is concerned). I refer of course to confidential letters of reference. These convey the teacher's impressions of the student's traits and qualities, merits and shortcomings, that may not be apparent in his examination marks. In some institutions they are transmitted only at the request of the student; in others they go out regardless of his wishes. Either way, he does not know what is in them. This is their great virtue as compared with open testimonials. Because the writer has not had to worry about his student's feelings when seeing himself thus described (bad points, as well as good) he is presumed to be frank and truthful. Truthful assessment is presumed to be fairer to more people than untruthful assessment would be.

Nevertheless, there is a feeling of unease among many students that they do not know what people are saying about them. This feeling flares up now and again in anxiety over 'secret files'. In the U.S.A., Congress has abolished the confidentiality of assessment in colleges and universities: the Family Education Rights and Privacy Act of 1974 gives students the right to examine whatever records and documents referring to them are to be found in the files of their college or university and to challenge the content if they see fit. It is difficult to believe that this denial of confidentiality will produce assessment reports that are more truthful and credible. Teachers might begin writing open testimonials so perfunctory and inconsequential, sticking to facts like examination results and avoiding all opinion, that they would soon cease to be asked to write any at all. Ultimately, perhaps, as Edward Shils (1975) predicts:

> [Employers] would seek other means of discerning the merits of those who apply to them. The telephone, which has already done so much to destroy the epistolary art, would add another conquest

to its list. The assessments which count would be oral assessments. A sort of black market in assessments would come into existence alongside the official market of bland, uninformative assessments.

But, at present in this country, assessment results continue to be confidentially 'reported'. Students jealous of their credibility will continue to ask for it. Teachers will continue to supply it. Of course, it might help alleviate some of the side-effects of reporting if industry and further education were to establish valid and humanistic ways of their own to select the best people they can. Yet they will still want information from others who have known the students longer. But what information is relevant? How many teachers, for instance, in response to an employer's request for a reference, will ask him to provide them first with a detailed statement of the specific duties and demands of the job in question and of the specific qualities to be expected from a suitable candidate? I ask in view of a ruling by the U.S. Supreme Court (1971), in the case of Griggs *et al* vs. Duke Power Company, against the use of 'broad and general testing devices' for job selection on the grounds that '. . . any tests used must measure the person for the job and not the person in the abstract'.

So what can teachers do to ensure that what they have to say about the student (if indeed there is anything of relevance they can say) is well founded, careful in underlining the distinction between indisputable fact and personal opinion, and inviting of discussion over how the assessment might be interpreted? At the very least, they must understand the processes of assessment which we shall consider in the remaining chapters.

CHAPTER 4

WHAT TO ASSESS ?

Having considered the purposes and side-effects of assessment, we now have all the context we need to begin thinking more critically about the *processes* of assessment. This involves us in grappling with the cycle of questions I posed at the end of Chapter 1:

What to assess? Deciding, realizing, or otherwise coming to an awareness of what one is looking for, or remarking upon, in the people one is assessing.

How to assess? Selecting, from among all the means we have at our disposal for learning about people, those we regard as being most truthful and fair for various sorts of valued knowledge.

How to interpret? Making sense of the outcomes of whatever observations or measurements or impressions we gather through whatever means we employ; explaining, appreciating, and attaching meaning to the raw 'events' of assessment.

How to respond? Finding appropriate ways of expressing our response to whatever has been assessed and of communicating it to the person concerned (and other people).

So, we'll devote one chapter to each of these questions, beginning with:

What to assess? Now it is by no means obvious that this should be the first question to ask. Many teachers might well say: 'Let's teach first; next, having taught, we'll decide how to assess; then we'll decide what to assess in the light of what our students produce.' Something of this attitude can be sensed among teachers who favour 'impression marking' of student essays rather than 'analytic marking' — that is, relying on the marker's impression of what is worth credit in the piece of work as a whole rather than awarding marks for each of several distinct qualities he has decided to look for *in advance* (Pilliner, 1968). It can be seen on an even larger scale — applied to the assessment of a student's work *in toto* rather than to individual pieces — in what Max Marshall (1960, 1968) calls the 'flotation technique'. Marshall suggests that the teacher should record his opinions of a student not by working through a checklist of characteristics (prescribed in advance and applicable to all students) but through concentrating on what 'floats to the top' of the teacher's awareness as being salient with regard to that one student.

We must heed the message in this approach. It counsels us against prescribing too early what is to be valued in the student's work. To do so would be to risk closing our eyes against evidence of valuable student learning that happens to lie outside our prior specifications. However, to suggest that this danger will be averted if we postpone thinking about what to assess until we've started interpreting the outcomes, is a trifle naïve. In fact, the very choice of one technique rather than another is usually to enable the display of one kind of student ability or quality rather than another. Thus, for example, if we decide to assess through essays we are implicitly valuing qualities of written communication rather than, say, the skills of debate or of co-operative interaction with colleagues.

Even if we have not begun earlier, we should certainly be thinking about the qualities to be assessed *while* we are deciding how. If we were uncritically to take for granted a particular form of assessment (because 'that's the way it's always done here' or 'it seems to give plausible results') then we would be losing the opportunity to examine and, if necessary, reject as irrelevant or insufficient the kind of qualities it draws attention to. Furthermore, we would be missing the chance to design an assessment situation in which the most valued qualities are likely to emerge, let alone of making it *open* enough for some of those valued qualities to be unspecifiable in advance. For example, let's say we take it for granted that students' work in local history must be assessed by means of an end-of-term essay exam, perhaps like all other arts subjects in the school. We would thus neglect to consider the possibility that more germane aspects of ability in local history might reveal themselves if we assessed instead in the course of a *project* in which students investigate an episode of local history using primary source material they track down themselves. Nor, therefore, would the possibility arise of having each student choose *his own* episode of local history to investigate, thus opening the assessment situation to allow the display of individual student qualities and response, unpredictable but worth looking out for, in addition to the skills and attitudes we are expecting in some degree from all students.

So thinking in advance about the kinds of qualities we are looking for in students is no more likely, and if done properly is less likely, to blinker us to idiosyncratic qualities than is leaving such considerations until the assessment event is already under way or even concluded. Even with informal assessment, where we may find ourselves assessing without having particularly set out to do so, e.g. in a conversation with a student, some previous thought about what we are expecting from our students, in general and as individuals, would not necessarily prejudice our perceptions. Indeed, it might open them up, especially if we had discussed those expectations with differently-minded colleagues.

The truth is, we are rarely so open and accepting as we think we are, even in classroom discussion or conversation. No teacher can enter such a situation without assumptions and expectations — about personality; about the teacher-student relationship; about the nature of knowledge and the demonstrability of understanding in general; about expertise in the particular craft or discipline he is concerned with; about the relevance of 'non-academic' traits; and so on. All of these affect the teacher's sensitivity to what the student says and does. Further, if the student is interacting with the teacher rather than being unobtrusively observed, these assumptions and expectations will, by affecting the teacher's behaviour towards the student (e.g. the name he addresses him by, the language and tone of voice he uses, eye contact etc.), actually influence what the student says and does.

Thus, the qualities and abilities 'revealed' by the student may be an artefact of the teacher's implicit anticipations — certainly in the weak sense that the teacher notices only those qualities that chime in with his anticipations (recall Nell Keddie's comments about teacher expectations for A-stream and C-stream pupils, p. 37); but also perhaps in the strong sense that his assumptions and expectations actually inhibit the student from revealing some true qualities, and force from him less typical ones.

Some thought about what one is looking for, in students in general and this student in particular, seems essential before one begins assessing. But the thinking must not stop once the assessment method has been 'chosen' and embarked upon. Students may give us more (or at least different!) than we bargained for. We must be sufficiently alert to respond to this and alter or focus both our expectations and the assessment method even while we are engaged upon it. As R. A. Markus (1974) suggests: 'The capacity for being surprised by unexpected qualities is one of the essentials of examining.' Notice, in the 'How to Assess?' question posed at the beginning of this chapter, that 'realizing, or coming to an awareness' is given equal importance with 'deciding' what one is looking for. Some assessment goals can be specified in advance, more or less precisely; others emerge. This is pretty much what I recommended (in Rowntree, 1974) when treating the closely related arguments and anxieties about 'learning objectives'.

Assessment Constructs and Learning Objectives

In the previous paragraph I used the phrase 'assessment goals' to stand for the qualities and abilities and traits we are looking for in students. Really, however, 'goal' is too purposeful a word and, at the risk of sounding jargonish, I'll replace it with the word 'construct', borrowed from the Personal Construct Theory of G. A. Kelly (1955). Once we get used to seeing 'construct' used as a noun, it does have the virtue of reminding us that 'what we see' in students is to some extent a fabrication of the mind of the beholder — a figment of his imagination.

We are not always totally aware of what assessment constructs we are exercising. Often we can say what qualities or understandings we are looking for in the student, e.g. 'I'm assessing her ability to convert vulgar fractions into decimals' or 'I'm interested in his attentiveness to other children's contributions in class'. However, especially when we are assessing some predetermined quality, we sometimes fail to notice that we are also making and conveying judgements about certain other qualities. Thus, we may say, 'I'm trying to assess the children's recall of the homework assignment', when it is clear to observers (from the way we selectively encourage and discourage, chide and ignore children during the assessment episode) that we are also assessing compliance with our classroom rules about shouting out answers, hand-raising, listening to others, keeping quiet when teacher speaks, avoiding local dialect, and so on. So we can have explicit and implicit assessment constructs. The implicit assessment constructs may be implicit only because they are so omnipresent and taken for granted that we forget, until reminded, that we are pursuing them as well as our conscious assessment constructs. Or, secondly, they may be implicit because we are unaware that we have ever paid attention to such qualities in the student. Those assessment constructs I spoke of as 'emerging' are probably ones we respond to implicitly before we become consciously aware of them. Sometimes, however, we might be perturbed at our implicit assessment constructs, feeling perhaps that it was none of our business as teachers to make and reflect back value-judgements about certain aspects of the student's behaviour or personality (e.g. his manners or his mode of dress), especially if we suspect a halo effect may have been influencing our judgement of his other more 'legitimately' assessable qualities. For instance, Holloway *et al* (1967) suggest that examiners' judgements in oral tests may be influenced more by the student's personality, particularly as affected by anxiety, than by what he knows. Kelly (1958) also observed students with personalities favoured by their teachers being given better grades than their 'objective' performances seemed to justify.

We may feel even more perturbed if we become convinced that we are pursuing implicit constructs instead of our explicit ones, deluding ourselves perhaps that we are assessing one set of qualities while actually assessing another less valuable set. Thus, for example, the compilers of the examination papers in 'A'-level physics investigated by Spurgin (1967), and of the university 'finals' physics papers investigated by Black (1968), presumably believed they were testing scientific thinking and various kinds of higher-order information-processing. Yet more than 80% of the 'A'-level questions and more than 40% of the university 'finals'-questions could be answered from memorization alone. (The man-in-the-street is only partly deceived when he assumes from television general-knowledge quizzes like *University Challenge* and *Mastermind*, which universities provide with contestants or venues, that university-learning consists in cultivating a memory for esoterica.) In short, we often pursue assessment constructs we are unaware of, sometimes at the expense of those we think we are pursuing. Implicit constructs are perhaps the sharp edge of the 'hidden curriculum' (Snyder, 1971), which students ignore at their peril.

Now what is the connection between assessment constructs and learning objectives? In the last few years teachers have got used to being asked, 'What are your objectives?' (see Tyler, 1949; Mager, 1962; Beard *et al*, 1968; Kapfer, 1971; Baume and Jones, 1974). By this, the questioner commonly means, 'What skills or abilities or knowledge or understandings do you want your student to possess after you've taught him that he did not possess, *or at least not in the same degree,* beforehand?'

Sometimes the teacher will be able to mention several fairly explicit objectives, e.g. 'This term, I want my history students to learn to:

1.   Distinguish between examples of primary and secondary sources.

2.   Suggest possible primary sources for various kinds of required historical information.

3.   Arrange various types of primary sources in a sensible order of credibility.

4.   Ask appropriate questions to determine the usefulness of any source.

5.   Distinguish between valid and invalid inferences that might be made from a source.' And so on.

But, even with the most explicit of objectives, there is often a gap between the intention and the testing. As Fairbrother (1975) has revealed, even with multiple-choice questions, teachers often disagree among themselves as to just what abilities are being assessed. So, more subtle questioners may ask as well, or instead, though probably not of the teacher directly: 'And what skills, understandings, etc. do his students believe they need to develop, or actually need to develop, in order to satisfy him?' Thus the teacher may say, 'By the end of this lesson I want my students to have explored their own and society's feelings about unmarried mothers and reached some conclusions as to why they feel the way they do.' And the observer may add to himself, 'Judging by the way he actually behaves towards the students during the lesson, and the way at least some of them seem to be interpreting his behaviour, he seems also to want (perhaps more so) that students should understand *his* feelings about unmarried mothers.' Both kinds of learning objectives — both the ones the teacher professes to want the students to reach and the ones he is believed, either by students or by an impartial observer, to be influencing them towards — can be considered assessment constructs so long as either his intentions or his actions suggest them so to be. His unacknowledged objectives are, of course, implicit assessment constructs.

Though all learning objectives can be seen as assessment constructs, not all assessment constructs are learning objectives. Most teachers would agree that objectives refer to aspects of the student's knowledge, behaviour or understanding that they are trying to change. They would not normally think of a student's 'likeability' or 'maturity' or 'sense of humour' as giving rise to learning objectives, it being no business of the teacher to improve these features. Nevertheless, these are all features about which teachers make assessments. For instance, when Junius Davis (1966) invited teachers at certain prestigious U.S. colleges to rate each of their students on several characteristics, teachers proved just as aware of their students' pleasantness and likeability as of their academic performance and ability.

Teachers are aware of, and respond differentially (i.e. evaluatively) to far more student attributes than is commonly supposed. In a study of sixteen secondary school-teachers, Wood and Napthali (1975) revealed more than fifty constructs by which teachers differentiate between pupils. Even after similar constructs had been grouped together, twenty-two separate constructs emerged. The most frequently used, and the number of teachers using each, were as follows:

Natural ability	(9)
Ability in subject	(9)
Interest in the subject	(8)
Class participation	(6)
Confident approach	(6)
Quietness	(6)
Behaviour	(5)
Tidiness	(5)

But many others, such as 'maturity', 'aggressiveness', 'extraversion', 'honesty', were important to some of the teachers with regard to some of the students. We cannot draw a sharp line between those student attributes the teacher is trying to improve and those he is not. Clearly, he is trying to develop the student's ability and interest in his subject. This he does by teaching him. Equally clearly he is *not* aiming to improve the student's likeability or sense of humour; partly, perhaps, because he

Figure 4.1:

Some Assessment Constructs of a Group of Science Teachers

Do the pupils have real interests of their own?

Do they persist over a period of days, weeks or months on things which capture their interest?

Are they capable of intense involvement? Have they ever had a passionate commitment to something?

Do they have a sense of humour which can find expression in relation to things which are important to them?

Do they continue to wonder?

Do they initiate activities which are new to the classroom?

Do the pupils talk to each other about their work?

Can they listen to each other?

Are they willing to argue with others?

Are they stubborn about holding on to views which are not popular?

Can they deal with differences of opinion or differences in results on a reasonably objective basis, without being completely swayed by considerations of social status?

Do they challenge ideas and interpretations with the purpose of reaching deeper understanding?

Are they charitable and open in dealing with ideas with which they do not agree?

Do they recognize conflicting evidence or conflicting points of view?

wouldn't think it proper, partly because he wouldn't know how. But what about students' confidence, or self-discipline, or honesty, or leadership, or diligence, or independence? By and large, such personal and social qualities are likely to seem of more professional concern to teachers of primary schoolchildren than to those of older students. But even with older students, who may be thought much less malleable in personality, one or more of these qualities may so impinge on the teacher that he feels impelled to try to exert influence (teach), if only minimally by having the right word for certain students when the occasion arises. This may apply equally to the teacher of, say, history or biology who notices (assesses) that the written work of certain students is poor in sentence construction or spelling and who therefore translates those assessment constructs into objectives about which he will try to do something with those students — even though he might feel that they

Can they suspend judgement?

Are they intellectually responsible?

Are they capable of experiencing freshly and vividly?

Are they able to make connections between things which seem superficially unrelated?

Are they flexible in problem-solving?

Can they afford to make mistakes freely and profit from them?

Do they reflect upon their errors and learn from them?

Are they able to say 'I don't know' with the expectation that they are going to do something about finding out?

Do they exhibit any initiative? Have they developed any skill in finding out what they want to know?

Do they know how to get help when they need it and to refuse help when appropriate?

Do they continue to explore things which are not assigned — outside school as well as within?

Are they self-propelling?

Can they deal with distractions, avoid being at the mercy of the environment?

Do they recognize their own potential in growing towards competence?

(from EDC, 1969, p.10,12)

are more properly the objectives of the English teacher. Thus, many assessment constructs that the teacher (perhaps implicitly) attends to with all students could emerge as *potential* learning objectives for some. Figure 4.1 shows a set of constructs developed by teachers on a science curriculum project; are they not all potential objectives?

Objectives in Assessment

There are many questions we can usefully ask about learning objectives as they relate to assessment: What are objectives? How are they used? What assumptions do they imply about learning and teaching and the nature of education? Where do they arise? Who decides which are most worthwhile? What form might they take? How might they be used? And so on.

By objectives we ordinarily mean the skills, abilities, knowledge and understanding in which the teacher *intends* that students should improve as a result of his interventions. As I mentioned earlier, however, we can also consider the skills, etc. that the student is constrained to learn as a result of the teacher's interventions, *regardless* of whether or not these all accord with what the teacher believes to be his intentions. Thus the teacher may purport to be, and believe himself to be, teaching children to analyse historical source materials; but the activities and assessments he devises may merely exercise the students in (and thereby teach them) prose comprehension. The possibility of conflict between intention and actuality will lurk behind our discussions of assessment methods in Chapter 5.

The use of objectives is grounded in an assumption that the purpose of education is to help people *change*. They are to become different from what they were, developing their existing qualities and abilities, and acquiring new ones. They are to change the way they think, act and feel. They are to become more knowledgeable, more skilful, more confident, more rational, more sympathetic, more insightful, more autonomous, and so on and so on. The underlying assumption is seen in school and college prospectuses and syllabuses, in speech-day orations, and in the writings of 'the great educators'. But nowhere is it seen more clearly than in the reports of government educational committees, e.g.:

Plowden Report (1967) Children and their Primary Schools Section 494-6 HMSO

One obvious purpose is to fit children for the society into which they will grow . . . for such a society, children, and the adults they will become, will need above all to be adaptable and capable of adjusting to their changing environment. They will need as always to be able to live with their fellows, appreciating and respecting their differences, understanding and sympathizing with their feelings. They will need the power of discrimination and, when necessary, to be able to withstand mass pressures. They will need to be well-balanced, with neither emotions nor intellect giving ground to each other. They will need throughout their adult life to be capable of being taught, and of learning, the new skills called for by the changing economic scene. They will need to understand that in a democratic society each individual has obligations to the community, as well as rights within it.

Newsom Report (1963) Half Our Future Sections 76 and 91 HMSO

Skills, qualities of character, knowledge, physical well-being, are all to be desired . . . certain skills of communication in speech and in writing, in reading with understanding, and in calculations involving numbers and measurement. . . . All boys and girls need to develop, as well as skills, capacities for thought, judgement, enjoyment, curiosity. They need to develop a sense of responsibility for their work and towards other people, and to begin to arrive at some code of moral and social behaviour which is self-imposed. It is important that they should have some understanding of the physical world and of the human society in which they are growing up. . . .

Like Plowden and Newsom, all teachers can offer statements of intent about how students should change. At the level illustrated above, such statements of intent are often called *aims*. These are very broad statements open to a wide variety of interpretations. Two teachers could easily agree that students should 'develop . . . capacities for thought, judgement, enjoyment, curiosity' but be completely at odds about what would constitute such development and how it should be assessed. So teachers and students between them interpret and construe the aims — which they may modify in the process — translating them into the actions and relationships and behaviours they expect of one another.

We can think of statements of educational intent being ranged along a general-particular or abstract-concrete continuum, with aims and objectives towards opposite ends. For example, one of the broad general aims espoused by a school might be 'to open out the child's imagination and sympathies'. A teacher of English might translate this broad aim into one slightly more particular: 'to foster an appreciation of twentieth-century literature', and for a certain class he might further specify 'some novels of D. H. Lawrence'. At some subsequent stage he might then decide that an appreciation of the novels is demonstrated in the attainment of such objectives as the student being able to:

Identify with Lawrence's characters.

Relate Lawrence's viewpoints to his own experience.

Analyse the literary elements that have provoked his involvement.

Describe an incident from his own experience as if seen by Lawrence.

Assume the persona of Lawrence in replying to hostile contemporary criticism.

Make and justify a personal statement as to Lawrence's 'meanings'.

Seek out and read more of Lawrence's writings than are set for assignments.

And so on.

Some such objectives could be suggested by the teacher in advance of meeting his class, perhaps because of his experience with similar classes in the past. Others would arise out of the uniqueness of the people in this particular class, yet still be seen to relate to the over-arching, but more general, aims. The teacher could move even further towards the particular, concrete end of the continuum by asking how he would assess attainment of the objectives. He might consider possible test-questions, e.g.: 'What would you have done if you'd been Mrs. Morel in such-and-such a situation (not actually described by Lawrence)'; or 'Reply as Lawrence to this review of your latest book in *The Times*'; or 'Why does Lawrence end the novel with that particular paragraph?', etc. He might also specify further by mentioning observational situations in which individuals' responses to Lawrence might be manifest, e.g. in conversations, dramatic improvisations, students' writings on other topics, and so on.

One of my chief contentions in this chapter (and the next) is that giving thought to objectives is essential if assessment is to be relevant and worthwhile. Many teachers, it is true, find it easier at first to decide what objectives they are pursuing *after* they have started to think about how they will assess. Nevertheless, having thought about the objectives to which those assessment procedures relate, they are then usually in a better position to analyse them more critically and develop many more of the same type or more relevant types. Students too are much concerned (especially the 'cue-seekers') to determine the basic objectives that lie behind, for example, the annually-changing cavalcade of questions in past examination papers. Where objectives are not made reasonably explicit and are left for the student to infer from whatever cues he can pick up, he is at the mercy of what Peter Elbow (1969) describes as: 'Judgements based on hidden criteria, judgements which he cannot understand and has little power over. If he is rewarded he feels he did the right things, but if the reward fails he never knows which step in the rain dance he missed.'

When the teacher is reasonably clear about what objectives his students need to attain, he should try to make sure those objectives are equally clear to the students — especially where not to attain them would be damaging in some way, e.g. by earning the student a 'bad mark' or by leaving him inadequately prepared for the next step in a sequence of learning. In the classroom, teachers can discuss objectives or purposes as they introduce each new activity. The primary school-teacher may do so concretely, e.g. 'Go and watch Molly and Raju sorting things into sets.' The secondary school teacher may expect more verbal sophistication from his students, e.g. 'Now what are we trying to learn from this experiment? Tell me what you expect to get out of it.' Where the student is not able to discuss the purpose of what he is learning with the teacher, as with any kind of pre-packaged, 'independent learning' materials for instance, a written statement of objectives may be helpful in orienting the student. Thus, many Open University correspondence booklets begin with a set of objectives, like these from a unit (one week's work) on Learning Styles and Strategies (Cashdan, 1971, p. 10):

By the time you have worked through this unit you should be able:

1. To list some of the main situations in which learning occurs.

2. To say how people are alike and how they differ in their approach to learning.

3. To specify some of the main factors determining these similarities and differences.

4. To define learning 'set' and to give your own examples of learning sets.

5. To define learning styles and strategies: to distinguish and give examples of Bruner's two main learning strategies.

6. To summarize Watkin's work on field-dependence/independence.

7. To summarize Kagan's work on reflection/impulsivity.

8. To discuss the main cognitive and personality correlates of 6 and 7.

9. To criticize and evaluate 6 and 7, both theoretically and in terms of children's actual performance (e.g. in school).

10. To suggest (and evaluate) links between 5, 6, 7 and 8.

11. To justify experimental method in educational psychology and to explain reliability, validity and correlation.

12. To interpret the results of simple correlational studies.

It is, of course, possible that some students will be (should be?) dismayed by the predeterminate completeness of such a list, which may sometimes run to perhaps thirty items. 'If the author already knows what I'm going to get out of it, what's the point of me working through it?' Ideally, this kind of list should be offered along with some suggestion that the student should at least be able to use these objectives in achieving purposes of his own or, preferably, that he should be able to get something personal out of the learning experience that transcends these objectives altogether. Again, it is likely that the student won't be able fully to grasp the import of such specific objectives until he is well on the way to having achieved them. But this does not detract from their value to the student who wishes to use them to check his own progress during or after the learning experience, especially if he knows he needs to satisfy others as well as himself. By their very preciseness they do also confront the student with the question of whether they are what he really wants from the learning experience; and so might provoke him to articulate more clearly and forcibly any alternative objectives he does want to achieve.

The idea that students as well as teachers can develop legitimate objectives must lead us towards a discussion of where objectives come from and who has the right to decide which are most worth pursuing.

Sources of Objectives

Objectives ultimately have their source in the perceptions of teachers, students, parents, employers and all who believe they have a stake in education. They come from the views we all have about the present and future needs of people living in society and about the skills and insights that have been developed through various arts, crafts, and sciences. Our beliefs about what is worth learning may find expression in broad curriculum aims like those of Plowden or Newsom or like this set (from Rowntree, 1974, p. 44):

> How far can we increase a child's intelligence? Can we maintain the growth? Can we teach him how (not what) to think? Can we teach him how to learn, and relearn? Can we teach him all man's ways of 'knowing'? Can we teach him how to share his learning and to communicate with others non-verbally and verbally, in speech, in writing, graphically, symbolically, using all media, old and new, as a producer as well as consumer?

> Can we teach children how to live with uncertainty and stress, how to avoid emotional damage and stunted growth, how to channel fear and aggression, how to believe in themselves and others, how to give therapy both to themselves and others? Can we teach children to empathize with others, to enjoy the diversity of people's life-styles, to get involved, to commit themselves to co-operative courses of action?

Can we identify physical skills that will always be useful to the student in adult life? Can he learn sufficient kinesic confidence to go on enhancing these skills and to take the risk of trying to learn new ones? Can we introduce students to sports and physical exercises that they can safely and beneficially practice throughout their lives?

Teachers sometimes adopt a three-fold classification when talking about aims and objectives: *cognitive* aims and objectives (to do with thinking and intellectual processes), *affective* (to do with attitudes and feelings), and *psychomotor* (to do with muscular activity). Thus, of the three paragraphs above, the first may be seen as largely cognitive, the second, affective, and the third, psychomotor. In practice it is less easy to separate the three. Even the Ph.D. student cannot write his thesis (however cognitive) without having both a commitment (affective) to the value of what he is doing and the ability (psychomotor) to type or write by hand. Again, the student who is learning all kinds of muscle-control and co-ordination in strenuous activity on the football field may at the same time be exercising his mind on questions of strategy and coping with strong feelings of frustration and aggression. Even teachers who spurn any but cognitive objectives must recognize that all objectives, however cerebral, have a vital affective aspect. That is, all teachers hope that a student will finish a course with at least as much (and preferably more) interest in the subject as he had to begin with. We are not concerned simply with what the student *can do* (his ability to perform so as to satisfy assessors); but, more importantly, with what he *will do* — his disposition to carry on from whatever he has learned, for his own satisfaction. It is the affective aspect that turns 'can do' behaviour into 'will do' disposition.

Broad curriculum aims like those in the three paragraphs above may be translated into what I have called *life-skill* objectives. These indicate what we might look for in the enhanced capacity and inclination for thought, action and feeling among students who have been exposed to a curriculum developed with such aims in view. For instance, Neil Postman and Charles Weingartner (1971) propose an 'inquiry' curriculum in which the teacher:

. . . measures his success in terms of behavioural changes in his students;
the frequency with which they ask questions;
the increase in the relevance and cogency of their questions;

the frequency and conviction of their challenges to assertions made by other students or teachers or textbooks;

the relevance and clarity of the standards on which they base their challenges;

their willingness to suspend judgements when they have insufficient data;

their willingness to modify or otherwise change their position when data warrant such change;

the increase in their skill in observing, classifying, generalizing, etc;

the increase in their tolerance for diverse answers;

their ability to apply generalizations, attitudes and information to novel situations. (p. 46)

Notice again that, although these objectives are essentially cognitive, an affective element is present in at least two, as is indicated by use of the word 'willingness'. This admixing of cognitive and affective can be seen also when John Wilson (1970) translates into 'life-skill' objectives the aim of 'helping the pupil to think morally'. This, he says, implies that the pupil should:

1. Demonstrate to an adequate degree the belief that the feelings, needs and interest of all other people are equally important to his own.

2. Be able adequately to discern what other people's feelings, needs and interests are, and also what his own feelings, etc., are.

3. Possess sufficient knowledge (e.g. of social norms and of things dangerous to humans) to be able to predict the outcome of his possible choices of action.

4. Possess adequate social skills with which to communicate, co-operate and interact with other people.

5. Be able to decide a course of action based on his own moral principles (and not on expediency, rules, impulse, guilt-feelings, etc.)

6. Possess sufficient alertness, courage and motivation to consistently carry out the moral actions he has decided on.

John Wilson goes to great lengths in considering the implications of these objectives, suggesting relevant learning activities and exploring the problems of assessment of morality (see Wilson, 1973).

In both sets of life-skill objectives quoted above, we see words and phrases like 'increase', 'sufficient', and 'adequate'. That is, the student is expected to 'increase' his power to do this or that. What would be 'adequate' attainment for one student would not be considered so for another or even for the same student at a different stage of his career. Such objectives are relativistic, needing to be specified still further with regard to the present and possible future states of particular individual students. It is important to note that while some objectives allow for mastery — 100% attainment — others imply *infinite improveability*. I have never seen this distinction made clear in debates about the usefulness of objectives and I suspect its absence is responsible for much unnecessary controversy. Nevertheless, even the relativistic objectives above, being, as it were, 'roughs' to be further tailored to what we apprehend of particular unique human beings, are likely to be a good deal more suggestive of assessment strategies than would be the high-minded but enigmatic aims from which we started.

Notice that I have made no attempt to relate such objectives to particular subject matter. They are content-free. But philosophers (see Hirst, 1968 and Hirst and Peters, 1970) may very properly point out that one does not develop abilities like 'critical thinking' or 'problem-solving' or 'collaborative enquiry' except in relation to some specific area of subject-content or body of knowledge. Furthermore, different areas of subject-matter or bodies of knowledge can be expected to demand different kinds of critical thinking and problem-solving and collaborative enquiry. Thus, the motorcycle mechanic and the lawyer might be expected to acquire these skills in different ways. So might the historian and the biologist. Hirst and Peters talk of distinct 'forms of knowledge', Philip Phenix (1964) of distinct 'realms of meaning', exemplified in but not restricted to the various curriculum 'subjects', which all demand specialized 'modes of inquiry' and 'ways of knowing'. Jerome Bruner (1964) suggests that our chief purpose in teaching a subject or discipline should not be to get the student to commit specific content to mind:

> Rather, it is to teach him to participate in the process that makes possible the establishment of knowledge. We teach a subject not to produce little living libraries on the subject, rather, to get a student to think mathematically for himself, to consider matters as a historian does, to embody the process of knowledge-getting. Knowing is a process, not a product.

This brings us to what I have called 'methodological' objectives (Rowntree 1974, 1975). By this I mean whatever cognitive, affective and psychomotor *processes* the student engages in and develops that can reasonably be held to be peculiar to the subject matter he is investigating: the differing methods of framing problems, the differing forms of investigation, the differing kinds of response to experience, the differing criteria for proof and truth, the differing modes of explanation and justification. I am talking here not of the concepts peculiar to various subject-matter areas but of the ways of generating and manipulating such concepts that are distinctive of that subject-matter and not to be easily categorized as special applications of generally useful abilities.

Such a distinction between methodological objectives and life-skill objectives should theoretically be possible whether the student is investigating part of some established discipline like astronomy or dentistry or economics, or a subject of his own devising like 'an analysis of television advertising' or 'designing things to help our handicapped neighbours' or 'life in our town during the Second World War'. In the inter-disciplinary project, of course, the student would need to borrow from the methodologies of several contributory disciplines as well as generate new ones out of his own style of enquiry. Thus, the student who wants to investigate the effects of the Second World War on the local civilian population may need to draw on the methodologies of history, statistics, sociology, economics, social survey, art history, political science, literary criticism and philosophy — among others.

However, it must be admitted that the distinction between life-skill and methodological objectives is more easily made in theory than when looking at examples. Here, for instance, are some objectives proposed by Alan Bishop (1971). Are they life-skills or methodological objectives and, if the latter, for which subject area(s)?

1. **Model construction and exploration:**

(a)   To search for, and find, similarities occurring in a variety of situations.

(b)   To isolate and define the variables underlying these similarities.

(c)   To determine and define the relationships that exist between the variables.

(d)   To establish the necessary validity of statements of these relationships.

(e)   To search for the axioms from which this model can be logically derived.

(f)   To vary the axioms in order to produce other consistent models.

2. Model application:

(a) To recognize that a given situation is one in which a certain model is applicable.

(b) To make assumptions about the variables defined in the model.

(c) To manipulate the model in order to solve the problem.

(d) To verify that the chosen model is the best analogue of the given situation.

(e) To use the model for making new predictions.

Actually these were proposed as mathematics objectives. But haven't they a relevance for inquiry in almost any single-discipline or inter-disciplinary area? Aren't they also applicable to 'everyday' problems like 'Why won't the damn car start?' or 'Isn't it time I considered a new career?' Aren't they, then, life-skills of very wide application? Remember, as another example, the history objectives we looked at on p. 86. How far are those methodological objectives peculiar to the historian and how far are they life-skills of relevance to lawyers, detectives, civil servants, business executives and, indeed,' any of us, when trying to reconstruct the past from evidence of debatable reliability? Again, look at the science teachers' constructs listed on p. 88 — life-skills or methodological objectives?

Indeed it is a moot point how far the methodologies of, say, a literary critic or psychologist differ from those of a chemist or historian except in applying different 'tool-kits' of concepts to different 'raw materials'. Richard Whitfield (1971, p. 25) goes so far as to suggest that 'our higher mental processes are surely more basically the result of cognitive processes acting upon content, which has been appropriately structured to bring out the essential principles, truth criteria, and generalizations, than a function of the content itself.' At the very least we must recognize that practitioners in various disciplines have more in common, both with each other and with the 'undisciplined' layman, than is commonly supposed. Indeed, if this were not so, if there were not some kind of overlap or at least generalizability between methodological prowess and life-skills, it might be difficult to justify the compulsory presence of 'subjects' in a school curriculum, considering how few people, apart from teachers, continue to pursue academic disciplines after leaving school.

Not surprisingly, some writers lump life-skill and methodological objectives together under the label *process* objectives (Cole, 1972). But this leaves us with a third category of objectives, relating to the knowledge — the concepts and principles — that this process produces and acts upon. These I have called *content* objectives. By this I mean the student's ability to recognize and expound the concepts, generalizations and principles that make up the substance and structure of his subject area. Notice, for instance, all the concepts and principles mentioned or implied in the objectives on Learning Styles and Strategies (p. 93): learning 'set'; style and strategy; reception; field-dependence; reflection/impulsivity; cognitive and personality correlates; reliability and validity; experimental method, etc. (But don't overlook the references to 'life-skills' like the abilities to summarize, criticize, evaluate, justify and interpret.)

Every subject or craft or discipline can be regarded as a network of many such concepts related together as principles and generalizations to form some kind of systematic, comprehensible structure. Often, several alternative structures can be identified according to the viewpoints of different observers — including the student.

So, apart from life-skills and methodological objectives, worthwhile objectives can also be derived by asking what concepts and unifying principles are essential to 'the' structure of a given subject and how we can assess the depth and extent of our student's understanding of them. But it is worth noting that the structure need not be one that exists prior to the student's interest in the subject. Rather than having him learn only some existing structure legitimated by 'experts', he may be encouraged also to develop structures of his own, building analogies and examples, and making new meanings and subject-content, as far as his own interests and experience allow. Without some effort in the direction of making new meanings and establishing new knowledge, his repertoire of methodological and life-skills is unlikely to be much enhanced. The student investigating civilian life during the Second World War, for example, may emerge able to describe, and suggest cause-and-effect relationships among such topics as social organization and adaptation; public disruption and personal loss; health, nutrition and living standards; employment, industrial relations and pressures for social reform; communication, propaganda and morale; and so on. The content objectives he thus achieves will integrate concepts peculiar to this particular subject-area, (e.g. evacuation, rationing, conscientious objection), with whatever more general concepts (e.g. socialization, norms, the price mechanism) he finds worth borrowing, along with the methodologies, from the many related disciplines.

Like any partitioning of such an area of human complexity, this classification into life-skills, methodological objectives, and content
objectives is open to accusations of overlap, omission, and confusion as
to which category a particular objective belongs in. However, as long as
we don't regard it as the only possible partitioning, it can be quite
useful in generating worthwhile objectives or deciding priorities
among objectives that have already emerged. Certainly, it is a classification scheme that does seem to relate to many public pronounce-
ments about aims and objectives. Thus, for example, John Dixon
(1969), in his influential reflections on an Anglo-American conference
on the teaching of English, outlines three widely-held models in the
teaching of literature — the personal growth model, the skills model,
and the cultural heritage model — which seem closely related to my
three categories of objective. Brian Lewis (1973) writes of the student
learning to recognize and recall, to explain and to justify in each of three
different problem-solving domains: '(i) the domain of individual
problems which arise within the discipline being taught, and which are
characteristic of that discipline [content?]; (ii) the domain of *problem-
solving procedures* which are used to solve the problems of
(i) [methodologies?]; and (iii) the domain of *higher-order problem-
solving procedures* which are implied in the use of (ii), and which can
be applied to seemingly-different problems in seemingly-different
disciplines [life-skills?].' And the same trio seems to pop up again when
Walter Elkan (1974) suggests that teachers of economics:

> . . . really have to do three things. First, to teach people through
> the medium of economics to *reason*, to learn to be *critical*, to
> express themselves *lucidly* [life-skills?]. . . . Second, I see our task
> as teaching students the very *basic notions* of economics, for
> example that there is a relationship between price and quantity
> demanded, the idea of choice and opportunity cost, the idea that
> consumption is ultimately determined by how much is produced
> [content-objectives?]. . . . Third, . . . some broad indication of
> *how* most of us would sub-divide and classify economics. . . .
> Students should also have some idea of what is meant by the
> *techniques* that are most commonly used by economists, like cost-
> benefit analysis . . . and national income accounting [methodo-
> logical objectives?]. [My italics throughout]

Too often in education, content-objectives are allowed to swamp out all
others. And even those content-objectives, perhaps adopted
unconsciously to facilitate testing and grading, tend to relate not to
content the student has established for himself but to content 'put across
to him' by the teacher. As Neil Postman (1970) combatively remarks: 'At

present, the only intellectual skill the schools genuinely value is memorizing and the student behaviour most demanded is *answer-giving* — giving someone else's answers to someone else's questions.' And so we lose sight, and the student never gains it, of the mental processes whereby such questions ever come to be posed, explored and understood within the discipline and in the world at large. Even students academically competent enough to gain entry to highly selective medical school can appear not to have achieved much in the way of relevant life-skill or methodological objectives:

> It was found that students who . . . were well-grounded in the facts of biology, physics and chemistry, did not necessarily use scientific ways of thinking to solve problems presented in a slightly new way. They might be able, for instance, to recite all the lines of evidence for the theory of evolution but yet be unable to use this material to defend the theory in argument with an anti-evolutionist. They might know what the function of a certain organ is believed to be but did not always know why, nor did they clearly understand on what kind of evidence a belief of that sort was based. When asked to describe what they saw in dissecting an animal or in looking through a microscope, they often did not distinguish sufficiently sharply between what was there and what they had been taught 'ought' to be there. It seemed that scientific ways of thinking did not automatically result from learning the facts of science. (Abercrombie, 1969)

Levels of Objective

Within each of our three types of objective, students may learn to move between several different *levels* of complexity. Some objectives will demand more, some less of them than others. The more difficult or demanding objectives often turn out to be so because the student needs first to have acquired several lower-level abilities which he is now deploying together in reaching some new peak. When assessing, it is very easy to find ourselves eliciting some of these lower-level abilities (e.g. 'What techniques are used to analyse this sort of data?') rather than the higher-level ability we are really interested in (i.e. 'Analyse this data').

Differences of level are very obvious among psychomotor objectives. Thus the goalkeeper who has learned to intercept a high cross by leaping above other players to catch the ball has (not just literally!) reached a higher objective than one who can only catch the ball while having at least one foot on the ground. To leap and catch the ball subsumes his being able both to leap and to catch, and to exercise considerable courage, the new 'whole action' being more than the sum of the parts. But so too we can see that cognitive objectives range from simply remembering factual data, up through skills like analysis and evaluation (using remembered data), towards the creative formulation and solution of problems, perhaps generating new knowledge, new meanings, on the way. Among affective objectives, the most basic may be to engage the student's attention or persuade him to 'reach out' towards new experience; at a somewhat higher level, this new experience may encourage him to value what he is learning; and at the highest level it may bring about a change in the student's life-style in that he is moved to adopt certain enduring attitudes: to the topic (e.g. optics); to the subject (e.g. physics); to the field (e.g. science); to relevant life-interests (e.g. criticizing pseudo-scientific advertising); and to the school and education generally; to teacher-figures and colleagues; to learning; to society; and to himself (see Scriven, 1967). Crucial here is the distinction between 'can do' and 'will do' behaviours.

Benjamin Bloom and his co-workers produced two 'taxonomies', one of cognitive, another of affective objectives. Each taxonomy arranged classes of objective in order from simple to complex, with the underlying principle that objectives at any one level build upon objectives at lower levels. The cognitive taxonomy (Bloom, 1956) has six main classes, each class being capable of further sub-division:

1. *Knowledge*. Ability to remember facts, terms, definitions, methods, rules, principles, etc.

2. *Comprehension*. Ability to translate ideas from one form into another, to interpret, and to extrapolate consequences, trends, etc.

3. *Application*. Ability to use general rules and principles in particular situations.

4. *Analysis*. Ability to break down an artefact and make clear the nature of its component parts and the relationship between them.

5. *Synthesis*. Ability to arrange and assemble various elements so as to make a new statement or plan or conclusion — a 'unique communication'.

6. *Evaluation*. Ability to judge the value of materials or methods in terms of internal accuracy and consistency or by comparison with external criteria.

Over the last two decades, this Bloom taxonomy has prompted many teachers to consider seriously, for the first time, the variety of mental activity they might be assessing in their students. (See Sanders, 1966, for an approach to classroom questioning based directly on Bloom.) This is not to say, however, that we can use it as a pattern with which to mould our teaching intentions. It has too many inconsistencies and incoherences for that. For instance, it is not always obvious that later classes build on or incorporate earlier ones: can't one evaluate, say, a work of art or literature without being able to 'synthesize' such a work oneself? Can't one synthesize a 'unique communication' before being able to analyse it or even comprehend what one is doing at the time? Equally, it seems possible that earlier classes sometimes depend on later ones — the reverse of the taxonomy's explicit intention. Thus, some types of comprehension might incorporate elements of application or analysis; some kinds of application are only possible through synthesis; and so on.

The taxonomy also glosses over the fact that while sixth-formers and post-graduate students can analyse and synthesize and evaluate, so too can infants and juniors. So how do the 7-year-old's evaluations differ in cognitive complexity from those of the 17-year-old's and the 27-year-old's? Are the older person's comprehensions, say, of higher level, than the youngster's evaluations? This confusion is aided and abetted, of course, by the content-free nature of the taxonomy. Patently, some things are more difficult to comprehend than some other things are to analyse or evaluate. Douglas Holly (1971) suspects an underlying ideology in the taxonomy's neglect of content:

> On this scale of things, ability to judge between arguments about, say, theoretical physics is of a higher order than the mere ability to comprehend the issues involved in, say, thermonuclear warfare, since the one is on 'Level 5 — Ability to Evaluate' while the other is only 'Level 3 — Ability to Comprehend'. This is what happens when one attempts to neutralize or equalize the *purpose* of knowledge and subordinate it to some notion of intellectual 'level', a familiar exercise among academics who would prefer not to be held morally responsible for the content of their studies. To take an extreme theoretical example, one presumes that Bloom and his colleagues would bravely stick by the rationale of their taxonomy if asked whether ability to judge between the merits of competing proposals for mass extermination ranked above ability to comprehend the Sermon on the Mount.'

Personally, I think they would want to argue that judging between arguments about theoretical physics subsumes the ability to comprehend such arguments and that comprehending the issues involved in thermonuclear warfare is a prerequisite to judging what ought to be done about them, leaving open that, once two specific contents are introduced, the comprehension of one may be more demanding than evaluation of the other. They might dare to suggest likewise with Holly's second 'extreme' comparison, and claim they are assuming teachers will guide students as to which activities are worthwhile and defensible. But it was a pity that several years elapsed before Bloom and his colleagues produced a taxonomy of affective objectives (Krathwohl, Bloom and Masia, 1964) and that this was not integrated with the previous one on cognitive objectives. Despite the authors' protests that 'each affective behaviour has a cognitive behaviour component of some kind and vice versa' (p. 62), the existence of two separate taxonomies fosters the illusion that 'head and guts' can be catered for independently and makes moral responsibility for cognitive content a kind of optional extra. The psychomotor domain was later explored in another separate taxonomy by Simpson (1967).

However, we must not be over-harsh in our criticisms. So long as we regard the taxonomies as suggestive, illuminative and stimulating, rather than as comprehensive, prescriptive and indubitable, there is much value to be had from them. Not so much from considering whether such-and-such an objective belongs in this category or that but from speculating as to what might be going on in the mind of the student as he tackles the many questions and activities given as *examples* in the taxonomies — and later, very helpfully, in Bloom *et al*, 1971. (For a review of other workers' taxonomies, see Glenn, 1977.) We should be particularly grateful that Bloom's work has focused attention on the distinction to be made between two broad categories of cognitive objective:

1. Knowledge (Class 1)

2. Intellectual abilities and skills (Classes 2-6)

This in itself, or at least when accompanied by the evidence as to how much differentiation is possible in the second category, would appear to be news to many assessors. Michael Scriven (1967) makes, in effect, the same two-fold classification: 'Knowledge' plus what he calls 'Comprehension' (to include analysing, synthesizing, evaluating, and problem-solving). The fine distinctions to be made among the higher processes will remain a matter for debate. Any such distinctions, perhaps made most clearly when grounded in a specific content, must at least recognize that all such processes somehow *transform* the remembered data to varying degrees and *go beyond* the information given. No one schema will satisfy everyone, but the following, though coarse-grained, is one I find quite useful in thinking about levels in relation to any particular content area:

1. *Recalling* facts or principles (e.g. What is an x?).

2. *Applying* a given or recalled fact or principle (e.g. How does x help you solve this problem?).

3. *Selecting* and applying facts and principles (from all that are known) to solve a given problem (e.g. What do you know that will help you solve this problem?).

4. *Formulating* and solving own problems by selecting, *generating* and applying facts and principles. (e.g. What do I see as the problem here and how can I reach a satisfying solution?).

At level 3, the student is choosing the means to a given end. At level 4, he is exercising at least some choice also about the end. Level 4 represents the student making his own meanings within his structure of ideas rather than performing tricks with other people's meanings. This relates to a useful distinction made by Eliot Eisner (1972) between *instructional* and *expressive* objectives. Instructional objectives — those that provide the essential, technical grounding (Items 1-3 above) — can be exemplified fairly specifically in advance. Expressive objectives, however, manifesting themselves in the personal and idiosyncratic performance of the student once he has mastered enough of the common technical grounding, can only be anticipated in general terms like 4 above. Eisner illustrates the distinction by comparing the student who has learned to speak Swahili with the student who is able to say something interesting in it. Joan Tough (1967, p. 33) seems to be implying a very similar distinction when recommending observation rather than tests in appraising a child's language because, 'Tests can tell us about the extent of the child's vocabulary, but not about the way in which he will use it.'

It may be that we teachers are sometimes too busy assessing instructional objectives to pay much attention to expressive behaviours. As long as Johnny is technically able to read, it may escape our notice that what he reads is fuelling dangerous fantasies, or that he spends so much time reading that he is gradually losing all contact with his peers, or that he actually chooses not to read at all unless it is demanded of him. To offer a Holly-type 'extreme theoretical example', it could be that two students would be given equal 'credit' for their attainment of instructional objectives in the area of 'Heat', without any recognition of the fact that one of them was expressing his knowledge by designing gas ovens for incinerating 'undesirable' aliens while the second was using it to combat the effects of hypothermia among old people.

Often expressive objectives are not assessed because none are reached. The student is constrained to learn the language rather than say something new in it — to demonstrate his immaculate reception of knowledge rather than his ability to add himself to it. When expressive behaviours are in evidence, they can be exciting, largely because so personal and unpredictable. They may impinge upon the assessor as new insights — with something to teach *him*. One of my colleagues says he hopes to encourage in his literature students the capacity 'to say something which makes *the tutor* radically rethink his own conception of an author or literary work'. Graham Holderness (1973), rebuking those teachers who regard students' personal viewpoints and anecdotes as an 'irrelevant' interruption to their teaching, illuminates the process:

> Discussing *The Rainbow* with a group of [Open University] students and hearing the personal responses, the individual contributions of a wide variety of ages and occupations — the 'irrelevant anecdotes' of a farmer, an ex-miner, an engineer, a schoolteacher, a single woman, a married woman — to my mind enriched the reading of that book infinitely. It came to life as I had never seen it before — and I had taught it many times.

This seems to lead us towards the question: Whose objectives should we be assessing?

The Negotiation of Objectives

We have considered where objectives come from and the variety that might arrive. But who decides which are most worthwhile? Who decides which to pursue? Is it the teacher? Or the student? Or some 'Them' outside the immediate teaching situation? What is and what ought to be the case?

Different answers will arise in different circumstances. One might ask, for example, where the particular teaching encounter lies along a spectrum from education through training to indoctrination. The 'indoctrination' end of the spectrum would be characterized by the learner being manipulated to achieve someone else's expectations of him — unwittingly, and unaware that he might be learning to do otherwise. Entering the 'training' band of the spectrum, we find that the student knows he is preparing to meet other people's expectations of him, but he broadly concurs with this and, provided his personal 'style' is to some degree taken into account, is content to shape himself to the normal demands of whatever trade or profession he is aspiring to. Towards the educational end of the spectrum, 'facilitation' predominates — the student's individual needs and purposes and rational autonomy are respected and he is being helped to enhance and fulfil expectations of his own. Another way of viewing this spectrum is to say that, at the educational end, the student is treated as the 'client' for a service, while towards the other end he is treated as the 'product' of a service.

In practice, of course, the distinctions are not clear-cut. Most educational systems contain some undertones of training, if not of indoctrination. Obvious perhaps when we think of doctors and lawyers; slightly less obvious when we consider how curricula in say chemistry or engineering are influenced by the supposed expectations of the professional institutions in those fields, regardless of whether all students intend to enter them; and minimally obvious but no less true when we think of thousands of students being identically groomed for standardized school-leaving exams. Yet, conversely, many training institutions bend over backwards to individualize what they have to offer and enable different students in different ways to get more than the required basics out of the course. I was amused recently, while teaching a course on curriculum development in Montreal, to find that, among my class of mature students, the most educational utterances came from the student concerned with the training of managers at a large Canadian bank rather than from the Quebec high school teachers who formed the bulk of my class. His perspective, both on management development and in the bank's 'disadvantaged youth' training programme, contained facilitative concepts like 'personal growth', 'interpersonal awareness' and 'positive self-image' — explicitly accepting that managers might grow out of the company and assuming that the high school dropouts were unlikely even to join it. This perspective contrasted quaintly with that of the schoolteachers whose quite understandable concern was with how to work as many students as possible through the all-important provincial examinations.

Mostly, teachers and students move to and fro over the middle ground between education and training, with occasional shifts towards indoctrination, often inadvertently and unintentionally through the medium of the hidden curriculum. Humanistic ideals pull the participants one way; the pressures for standardized qualifications and credentials pull them the other. But rarely, if ever, do objectives emanate solely from the desires of students or solely from those of others. Choice of objectives is a complex 'transaction' in which all parties concerned reach tacit agreement as to what is to count as valid educational knowledge. Through persuading and influencing one another, through bribery and coercion, through trust and mutual responsiveness, teachers and students negotiate an acceptable compromise between what 'the system' requires, what the student wants to learn about, and what the teacher feels capable of teaching.

A fascinating account of how such negotiation works out, even in a 'training' milieu like a medical school, is provided by Everett Hughes *et al* (1958). They describe how the students, as a group in intensive contact with one another, reach general consensus that they will concentrate their academic efforts on those parts of the curriculum that seem to them relevant to their futures as general practitioners. Thus, for example, they pay most attention to common and curable diseases, they take short-cuts in laboratory work knowing that they will not do such work as doctors, and in the final years they put their effort into clinical activities, examining and taking histories from patients, rather than into swotting for the formal examinations. The assessment system appears flexible enough to validate such emphases by not penalizing deviance from what might appear to be the institution's formally stated objectives. The authors stress the social nature of the transaction:

> . . . student culture provides the students with the social support that allows them, in individual instances and as a group, independently to assess faculty statements and demands so that they can significantly reinterpret faculty emphasis and, in a meaningful sense, *make what they will of their education.* [My italics]

Of course, it may be said that in schools and universities as they are at present, students who are allowed to choose one activity rather than another, or one course rather than another, are implicitly electing to pursue one set of objectives rather than another. However, the objectives of a course are often obscure or liable to misinterpretation: witness the many students who come to subjects like psychology or sociology only to find them less relevant to their 'interest in people' than they had anticipated. In any case, students may well choose not the courses and activities that are going to stretch and challenge them and allow for maximum personal growth, but those that promise to be least demanding and least likely to end in loss of face, or a sub-optimal 'grade-point-average', or whatever is the local equivalent in the summative totting-up system.

Once embarked upon a course, it can be only too easy for the teacher to fall into manipulating students towards his, or 'the system's' objectives rather than facilitating them in developing objectives of their own. The teacher with a syllabus to 'cover' at all costs is particularly prone (remember Norman Conway, p. 56 and Charles Blount, p. 62?), but other factors also (e.g. large classes) often make it difficult for a teacher to build on individuals' interests as he might like. Frederick Macdonald (1971) gives an everyday example, quite run-of-the-mill stuff, of a teacher introducing a project on 'pioneer life' to a class of ten-year-olds:

> He asked the students what they wanted to study about 'Pioneer Life' and what kinds of questions they should raise concerning the subject. As the discussion proceeded, the children suggested the usual categories for studying a history unit — namely the pioneer's food, shelter and clothing. One child mentioned that he had seen a Western movie in which a man accused of horse stealing was immediately hanged. This comment on the movie evoked considerable interest in the group and one of the children asked why the man was hanged right away. The teacher dismissed this question as irrelevant to a discussion of pioneer life. The decision not to utilize this question in effect set the stage for the kinds of things that the pupils would talk about. Had the teacher chosen to capitalize upon this question, topics concerning pioneer conceptions of justice and due process of law, the function of law-enforcing bodies, and the validity of citizens' arrest could have been developed. The teacher's decision at this point then determined the character of what the children could learn.

For whatever the reasons, this teacher has resisted student attempts to negotiate what is to count as knowledge worth having. (Look ahead to see how a student's gesture towards new objectives is ignored in the pair of assessments quoted on page 145/6.) He has failed to recognize the validity of the objectives that students are reaching out towards. He thus loses the richness of the kind of 'transaction' described by my colleague Nick Farnes (1973) where:

> . . . 'trade-offs' can be made between the child's purposes and the teacher's purposes, so that some from both sources can be incorporated into an activity that has meaning for the child because it is rich in those things he is interested in doing and at the same time fulfils many of the teacher's own purposes. Activities that the teacher considers important and perhaps the 'real' purpose of education are best achieved when the child sees them as

a means of achieving purposes that he considers important.

Awareness of the distinction between process objectives and content objectives seems to be essential to such benign opportunism. The teacher needs to have a keen eye for priorities among existing and potential objectives. He needs to see how they relate to over-arching aims. He needs to recognize that many alternative methodological objectives can equally well support the most valued life-skills and that, even within his own subject, many alternative content objectives (not just the ones that happen to appeal to him) can equally well help towards the more important methodological objectives. The teacher who thinks super-ordinately in terms of process objectives will appreciate that they can be rigorously pursued through an infinite variety of content, allowing students plenty of scope to achieve their own objectives as well as 'his'. The birth of such objectives, at which the teacher will often be acting as midwife, contributes to the student's autonomy and gives him more chance of finding himself in his work. A sense of the many-to-one relationships between content objectives and process objectives (and between process objectives and 'a worthwhile education') enables the teacher to be accepting, and open, as an assessor, to a wide diversity of student purposes.

Transcripts of classroom interactions in college courses given by such educators as Carl Rogers (1951) and Nathaniel Cantor (1972) show how objectives and content can be negotiated during a series of discussion classes so that, as Cantor puts it: 'Every individual will take out of the course what he feels he wants or needs and will put into it whatever efforts his capacity and willingness to learn allow. . . . As long as the student is sincerely trying to do something with himself and struggling to learn, he should be permitted to move at his own speed and on his own level.'

Even with the pre-packaged, teaching-at-a-distance correspondence courses of the Open University, certain course teams are now attempting to give the student some latitude in how he interprets the course. For example, while each student is expected to return essays or reports for assessment at particular points in the course, the topic need not be one that hundreds or even thousands of other students are all tackling at the same time: rather, he may be invited to agree with his correspondence tutor a topic of his own devising that allows him to explore whichever aspects of the course appeal most to him. Some courses go even further by building in a substantial *project* component, accounting for perhaps half of the student's time or more on the course, in which he is free, with guidance from his tutor, to apply the methodology he is learning from the more structured sequences of the course to a problem he formulates for himself. This he researches using whatever resources are available locally. In a course on architecture and design, for instance, the student can spend about one-fifth of his time in studying a locally-accessible building or artefact of his own choice, backing this up with work on primary documentary material and relevant secondary sources. This kind of project, demanding that the student define his own goals and select his own resources, is to be distinguished from those 'projects' in other courses that require the student to use local resources but stipulate the topic he is to collect data on (e.g. pollution levels or children's attitudes) and give him a 'recipe' to follow. Plans are now afoot within the Open University for at least one 'course' to consist entirely of a student-initiated project. This has already been pioneered in, for instance, the School of Independent Learning at Lancaster and, covering an entire degree programme, by the University Without Walls in the U.S.A. That the student should learn to plan his own education can be said to be one of the teacher's prime objectives in such courses. Roger Harrison and Richard Hopkins (1967) illustrated this dramatically in their training of Peace Corps volunteers. Since they wanted to wean recruits away from dependence on experts and enable them to cope in highly fraught situations on their own, what they looked for in their students, right from the start, was nothing less than the willingness to plan and assess their own training.

Naturally, the need to encourage students to develop objectives of their own is not confined to universities — nor even to universities plus primary schools. Unless secondary schools take this aim seriously also, they may be ensuring that their students will never, in future, feel they have learned anything worthwhile unless they have been told what to learn and had it taught to them. Fortunately there are teachers alert to this danger and ready to encourage negotiation in the curriculum. Colin and Mog Ball (1973) discuss many examples of how groups of secondary schoolchildren have been able to develop purposes of their own through projects in the local community like preserving a sphagnum moss bog in danger of drying out, or renovating an old wind-mill and operating it as a museum. Postman and Weingartner (1971) also give many examples of how students can formulate their own objectives if they are encouraged to learn through asking and elabora-ting their own questions rather than simply answering other people's.

Undoubtedly, this may all demand a great deal from students. Not all will have the maturity, certainly at first, to cope with the responsibilities of personal knowledge — even at university level. Liam Hudson (1970) distinguishes between two types of students: the 'Sylbs', who are syllabus-bound, and the 'Sylfs', who are syllabus-free. Some like to be told what to study; others like plenty of choice in the matter. William Perry (1970), whose description of the intellectual and ethical development of students during their four years at Harvard echoes Piaget's observations of young children, notes a progression of much consequence here. He illustrates, with extensive interview transcripts, how a student often begins with the expectation that knowledge consists of right answers, one per problem, and his teachers will tell him what they are. Later on he may recognize that teachers appear to be presenting several right answers to the same question but he assumes this is a teaching technique to help him find the real right answer for himself. It is some time before he conceives of knowledge as relativistic and dependent on context, and comes to see that several answers can be right, not because 'everyone's entitled to his opinion' but because they can be justified in particular frames of reference. Only those students who are well on the way towards this relativistic viewpoint are likely to commit themselves to objectives of their own. Perry does not explore the possibility that students may go through the progression earlier, but experience would suggest that wise teaching can ensure that a child can, at least intermittently, grasp much earlier, even in primary school, the idea that his own viewpoint or interpretation may be *justified* as an alternative to other people's.

Naturally, the implications for assessment are enormous. If students are admitted to have worthwhile objectives of their own, then presumably the assessor, the teacher or examiner, should be looking out for these, with a view to 'giving credit where credit is due', as well as for attainment of 'his' objectives. And if these objectives are going to be different for different students, what happens to our ideas about fair comparisons between students? And if the student's objectives take him into content areas that the teacher himself has not explored, what forms can diagnostic assessment take and what sort of feedback is he going to be able to give to the student? (It must be possible, or post-graduate thesis supervisors would be superfluous.)

Apart from Objectives

Let's end this chapter where we began, by reminding ourselves that the teacher will work with many assessment 'constructs' that are *not* objectives. That is, he will be alert to many aspects of the student's personality and behaviour which he does not intend to change. These may or may not influence his response to other aspects of what the student is and does — through the halo effect and biased perception, for instance, or through using *all* he knows about the student in helping him towards objectives.

We must notice, in passing, that many assessors not acting as teachers and having no interest in changing the student, assess through constructs that do not include objectives at all. Thus psychologists with an interest in 'personality' may measure people's extraversion, anxiety, aggressiveness, neuroticism, etc., not with a view to using the resulting data in treatment but perhaps in order to establish how such personality variables correlate with other variables. In similar vein, a well-fortified tradition has developed for assessing people using the construct 'intelligence'. (Or, more properly, 'constructs', as the multiplicity of different tests for 'intelligence' reveals — *The Mental Measurements Yearbook* [Buros, 1972] lists 147 different tests of 'personality' and 121 of 'intelligence'.) Only recently has it been seriously urged that this construct too be translatable into objectives — on the assumption that appropriate teaching can help the child's intelligence *increase*. Again, employers, in screening applicants for posts, are exercising a number of constructs — ability, experience, industriousness, reponsibility, ambition, etc., which they do not intend to make into objectives, or certainly not for any but the selected candidate (Webster, 1964). What they are looking for is the best possible match between each of the people who present themselves and the 'ideal' person for the job in the terms of their corporate 'construct system'.

In our everyday dealings with other people we rarely take it upon ourselves to change them in any enduring way. We may act so as to alter the way they behave or react to us at a given moment but we don't usually aim to alter the person's *disposition* to act thus in future. The constructs we exercise in such relationships are those that enable us to predict and cope with the other person's responses, to build upon them in pursuing the relationship, rather than to change the person.

Teachers, too, in dealing with children will often view them in terms of constructs which they take to represent dispositional features. They will act as though some perceived traits, abilities and qualities in the child are to be accepted as 'given'. Thus, Bill may be seen to be 'a slow starter'; Joan may seem happy to leave the planning of an activity to the rest of her group but be enthusiastic in carrying it out; Alan may show an early fascination with architecture; Sushma may appear to be the kind of girl who always manages to bring out the best in other children with whom she works; Martin may seem to reveal unexpected depths of feeling in his powder-painting of his Mum; Barry may like leaping about from one part of a problem to another, while Colin prefers to trundle systematically along one path leaving no stone unturned; and so on. However, teachers do use these accumulating, developing assessments differently from the rest of us — indeed differently from the way they themselves use such appraisals when not acting in their teaching role. The knowledge they acquire of their pupils is used not only in promoting amicable and supportive social relations (which are valuable and rewarding in themselves, of course) but also in pursuing their professional intentions with their students.

The teacher's knowledge may be used with prejudice — positively or negatively. If he receives generally 'good vibrations' from a student, he may over-rate that student on many constructs that contribute in no way to the 'vibrations'; conversely, the student for whom he has conceived a distaste or lack of affection, may be unfairly 'marked down' on constructs that were not influential in shaping the early poor impression. In this connection, Philip Jackson (1968, p. 22) raises an intriguing possibility about whether friendships among children follow from perception of approved qualities in the other person or *vice versa*: 'One begins to wonder whether friendship is determined by the possession of special qualities or whether the qualities are ascribed as a rationalization of friendship or enmity that exist already . . . my friends are good guys and my enemies are tattle-tales and cheaters, rather than good guys are my friends and tattle-tales and cheaters are my enemies.' Do teacher-assessments ever arise in this way, I wonder?

Hopefully, however, the teacher should be able to use his appraisals to guide and enhance his students' learning. Thus he may take care to give Bill extra help or stimulation at the beginning of a project; to put Joan with a group who are capable of planning themselves but likely to draw her into it; to point out for Alan any links with architecture to be found in a new project; to put Sushma with a group who could benefit from her gifts as an *animateur*; to structure problems and tasks so that Colin and Barry can both pursue their most effective learning styles; and so on. In summary, we can say that the teacher will depend on his assessments of a student's personality, social skills, interests, learning style and so on, in individualizing his treatment of that student. He cannot treat the student as differentially as he ought unless he does know him as an individual. This demands that he sees how that student differs from others. He can then build on his strengths and avoid getting him snarled up in his weaknesses.

But if the teacher is not prepared to put up with the student's weaknesses (as he 'constructs' them), he may begin urging the student towards eradicating them. Thus we come full circle once again to recognize that assessment constructs, used originally in developing experiences leading to *other* objectives, may at any time become salient as objectives themselves. How far the teacher will regard his assessment constructs as indicating qualities in which he should help the student develop, as opposed to simply observing and responding to developments, will depend on how far he sees it as his business to intervene and what chance he thinks his interventions would have of making a worthwhile difference.

CHAPTER 5

HOW TO ASSESS ?

How do we come to know other persons (or they us)? Through what means do we come to hold beliefs about them which we take to be justified? Often we learn about them without really trying. In the course of our everyday interactions with them we form impressions, tentative at first perhaps, which subsequent experience of them either increasingly confirms, complicates, or else negates. Jack, Jill and Julie all seem very vivacious when first we meet them; but longer acquaintance indicates that while Jack is always so, Jill is so only when in the company of Jack (though in quite a different way from him), and Julie is never observed to be so again.

Our everyday assessments of other people come mostly through observation of, and reflection on, events and episodes that arise in the course of living, working and playing together. In these, the other person reveals something of himself, or (recognizing the 'beholder's eye' in this) we notice some aspect or other of that person's speech or actions and tie it in with some 'construct' we are exercising in relation to that person. (Naturally, 'the other' will be doing it to us also and indeed both of us must do it if we are to relate to one another.) The film seen and discussed with a friend, the shopping and holidays experienced with the family, the tasks performed jointly with workmates, board games played with visiting relatives, over-the-garden-fence exchanges of surplus vegetables with a neighbour, weekend political discussions in the pub with acquaintances: these are just samples from the infinite stream of episodes in which assessment is informally at work.

In such episodes even the most guarded person reveals to us something of himself. His very guardedness is one thing we feel we know him by; though if we cannot explain it or suggest how it ties in with other qualities he may possess, we may not remain satisfied with this level of knowledge. Perhaps we somehow sense he is 'worth getting to know'. Perhaps we fear it would be dangerous not to know him better and therefore become more able to predict his reactions. In either case, we may be interested in what other people have to say about him: 'What do you make of old so-and-so? How did you get on working with so-and-so? What did so-and-so have to say about it?' We can also ask questions directly of the other person. If we want to know about his history or his beliefs or his knowledge, we can ask him to tell us. How we interpret his answers will depend not only on what he says but also on how they tally with what else we think we know of him. We'll no doubt be looking for consistency. Any dissonance between what he seems to be saying and what we've come to expect will need to be resolved — either by throwing his veracity into question or by adjusting our image of him.

We don't normally fabricate situations for the sake of making assessments or revealing hitherto hidden sides of a person's nature. Children do it, of course, from time to time — 'trying it on', seeing how far they can push us, establishing for their own satisfaction the boundaries of our tolerance or credulity. If, occasionally, we do think of a situation as 'testing' we usually do so *after* the situation has arisen — 'Now we'll see if he puts his money where his mouth is!' or 'This will show what she's made of.' Mostly, our everyday assessments of others are *ad hoc*, informal, and often unconscious.

Assessment in Education

In education, however, assessment is intentional and of the essence. All participants rapidly become aware of it, recognize it as a necessary and continuous component of their situation, and make decisions as to the role they will play in it. The teacher, certainly, must *plan* and *evaluate* his assessment methods in relation to the *purposes* he is pursuing. As soon as he does so he will find himself caught up in balancing the claims of various conflicting modes of assessment, e.g.:

formal	vs.	informal;
formative	vs.	summative;
continuous	vs.	terminal;
course work	vs.	examination;
process	vs.	product;
internal	vs.	external;
convergent	vs.	divergent; and even
idiographic	vs.	nomothetic!

This pile of terminology (which I'll sort out in the following pages) is far more differentiated than we are used to in everyday life. So too is the attendant technology. People in education contrive many more ways of finding out about students than they would dream of using on their family and friends. All the more reason why the teacher should keep asking himself whether he is truly gaining the sort of knowledge he says he is looking for and who will benefit from its being known anyway.

Formal vs. Informal Assessment

This distinction arises directly out of the observation that assessors in education may *contrive* assessment incidents. That is, they may arrange for students to perform tasks that have no direct instructional function and whose sole function is to provide knowledge about the student. Students are almost certain to be aware of the purpose of the exercise (e.g. a standardized test or an examination): if they are not, some deception may be afoot! This I would call *formal* assessment, distinguishing it from the informal assessment that the teacher carries out on the basis of what students are doing anyway as part of their classroom and communal activities — having discussions, working in laboratories, writing papers, collaborating in field studies, and so on — where, hopefully, assessment will not be paramount in the students' minds, nor even in the teacher's perhaps. You may see what is virtually the same distinction expressed by the terms 'obtrusive vs. unobtrusive' which put the emphasis on whether or not the student is aware that he is being assessed.

Eugene Webb *et al* (1969) provide a fascinating compendium of unobtrusive assessment techniques. Making a further useful distinction within this category, they consider observations (e.g. of how different children react to a ghost story); archives (e.g. local juvenile court records); and physical traces (e.g. the student's written work or how well-thumbed his textbooks appear to be). The use of archives (another teacher's records on the student we're interested in would be a further example) somewhat clouds the similarity between unobtrusive and informal assessment. For although our inspection of such archives is unobtrusive — the student is not aware we are thus collecting assessment data — the data itself may well be a product of formal and obtrusive assessment by that other teacher. Indicating just how ubiquitous, and hopefully subtle, informal assessment can be, Pierre Bourdieu and Jean-Claude Passeron (1970) quote an ironic remark of Stendhal's: 'In theological college, said Stendhal, there is a way of eating a boiled egg which reveals the progress made by the candidate in his pious life.'

But perhaps you are beginning to feel ethical twinges. Informal, unobtrusive assessment can indeed slide easily down the slippery slope towards the covert, the surreptitious, and the downright sneaky. For instance, James Popham and Eva Baker (1970) describe how a class of twelve-year-olds were secretly trained to assess and report on the student-teachers who came to them for 'teaching practice'! There are several lines of self-justification for the unobtrusive assessor. He may, very properly, say that for students to realize he is assessing would be to distract them and interfere with their learning. He may go further, with the Heisenberg Uncertainty Principle, explaining that students may clam up or mislead him, especially if they realize it is some sensitive moral or social quality that is being remarked upon. The classic work by Hugh Hartshorne and Mark May (1928) on the investigation of 'character and moral attitudes' in children gives rise to the intriguing paradox that in order to test someone's honesty you may need to be dishonest yourself. They mention, for example, the 'over-change test' where the child is sent with a coin or banknote to buy from a shop some article whose price he knows: it has been arranged for the shopkeeper to give him too much change and the test is whether the child reports the surplus or keeps it for himself. Another example is the 'let-me-help-you test' where the child is sent off to perform a task without help and the test is whether or not he accepts help from a confederate of the assessor and whether he reports the fact if he does. The mutual deceptions of assessor and child lend a special irony to the book's title, *Studies in Deceit*.

Notice that these assessments of a child's honesty are, in the sense I defined it above, *formal*: that is, they are based on specially engineered 'happenings' rather than on experience of how 'honestly' the child behaved in his regular activities. They are nevertheless unobtrusive because, although the child may appreciate that something is being tested, he is misled as to *what* is being tested. This conjuror's trick of drawing participants' attention to one aspect of a situation while actually assessing quite another is common among social psychologists (e.g. the Pygmalion experiment, p. 42), but not among teachers. Well, it may be deceiving, but is it unethical? Again, we must go by the *intention* and not the action. Again, 'who benefits?' Suppose your intention is to learn the truth about the student in order to help him in some way — perhaps by more individualized teaching. Suppose also that you believe the truth would be hidden if he knew of your assessment interest, even if he approved of your intention. Then you would probably be justified in keeping your intention from him. Whether you would be further justified in *misleading* him as to your intention is not so clear and might depend partly on whether this might harm him in any way. If you truly do intend to benefit the student, and if you're sure he truly would recognize what you'd propose as a benefit, and if your relationship is amicable enough to ensure that he would feel amused rather than betrayed if he did become aware of what you'd been up to, then you are probably in a fairly defensible ethical position.

Ordinary, common-or-garden informal assessment of students in everyday activities needs no such rigorous justification — it is too much a component of what all participants accept as education to involve any dishonesty. And as for who benefits, it is probably even more likely than formal assessment to be used diagnostically in helping the student. Certainly informal assessment is unavoidable and often must be unobtrusive unless the teacher is to get answers designed to protect his feelings or the student's rather than to 'tell it like it is'. Asking what his students know and profess will not always give the teacher the same information as observing what they actually do.

Formative vs. Summative Assessment

Both formative and summative assessment can be either formal or informal, obtrusive or unobtrusive. We've used the distinction between formative and summative assessment several times already. Is the teacher intending that the knowledge he gains about the student should be used diagnostically in helping the student grow? Or is he intending to obtain information about the student's present state that can be reported to a third party who may use the knowledge in deciding what to do with the student? Some institutions can be seen to be concerned with one of these aims to the virtual exclusion of the other. Thus, the external degree wing of London University is exclusively concerned with summative, classificatory assessment, while the assessment experienced by most students in 'adult education' classes is exclusively formative. Teachers in most institutions, however, recognize that they will be involved with both kinds of assessment.

The boundary between formative and summative assessment is not always clear-cut. Certainly an examination at the end of a student's course, which is being used to decide what the student, as he is now, 'adds up to', and where the assessor has no intention of basing further teaching on the knowledge so gained, is a tool of summative assessment. Certainly the teacher's comments on a student's homework or his response to remarks in class seem to indicate formative assessment — implying some kind of teaching intention. But what of an examination at the end of a term — which might provide insights about the student that would assist in teaching him in the following term? What, on the other hand, of traits the teacher ascribes to the student during conversations if these seem to the teacher to be traits in which he cannot be expected to influence the student but about which he still feels impelled to communicate to the student's parents on his report card or to a potential employer in a reference?

The distinction between formative and summative assessment (pedagogic vs. classificatory as Vandome *et al*, 1973, put it) is not to be seen in the *form* of the assessment but, yet again, in the *intentions* and interpretations of the assessor. Even the most formal and infrequent examination can be used for the benefit of the learner by revealing to him where he needs help. Even the most casual of chats, a form deceptively taken by many an interview, or the comments on an essay, can be used to provide others with the decision-making information they are presumed to need about the student. The criterion is whether the teacher sees himself as getting to know the student in order to teach him better or in order to help others feel better informed about him.

Continuous vs. Terminal Assessment

This distinction usually refers to the frequency rather than the purpose of the assessment. The terminology is neither self-explanatory nor elegant. (Some medical educators with whom I was recently discussing these issues gently pointed out that to them a terminal assessment meant a post-mortem! Yet this little jibe is not too distracting for it brings to mind the 'psychological autopsies' constructed by Edwin Shneidman [1964] and his colleagues at the Los Angeles Suicide Prevention Center in order to obtain 'psychological data about the behaviours and statements of the deceased in the days before his death, from which information an extrapolation of intention is made over the moments of, and the moments directly preceding, his cessation'.) Other terms have been used instead of both continuous (e.g. intermittent, regular, cumulative) and terminal (e.g. periodic, final, end-of-course).

What the distinction seems to come down to is whether the student is being assessed off-and-on throughout his course, or his association with a given teacher, or whether he is to be assessed only at the end of it. Naturally, the length of course makes a considerable difference to the significance of this distinction. If 'the course' is taken as a three-or four-year degree programme then a terminal assessment relating to the whole programme when completed would be a very different assessment experience than if the student were assessed after each individual and sequential component course he completed. Thus 'terminal' assessments, say every three months, might seem more continuous than terminal; and if we think about assessments covering each section within a course as the student completes it (and some teachers do go in for monthly, or even more frequent quizzing) the distinction might seem even further eroded.

But, in fact, the conflict is not really between continuous and terminal *assessment* at all. Most teachers will recognize that, in order to claim they are teaching, they must assess not only at the end of a course (which establishes merely whether or not and to what extent the student has learned) but also during the teaching — continuously — so that they can continuously adjust their teaching tactics according to how the student is developing. In fact, the conflict is between continuous and terminal *grading*. That is, does the continuous assessment, which may be taking place anyway, actually count? Does the summative grade or classification or description ultimately accorded to the student depend purely on his performance over a short period of time at the end of a course or are his previous on-course performances taken into the reckoning also? Sudden death play-off or cumulative track record?

In this context it becomes clear that formative assessment cannot be exclusively identified with continuous assessment, nor summative with terminal. Continuous assessment may be used formatively around the time it is taking place but subsequently go to contribute to a summative assessment. A teacher might dispense with terminal assessment altogether, as a separate exercise, if he thought that a satisfactory summative assessment could be compiled from the series of continuous assessments.

Indeed, if continuous assessment is happening anyway, what need is there of some exercise or episode that can be labelled terminal assessment? Well, with many courses, a final assignment can be seen to differ from those that have gone before in that it gives the student an opportunity to bring together a variety of skills and perceptions which could only have been exercised and assessed separately hitherto. George Miller (1976) gives the example of medical school graduates whose certification it would be inappropriate to base 'on the ability to list the signs and symptoms of rheumatic fever, or the characteristics of presystolic murmur; it might better be based upon the ability to identify, through analysis of data derived from real or simulated patients, those individuals with the highest probability of suffering from rheumatic heart disease... medical education requires the integration of bits, not merely their possession in isolated form.'

Just as a case may be made for terminal as well as continuous assessment, so there is a case to be made for continuous as well as terminal grading. That is, *if* the student must be labelled, the nature of his label should be determined by what he has done on the way as well as at the end. If the label is to tell some kind of truth about the student, more truth may accrue from asking how he has done in essays, class tests, projects, field work, practicals, tutorials, and so on throughout a year than from asking how he did during, say, a few hours of examination at the end of it. Partly this will be because the student's behaviour is being more widely sampled — and usually the longer we know a person the more we know of him. Partly it will be because the behaviour may be more typical of the student — one of the students quoted by Gerda Siann and Kate French (1975) explains why:

> I work hard and consistently well all year, I am frequently commended for my tutorial contributions — I also know that my hard-earned ideas are noted and stored away by less vociferous students, yet, because of the truly fearful stress which I feel each time, I know my exam results cannot reflect the best.

This student's mention of stress reminds us that continuous grading is sometimes claimed to be less stressful than 'one shot' examinations and other forms of terminal assessment. As a consequence, students can be expected to enjoy their work more and reach higher standards. Against this must be set the pessimistic view that continuous grading will be *more* stressful since the student will feel himself perpetually under surveillance. One student in a letter to the *Times Educational Supplement* (Cowell, 1972) wrote that comparing continuous assessment with examinations 'is like comparing months of nagging toothache with the short sharp pain of having a tooth removed'.

It is true that students who have experienced continuous assessment are often reported as believing it to be less stressful than all-or-nothing final assessment (Bassey, 1971; Siann and French, 1976). Yet it is possible to speculate that this may be simply because one gets used to regular stress and fails to notice that one's behaviour has been changed — perhaps for the worse. Constant reminders that one is being judged and, more significantly, the judgements recorded simplistically for others' eyes, may well encourage instrumental at the expense of expressive attitudes. Will the student be too busy maximizing his grades to relax and enjoy his studies? Recall 'the grade-point-average perspective' explored by Becker *et al* (1968). In my Open University experience of continuous assessment, students will rarely be persuaded to tackle an assignment, however interesting or worthwhile, unless they are assured it will be graded. When they are given so much work to do that *is* graded, and the university sets such store by the results, we should not be surprised if most prefer to devote their limited time to the work that will affect not only the kind of degree they get but even their right to continue in the university. George Miller (1976) gives an illustration of how this instrumental preoccupation worked out in a medical school when the Pharmacology Department found itself with falling attendance at its Thursday afternoon laboratory sessions because the Department of Physiology had instituted a weekly quiz on Fridays. Pharmacology successfully retaliated with laboratory examinations on Thursdays! Again, Jennifer Platt (1972, p. 20) records how, in a new pattern of final-year assessment at the University of Sussex, students neglected non-assessed course work in favour of work that was assessed: thus the university's hope of freeing more time in the final year for constructive academic enquiry was thwarted. Selective neglect of courses introducing 'Pass-Fail' grading has likewise resulted in the failure of that innovation in U.S. colleges where a student's vital grade-point-average has continued to be determined by A-F grading on *other* courses (see Bain *et al*, 1973; Quann, 1974).

One may feel equally ambivalent about another advantage commonly claimed for continuous grading — the pacing effect. Students are held to benefit from the way in which regular assignments and other gradable events structure their time for them. No more 'swanning around' and 'goofing off' for two months of a term or two years of a degree programme followed by a final flurry of intensive effort prior to the terminal assessment. Rather a steady, regular application throughout the course. This may seem a mild form of coercion, and one that many students will appreciate as encouraging them in systematic work habits. And yet one wonders how such students will fare when no-one else is structuring their efforts for them. If one of our objectives were to enable the student to make his own decisions and take responsibility for the outcomes, we would need to consider whether we were truly helping him towards this end by imposing a pattern of work — however valuable this might be for *other* objectives. How far does the anticipation of regular grading prevent the student from developing his own rhythm of trotting, cantering and galloping, from exploring academic areas not demanded by the assignments and, indeed, from devoting as much time as perhaps he should to the extra-curricular — to sports and societies and enjoying the company of his colleagues?

As with most educational phenomena, some students will be affected in one way by continuous assessment, some in others. What investigations there have been indicate that students who've experienced continuous assessment generally welcome it: e.g. 89% of Edinburgh students (Siann and French, 1976); 92% of Sheffield students (Cox, 1973). However, our knowledge of how they use it and what it is doing for them remains at the level of anecdote and armchair rationalization. The most recent study of continuous assessment in British schools (Hoste and Bloomfield, 1975) has a section on teachers' views of continuous assessment, another on moderators' views, yet none on pupils' views and, indeed, has little but speculation about its effects on pupils. George Miller (1976) suggests that many students see continuous assessment as a fail-safe means of avoiding unfairness rather than as a positive aid to learning:

> With careers on the line most would prefer to heighten the probability of success by spreading the certification assessment over time. But this is probably a manifestation of how success is perceived and is a direct result of the pernicious academic practice of grading and ranking. If future appointments or career choices are significantly influenced by marks in course or ranks in class

then it is understandable why students might be reluctant to allow this significant criterion of achievement to depend upon a single terminal performance before examiners who may have special interests, use unknown criteria, probe a limited range of content or professional skills, or be encountered at a time when either candidate or examiner is for some unrelated reason not functioning at optimum level.

Certainly continuous assessment can be arranged so as to avoid both the unfair 'untypicality' of terminal examinations and the anxiety that every false step along the way could count against one. Some continuous assessment schemes (e.g., the Open University's) count for grading purposes only the *best* pieces of work done by the student — say his six best essays out of eight during a course. This stratagem can take a lot of the stress out of continuous grading, especially if, as in the German Department of the University of Warwick (Thomas, 1976), students are expected to revise their first drafts after discussion with tutors. Students may feel freer to explore and to take intellectual risks, knowing that brave attempts that have failed to come off will not necessarily be held against them. Teachers too may see how 'best work only to count' may allow them to pursue a policy of 'mastery learning' (Bloom, 1971; Block, 1974), aiming to have all their students produce sufficient work of quality, whatever else they may produce besides and along the way.

Somewhat in the same spirit — of recognizing only the best a student has to offer — is the policy of having students sit a terminal exam as well as be continuously assessed, but reassuring them in advance that their exam result will be counted only if it *improves* on their continuous assessment results. This, of course, would enable a college to avoid discriminating against those students who wish to be free of the externally-imposed constraints of continuous grading and to rely on working at their own pace, and in their own way, 'getting it all together' in time for the exam. In the Chemical Engineering Department at the University of Aston, continuous assessment and examination marks are combined by weighting them 60:40 in whichever direction gives best advantage to each individual student. The History Department at Leeds University classes students on their final examination score but allows for the class to be raised if the tutor's previously recorded continuous assessment grade is more than one class higher: the class cannot be lowered by a poorer continuous assessment grade, however.

So, by giving the student more opportunity to demonstrate his quality, and then concentrating on his best work, continuous assessment can do much to counteract stress and anxiety. Since he knows his least successful pieces of work will not be held against him, he can afford to push himself to the limits of his capability without the constant dread of 'blotting his copybook'. I believe that most teachers will see the merit of basing continuous assessment on the students' best work, even if it doesn't picture them 'warts and all', because *it is less likely to inhibit good work actually being produced*. Notice that compromise is impossible. To grade all pieces of work, for example, but withhold the grades from students is likely to increase rather than decrease their anxiety and their instrumental scrabblings to 'psych-out' the system. Robert Pirsig (1975, pp. 187-96) describes the confusion that ensued when he withheld grades (under the impression he was thereby abolishing grading). The prestigious Reed College of Portland, Oregon recently reported (Reed, 1973), with only a cryptic reference to 'students who feel a real need for more specific information', that they have abandoned their sixty-year-old practice of withholding continuous assessment grades until graduation (except for students doing badly).

Course Work vs. Examinations

Perhaps you feel we've just dealt with this distinction in the previous section. But we must resist the temptation to equate continuous assessment with course work, and terminal assessment with examinations. Admittedly, they usually go together in practice; but logically they need not. It's worth separating them out, not as an exercise in nit-picking but because doing so opens up new pedagogic possibilities.

Let's start by defining our new term: 'course work'. This can be defined in terms of process — what the student does during the course of his studies or in terms of product — things he produces during his studies. (More of this distinction later.) Continuous assessment must take account of one or other (or both) of these, because there is nothing else that can be so assessed. So we would normally think of continuous assessment being based on what students do or produce in tutorials, classes, practicals, field work, written assignments and so on. But it does not have to be. It could be based on what they produce in a series of monthly three-hour examinations each assessing what they have learned since the previous exam. A teacher might argue that he could best build up an understanding of his students, whether for formative or summative purposes, by analysing their examination work. This might seem especially reasonable if he claimed that one of his objectives was to help the student learn to work under pressure.

In some circumstances, then, continuous assessment could, and perhaps should, take account of examination performance. Conversely, terminal assessment does not have to be based on examination but instead can take account of course work. That is, the student can be assessed at the end of his course, in the light of what he has done *during* the course. He can, for example, ask his teacher for a 'reference' commenting on what he knows of that work. He may also present an external assessor with a 'portfolio' of his best products: essays, stories, poems, research reports, field notes, drawings, photographs, paintings, or whatever. Or, especially if he has been working in three dimensions, he may invite the assessor to an exhibition of his sculpture, brickwork, jewellery, engineering prototypes, or whatever. Terminal assessment is possible, then, without any new task being specially carried out to provide information that could not have been made available earlier. (Compare the terminal assessments that, to revert to the sombre meaning I mentioned earlier, are made of an author or composer's work immediately on his decease.) Even if a final, terminal task is required, it could still be something very different from what we normally think of as an examination: e.g. a thesis, a report of a prolonged field study, a film, a paper presented at a symposium, and so on.

The point of making this distinction is that the use of examinations cannot be justified merely on the grounds that summative and therefore terminal assessment is necessary. Since terminal assessment can take place without examinations then the decision to do it with examinations still needs explaining.

So what is special about examinations? How do they help us learn about the student, come to know him or about him, in ways that other assessment methods do not? Clearly, this depends on what we mean by 'examinations'. To most people, 'examinations' connote the following features:

1.   All students are given the same task to perform (e.g. writing a set of essays, driving a motor car along a set route, examining a patient with a view to diagnosis).

2.   Although students are expected to have 'prepared' for the task, its precise nature is not made clear until the moment they are asked to embark upon it.

3.   The task is performed in the presence of a non-collaborating person with the policing role of 'invigilator'.

4.   All students are given the same limited period of time to work on the task even where the task is one which they might be expected to perform better if given no time limit — as they might well be with similar tasks outside the examination situation.

5.   Students are not allowed to consult references and information sources while performing the task — even though it might be normal practice to do so on similar tasks outside the examination situation.

6.   Students (or candidates as they are often called in this situation though they would not be when performing similar tasks as part of course work) are not allowed to consult with one another.

7.   Students are expected to experience at least some sense of stress and urgency while performing the task — again, regardless of whether such would necessarily accompany their performance of similar tasks elsewhere.

Other features are detectable, e.g. that examinations may be held infrequently, that performance may be assessed by people who do not know the students, that considerable time may elapse before students will be told how well they performed, and so on. But the seven features above are perhaps the hard-core. So, we must ask, how far does a situation remain an examination, and what difference does it make if we start chipping flakes off this hard-core?

To begin with, even in the most traditional three-hour examination paper, it would be unusual for all students to tackle exactly the same task. They may all have to write four essays but usually this will allow each student to choose four from perhaps ten subjects. Now there are 210 ways of choosing four from ten. (1540 ways if we count the different orders in which students might choose to answer the questions.) So even with more than 200 candidates taking the same paper it is still possible that no two have answered the same set of questions. Unless it can be shown that each question demands exactly the same knowledge and skills as every other (which is inconceivable), the students may all, in effect, be taking a different examination. Any attempt to compare students' overall performances would thus be questionable.

Usually, of course, the situation is not so extreme. Some questions are so popular, and some so neglected, that the number of combinations actually chosen is much smaller than that theoretically possible. So even among the 200 students mentioned earlier, we might be able to see that, apart from a few mavericks, practically every student can be compared with, say, half a dozen or so others who chose to answer the same set of questions as himself. What if we want to compare more widely than this? Suppose we want to argue that a student who scores, say, 50% on the set of geography questions he answered is level in geographical attainment with another student who scored 50% on another set of questions from the same test. To do so successfully we must be able to convince ourselves that there is some underlying geographical 'nous' of which all the questions, regardless of the different knowledge and skills they may draw on, are equally revealing. The hopelessness of this requirement led psychometricians to urge that scores on separate questions within a test should not be added up and averaged (so as to allow comparisons) unless it can be shown that all questions are tapping the same underlying ability. Thus, if a particular question proved generally much easier or more difficult than average, then they would drop it from the test.

Even were an examination to allow no choice of questions, students would still interpret the set questions in a diversity of ways. Examiners the world over, at all levels and in all subjects, complain that too many candidates have avoided the exact questions set and have, in effect, chosen instead to answer related questions of their own. (Like the candidate who was asked to evaluate the relative contributions of Jewish and Greek ideas to the development of Christianity and who wrote, modestly, 'Who am I to offer judgements on an issue about which the leading authorities cannot agree? Instead, I hereby append a list of the twelve tribes of Israel.') Of course, one might like to see such a practice as a sign of students negotiating their own objectives. How fair is it, after all, when an examination for which the student has prepared for months does not offer him the opportunity to demonstrate what he can do well and asks exclusively for things he feels less confident about? However, I suspect the tendency to answer the 'unset' question is usually less rationally motivated. Indeed it may be just another response to stress. The research of G. V. Hamilton (1916) indicated that both humans and animals under stress were often unable to perceive more than one line of behaviour and would pursue it rigidly even if inappropriate. This might help explain some students' inability to notice that the question they are asked is not the one they came prepared to answer.

Furthermore, examiners themselves inadvertently manufacture task diversity. Countless studies have shown how the same essay will be given quite different marks by different examiners. This seems to indicate that examiners also interpret the question in a diversity of ways and hence what is expected from the student by way of performance depends on which of the examiners he draws. (See the review article by Ruth Beard in CVC, 1969).

Where an examination takes some form other than a written paper, it can be even more obvious that the task is not the same for all students. Two students taking a driving test will experience different traffic conditions even though they may be driving along the 'same' route within a few minutes of each other. Even if the same patient is examined by several medical students they are unlikely to all get the same pattern of response from the patient. One cannot step in the same river twice!

Finally, we might look to one effect of the time-limit that operates in most examinations. Whatever the task, many students simply do not have time to finish it. Many psychological tests, intelligence tests particularly, are designed so that very few candidates will complete all the items. These are often called 'speed tests' to distinguish them from 'power tests' in which the emphasis is on having the student tackle everything. The typical examination will be a power test for many students and a speed test for others.

So, the most obvious feature of examinations — uniformity of task — has long been less than universal. So too with the second feature — knowledge as to precisely what task is to be performed. In the fourteenth-century University of Bologna, students were given examination questions two days before having to submit written answers which they had to defend before assessors who voted on their performance. Today, 'seen' examinations are making a come-back in colleges and universities. Students are given advance notice of one or more of the tasks they will be expected to perform under 'examination conditions'. Roy Cox (1967), for example, reports on second-year sociology exams at Essex University where the questions on part of each paper were given out two weeks in advance. These 'pre-set' exams were clearly testing different student skills than were either regular homework assignments or 'unseen' exams. Although 27 out of 40 students preferred the pre-set to the unseen, the majority had reservations. Some students appreciated the opportunity to 'consider the questions coldly', to think out 'original ideas' and to let them 'simmer'. But others worried about getting 'bogged down in detail searching for the perfect answer' or suspected higher standards would be expected for the pre-set questions and felt there would be 'no excuse if you make a mess'.

Whether or not students perform different tasks in the examination and whether or not they know in advance precisely what the task is to be, it is not uncommon, as another relaxation of the seven strictures with which we began, for them to be allowed to consult references or information sources. Thus the candidate in pharmacology may be allowed to consult his *British Pharmacopoeia* for details of drug handling. The candidate taking a mathematics paper may be allowed to use mathematical tables, which may or may not contain statistical formulae, conversion tables and so on. (Not being allowed such aids in my day, I remember waiting outside the doors of my statistics exam room staring at a sheet of paper containing all the essential formulae, then, as soon as the doors opened, throwing away the paper and sprinting to my seat to recreate its contents on scrap paper before the image faded from my mind!) But should the student be allowed to bring into the examination room his textbooks or his notebooks? It is not unusual now for students to be allowed to bring certain specified books into what has come to be called an 'open book examination'. Again we must note that such an examination makes different demands on the student than does the 'closed book' exam: he may be saved the trouble of memorizing 'useful quotations', dates and quantities, and other details; but he now is taxed by the problem of rapidly tracking down only the detail he needs to support his case and avoiding the temptation to paraphrase his texts or string together massive quotations on a thread of waffle.

The late Chairman Mao favoured both of these latter two relaxations: 'Our present method of conducting examinations is a method for dealing with the enemy, not a method for dealing with the people. It is a method of surprise attack, asking oblique or strange questions. . . I am in favour of publishing the questions in advance and letting the student study them, and answer them with the aid of books' (Schram, 1974).

We see, then, that teachers still feel justified in saying they are setting an 'examination' (as distinct from 'course work') though the task performed differs from student to student and even though students are given precise prior knowledge of what is expected of them or are allowed to take reference materials into the examination room. How many more of the original seven strictures can we relax and still call it an examination? Practically all, it seems. R. T. Jones (1969) sees no incongruity in talking of 'the two-week exam' — one of the assessment methods used in the English Department at York University — where students are given a normal-looking question paper but are asked to hand in their answers fourteen days later. Clearly the work is not invigilated, students can consult whatever or whomever they will, and they can spend as little or as much time as they wish over the task. Jones points out that this method is used, as well as the traditional three-hour 'unseen', because 'although much of our work, whatever profession we follow after graduating, has to be done against the clock, our *best work* generally isn't'. Richard Thomas (1976), from the German Department at Warwick University, describes how time-pressure militates against 'best work' in the exam situation: '. . . students can easily be forgiven if they feel it wise to play for safety. Attempts at originality or at an independent view may well be risky, all the more so since in the time allowed there is little chance of a proper working out of arguments — and, if you find half-way through your answer that it is, after all, on the wrong lines, you have not the chance to start again, except to produce a rushed result.' How many academics, I wonder, would happily be judged on the first draft of a paper they produced in such circumstances? Thomas explicitly denies that his alternative to the three-hour exam is continuous assessment, insisting that the 'examination' consists of a number of essays submitted at the end of each year of the degree course: these essays are reworked versions of papers which students may well have presented in seminars and which they will certainly have discussed in detail with tutors and, indeed, will have been encouraged to collaborate over with other students. The results, says Thomas, are 'often a real pleasure to read, and sometimes of striking quality — not infrequently, beyond what the student ever thought he was capable of'.

Of course, the time-constraints can be relaxed without letting everything else go as well: students can be sat down in an examination room, given an 'unseen' paper which they have to tackle in the presence of an invigilator and without reference to books or colleagues — but be allowed to take all day over it if they wish. This would be to make it more a 'power' test, less a 'speed' test. Joseph Schwab (1969) sees clearly that when the strictures are relaxed sufficiently, a terminal assessment becomes less of an examination and more a culmination of the curriculum. He suggests that a couple of weeks before the end of a course, students should be given a 'set work' (e.g. a new novel or engineering design problem) which they are to tackle in the examination room. It should be typical of those the student has worked with during the course, and accessible to the methodological skills he has learned, but should be quite *new* to him and not have been previously discussed by the teacher. Students may then choose their own ways of coming to grips with the set work, consulting whatever resources they please and working alone or in groups. They may bring books and notes to the examination and will be at liberty to confer with colleagues. Schwab points out that:

> This runs counter, of course, to the tradition of examinations. Students are collaborating; they are cheating in fact; borrowing ideas from each other, criticisms, tips and caveats, which is exactly what we have taught them to do. They are doing exactly what we do — unless we are poets or egomaniacs — when we undertake a similar work, for we too borrow ideas from colleagues and predecessors (and it matters very little whether we seek their help face-to-face or by way of their publications), and seek from colleagues charitable enough to give it, criticisms of our thoughts and formulations. The examination, in short, is a continuation of the curriculum as well as a certifying device.

The point of all this discussion, however, has not been to stipulate what is or is not an examination. Nor has it been to argue the respective merits of course work assessment and various kinds of examination. Rather it has been to reflect on the fact that students can be assessed under a variety of constraints and that different combinations of constraints will result in different skills and abilities being tested. The traditional three-hour exam tests the student's ability to write at abnormal speed, under unusual stress, on someone else's topic, without reference to his customary sources of information, and with a premium on question-spotting, lucky memorization, and often on readiness to attempt a cockshy at problems that would confound the subject's experts, e.g. 'Why is Lear's death so moving?' (Stevens, 1970, p. 45). The spoof question paper in Figure 5.1 (p. 136) is a wild illustration of how exams must often seem to the hard-pressed student.

Perhaps unusual stress is the sole identifying feature that is likely to adhere to any assessment exercise that is thought of as an examination. Such an exercise, coming usually at the end of a course and functioning somewhat as a *rite de passage* from one educational state to another, takes on a ritual significance that other assessment events, being less concentrated and ultimate, do not. (Remember Norman Russell's 'week of tests the season of fear' in his poem on p. 29?).

Figure 5.1

Candidates must attempt *all* questions:

1. *History*: Describe the history of the Papacy from its origins to the present day, concentrating especially but not exclusively on its social, political, economic, religious and philosophical impact on Europe, Asia, America, and Africa. Be brief, concise and specific.

2. *Medicine*: You are provided with a razor blade, a piece of gauze and a bottle of Scotch. Remove your appendix. Do not suture your work until your work has been inspected. You have 15 minutes.

3. *Public Speaking*: 2,500 riot-crazed immigrants are storming the local Citizens Advice Bureau. Calm them. You may use any ancient language except Greek or Latin.

4. *Biology*: Create Life. Estimate the differences in subsequent human culture if this form of life had developed 500m years earlier, with special attention to its probable effect on the British parliamentary party system. Prove your thesis.

5. *Music*: Write a piano concerto. Orchestrate and perform it with flute and drum. You will find a piano under your seat.

6. *Sociology*: Estimate the sociological problems which might accompany the end of the world. Construct an experiment to test your theory.

7. *Engineering*: The disassembled parts of a highpowered rifle have been placed in a box on your desk. You will also find an instruction manual, printed in Swahili.
  In 10 minutes a hungry Bengal tiger will be admitted to the room. Take whatever action you feel appropriate. Be prepared to justify your decision.

8. *Political science*: There is a red telephone on the desk behind you. Start World War III. Report at length on its socio-political effects—if any.

9. *Philosophy*: Sketch the development of human thought; estimate its significance. Compare with the development of any other kind of thought.

10. *General knowledge*: Define the Universe. Describe in detail. Give three examples.

Pass Mark: 85%

(Suggested originally by the Apex Club of Katherine, Australia as an entrance test 'not intended to be rigorous, merely a simple questionnaire designed to eliminate truly unsuitable candidates.)

Process vs. Product Assessment

For a student's work to 'count' for anything, it usually has to result in a *product* — a painting, a laboratory notebook, a three-dimensional model, or the perennial essay. It is not hard to see why assessors have concentrated on products — they are easy to manage. They stay still while you inspect them. They can usually be stored without deteriorating in case you need to assess them again later on. They can usually be sent fairly easily to other assessors. They appear to exist for all to see in the same tangible form, with some 'true value' that we feel we ought to be able to agree on. One is reminded of the ecologist examining the regurgitated pellets of owls or the faeces of badgers as a more convenient means of establishing the creatures' diets than hanging about trying to observe what they eat.

No, life is not so simple in the world of *process*. Take, for instance, a musical or dramatic performance or a child reading aloud. The assessor may experience these performances, as an observer, but he cannot preserve them. He must assess them in real time — while they happen. Nor can he get second opinions from colleagues who were not present. Furthermore, because the earlier parts of the performance are no longer in existence once the end is reached, he cannot check how closely his perceptions relate to what 'actually' happened. For instance, a brilliant beginning may have made him either more or less indulgent of what followed; conversely, an inspired conclusion may have created a retrospective halo effect causing him to forget some of the early fumblings. In some cases, say, with a dramatic or musical performance that is sufficiently out-of-the-ordinary, he may realize towards the end that he has been misinterpreting it or approaching it from quite the wrong angle; in the light of this realization he might experience it quite differently were he able to experience it again. The performance is clearly not 'out there', awaiting scrutiny, as an essay or a set of calculations appears to be.

In case you're wondering, I do *know* about audio- and video-tape recorders and about film-cameras. Plays and music can be recorded just as conversations and physical activities can, in principle. Novice teachers have learned much about themselves from watching and discussing tele-recordings of their work with children in 'micro-teaching' sessions; golfers have been able to see the faults in their swing; discussion participants have been able to get new insights into how they appear to others through seeing how the camera or microphone catches them. But to assess a recording is not the same as to assess a performance. In some ways it may be better — you can replay the recording until you are satisfied that you have perceived every nuance and checked every doubtful interpretation; your attention will be concentrated by what the cameraman or sound recordist (who perhaps was yourself) has focused on; other people who were not present at the performance can give an opinion; and so on. But these strengths may also be weaknesses. For one thing, if you recorded the performance yourself you may have been too busy with the technicalities to experience the performance while it was going on. Even if someone else recorded it, you may have put less of yourself into experiencing it than you otherwise would, knowing you'd have a recording with which to round out your impressions afterwards. The camera and the microphone are just as selective as the human eye and ear; with the result that the observer of the recording has much less to select from than does the observer of the actual performance — information is lost. This is especially so when you recall that sight and hearing are the only two of the six or more human senses to benefit from recording. We've long been used to the 'movies' and then the 'talkies' as extenders of our experience but the 'smellies' and the 'feelies' are still undeveloped and it takes a clever recordist to capture alive on tape or film the ambient energy — the 'sizzle' — of human interaction and to make the audience feel anything like the involvement they'd have felt if they'd been there.

The learning situation is awash with process — the on-going reality of students interacting with ideas, with one another, with the teacher, with the physical environment, displaying as they do the workings of their minds and spirits in how they define and respond to the situation they are living through. Some of this may be faintly echoed in whatever products they emerge with. But we can learn far more about the student, whether our aim is to use the knowledge to help him learn or to inform other people about him, if we observe *how* he learns and produces.

No teacher who seriously endorses process objectives (see p. 99) as well as content objectives can afford to neglect process assessment. If he wishes to influence, or even understand, the student's learning style and how he is developing, for example, in his capacity for problem-solving or for collaborative work with others, he cannot wait for the product to give him insights but must seek understanding while it is in process of production — intervening, where necessary, with guidance. Many outcomes of process learning, and many assessment constructs that have not given rise to objectives, do not get expressed in products. Look back, for example, at the list of constructs in Figure 4.1 (p. 88); how elusive would some of those be to the assessor of products? And, indeed, it may be something of a comment on our consumer-society that we even expect learning to result in a flow of *products*. Why should it? Why should it not result equally often in speech and action and valuable new relationships among people? One student, quoted incredulously by Arnold Beichman (p. 142) in Cox and Dyson (1970), puts the case for 'Action Ph.Ds' to be awarded partly on assessment of the student's social action rather than a dissertation:

> A lot of this stuff we take in political science, sociology or anthropology is so much crap, let's face it. You memorize a lot of bullshit, take an exam or do a paper and the dissertation is even worse junk. What we mean by an 'action Ph.D' is that a graduate student after he passes all his requirements, is going to go out, say, to neighbourhoods of the poor, the underprivileged, and work with them on their problems. For example, he could organize rent strikes in the Puerto Rican neighbourhoods or a march on the welfare office or City Hall or against high-priced food stores that exploit them. All this would be as much a part of the Ph.D program as passing the orals. In fact, the action would be the equivalent of the dissertation.

The Chinese would concur with this suggestion, of course. Roger Harrison and Richard Hopkins (1967) seemed to also: in training Peace Corps volunteers to work in developing countries, assessment was in terms of how the trainees coped with the rigours of organizing their own learning activities in the jungle training camp and how they coped with the daily crises that beset them when they eventually got working with their 'clients'. In some areas, medical education for instance, where the student's vital ability to relate well to patients cannot be inferred from his having produced convincing case-histories, it is common to observe the student in action as part of his assessment. Similarly, with many other interpersonal and indeed many psychomotor skills, one cannot expect to learn the truth about how a student would, let's say, collaborate with others on a design team, converse in Italian, or tie his own shoelaces, by asking him to write an essay or answer some multiple-choice questions about how he would do it. Charles Schulz makes the point very well in one of his Peanuts cartoons: Charlie Brown, kite-string in hand, lectures Lucy at length on the aerodynamics of kites ('the ratio of weight to sail area is very important . . . known as sail loading', etc.); obviously he could write a good essay on the subject but his process-weakness is highlighted by Lucy's crushing observation, 'Then why is your kite down the sewer?'!

So, although terminal, summative assessment usually concentrates on products more than does formative assessment, it need not do so; and in some cases must not do so. If the emphasis is on process objectives, there may be no product to assess (e.g. conversing in French). Even if the processes are meant to result in a product, it may be illegitimate to make too many inferences about the nature and the quality of the processes that went into it: perhaps because various different combinations of process skills could equally well have resulted in a product that looked the same; perhaps because the product, while giving a good idea of the process skills that went into its creation, fails to reveal anything about other, at least equally important, process skills that were being exercised in the same context. For example, a set of patients' case-histories may tell something about the ability of a student-doctor to elicit information but conceal the fact that he antagonized each and every one of them in the arrogant or insensitive way he did it. I suspect both of these factors operate at times in project-work, where, despite there being much emphasis on process objectives, most of the advice on their assessment seems to concentrate on how to infer the process-contribution from the finished product rather than how to observe processes in action (see Hudson, 1973; and Macintosh, 1974).

Though a product may fail to reveal all about the processes that produced it, these may be somewhat recoverable by discussion with the student who produced it. Some oral examinations concentrate on quizzing the student about how he developed the written work or other exhibits that the examiners have seen. Recalling and talking about processes, however, is not the same as demonstrating them. The student may be unable to find the words to let his examiner into what was going on in his head; he may have forgotten; he may have acted intuitively without ever reflecting on how he was setting about his production; or he may simply spin a yarn because he knows what sort of processes the examiner is likely to approve of. Conversely, even if the exercise of processes results in no tangible, assessable product, something of them can be made tangible, as we've already discussed, by recording the episode. Finally, if process-learning has no other product, it has the student himself. As Robert Pirsig (1975) said, in arguing that the duality between mechanic and machine disappears when the man 'cares' as a craftsman for what he is doing, 'the real cycle you're working on is a cycle called "yourself".' Processes leave their mark on the student. What does he feel he has learned from the processes he has engaged in; how has he grown; how have they affected his viewpoints? They have helped determine not just what he *does* and what he *knows*, but also what he *is*.

Internal vs. External Assessment

Here the underlying question is: Who shall assess? Shall it be someone internal to the teaching situation (e.g. the teacher) or some external assessor? Someone who knows the student or someone who does not? The answer must consider whose assessments are likely to be the most truthful and useful.

Everyday formative assessment will, almost by definition, be internal — performed chiefly by the teacher as part of his teaching. Though he is not the only one who contributes here: other teachers, the student, and the student's colleagues will all help him 'form' the student through their informal assessments. (More of this in a moment.) The teacher's pre-eminence in this area of assessment goes unquestioned. Who else is in a position to find out about how the student is developing with sufficient accuracy and frequency to help him along the way? In passing, however, we must recall that such assessment is prone to all kinds of prejudices, oversights, misinterpretations, and idiosyncrasy of standards; and, while this is the 'diagnostic interface' of teaching, student-teachers are not normally given training, or even supervised practice, in how to do it.

But misgivings about teachers having the predominant responsibility arise mainly when the assessment is meant to be summative, classificatory, and reported. Such misgivings have diverse causes. For instance, Joseph Schwab (1954) blasts off at the supposed effect on teacher-student relations:

> . . . ingenuity could not combine the inimical effects of bread-and-butter love and submission to the taskmaster and inquisitor more effectively than does the institution of the teacher-set examination. Without its removal, the possibility of establishing a sound teaching relation with the vast majority of students is well-nigh nil.

With external assessment, by contrast, the teacher and student can play the game of 'collaborating' to defeat the assessor (fairly, of course);

though this may seem a little unreal if the student becomes aware that the teacher can, if he wished, *become* the assessor (as in CSE).

But even stronger misgivings about internal assessment, representing very powerful interests in society, are expressed here by the Schools Council (1963, p. 25):

> In some countries . . . it is accepted that the teacher is likely to know more about his pupils than an external assessor, and that he can provide more information about them than a necessarily short examination can hope to do. He can also put his own pupils in an order of merit more accurately than any examination. What he cannot do is to be sure that he is accurately assessing the standards of his own pupils in relation to those of other pupils in other schools.

One might wonder why the teacher should need to relate his assessments to standards applied elsewhere. After all, any potential user of the information he has to offer about one of his students might be presumed to be interested in what that student knows, and can do, and is, rather than whether he is better or worse in some overall sense than some other students with whom the user has no direct concern. However, the ideology of classificatory assessment fosters the myth of comparability of standards, and asserts by its procedures that there is some sense in which GCE passes in English literature and in mathematics, or second-class degrees in Spanish and in aeronautical engineering, can be held equivalent. Since assessors are not expected to describe the students, but to produce simplistic, reductive labels instead, there arises the need to see that students are not treated unfairly by having the 'wrong' labels attached. Hence the attempts to arrive at a label which *other* teachers would agree with.

Whether teachers are entrusted with the labelling depends on the level of public confidence in their professional judgement. British university teachers have traditionally exercised enormous freedom to set and mark their own examinations. Admittedly it is the custom to appoint 'external examiners', usually teachers from other universities, whose role it is to ensure that standards of accreditation are similar to those in other institutions. Many of us who have acted in this capacity, however, would feel the role is heavier on symbolism than effect, since there is often no opportunity to do more than sample the work that has been marked and the 'external' who makes a practice of vehemently insisting on standards other than those of his hosts is unlikely to be asked back the following year.

In schools, teachers have not traditionally been trusted to the same extent. External assessors have until recently given the final verdict on their students. In the late nineteenth century this was done by Her Majesty's Inspectors whose annual visits to schools might, in those days of payments by results, un-nerve the teacher more than the pupils. In the twentieth century, psychologists began to take an 'external' hand in summative assessment of primary schoolchildren, e.g. through the development of standardized tests of reading and of general ability. Similarly, the universities became the centre of influence in the various examining boards for secondary school-leaving examinations. But recent years have seen teachers taking more and more responsibility for summative assessment, first of all for other teachers' students through membership of examining panels and latterly for their own students through arrangements whereby their marking will simply be checked or 'moderated' by external assessors, usually other teachers. Some moderation procedures are described by Hoste and Bloomfield (1975). Essentially, they aim to ensure that each student's work gets a grade that a consensus of teachers would agree with — by preliminary exercises to allow a teacher to compare his marking with that of colleagues and subsequently adjust his standards and/or by having his marks adjusted subsequently by an external assessor who has himself marked a sample of that teacher's students, and of other teachers.

So long as assessments are to be reduced to labels, some such external check on internal standards may be fair. But care is needed to ensure that assessment methods are kept relevant to the educational objectives and not distorted for the sake of administrative convenience, e.g. having students write essays about navigation which can be sent off to external assessors rather than expecting the external assessors to come and see how well students can sail a boat. Similar distortion could arise out of the desire to ensure comparability in project work assessment — especially when the work is individualized with different students pursuing different purposes in different ways. Assessment, and the implied comparison of highly individual theses, is handled at post-graduate level by having more than one assessor per candidate. The danger is that the expense of doing likewise for larger numbers at lower levels would drive out the assessment of individualized assignments, and hence, by natural selection, squeeze out individualized activity altogether in favour of standardized tasks.

Incidentally, formal examiners are not the only possible source of external assessment. During his school career the student will have interacted with many people in his local community: he may have been a member of a scout group or political party, done voluntary work for the old or disabled, delivered newspapers, or worked in a supermarket at weekends and holidays. Many people outside his school will know him as a person and could contribute to his 'profile'. (Parents too may be expected to know a thing or two.) Similarly with the college or university student whose range and depth of interactions with others in the community we might expect to be even greater. Teachers are not obliged to gather together such dispersed assessment data for summative purposes, though when from time to time the odd tit-bit reaches them, it can help influence their formative approach with the student.

The teacher may well find another source of useful semi-external assessment among colleagues who also teach his student. Unless assessment is discussed *collaboratively* among colleagues responsible for different areas of a class's curriculum, much potentially relevant information will be lost. Teachers are liable to overlook or misinterpret students' display of skills taught by other teachers of other subjects. Hence, evidence as to the student's ability to transfer and generalize his learning may be ignored. For instance, the student who has been encouraged to read widely by his English teacher may display this disposition not in English but in science or mathematics — without his English teacher ever getting to hear the good news. Again, the student who has been taught, perhaps by philosophy or religious studies teachers, to tease out the implications of fine-sounding slogans and assertions, may practice the skill in history or economics lessons, perhaps to the displeasure of his teachers. Ideally, each member of the teaching team should be aware of his colleagues' objectives as well as his own and should be prepared to observe students' exercise of them in his lessons and report back to colleagues when necessary.

Finally, there are two more sources of internal assessment — the student himself and his colleagues. How far can the student contribute to his own assessment? How far should he be taught to do so? Self-assessment is undoubtedly a valuable life-skill. Michael Simpson (1976), discussing this point in the context of medical education, makes the point that 'a doctor had better be his own most severe and most reliable examiner — for very often, in practice, he will be his own only examiner'. A person with limited talents but a realistic capacity for appraising them might cope better with life than his highly talented friend who lacks the capacity for self-knowledge. In formative assessment there are no barriers to promoting self-appraisal. Students may be encouraged to keep diaries, journals and weekly reviews of their work and to discuss both those aspects of their work they seem to be mastering and those they are getting stuck over. At the end of each learning assignment or project, the student may be asked to indicate his thoughts and feelings about it. What did he make of it? What did he get out of it? What did it do for him? How interesting was it? How difficult? How worthwhile? What was the best thing about it? What was the worst thing? What other experiences does it connect up with? What would he like to work on next?

If the students are using programmed learning or other structured learning materials they may be able to assess their own progress very realistically in terms of the objectives being pursued. Where students are partly responsible for their own objectives, self-assessment will not be so easy, for students will need to develop their own criteria for judging progress — not take them on tailor-made from the teacher. But the sensitive teacher can help the student externalize his criteria and urge him towards higher and higher standards. That such self-critical skills may long go wanting can be inferred from experience like that of John Cowan (1975): even in university examinations many students (whatever their general ability) are incapable of deciding to which questions they have given their best and worst answers.

Schools will find their own way of encouraging self-assessment if they value it at all. Bosworth College (Marcus, 1973) expects the student to contribute to the periodic report, thus allowing interesting comparisons of viewpoint between student and teacher. Here, for example, are the two reports on a student's progress in religious knowledge:

Student's Report

I don't think my work has got any better since my last report. This is really because most of the written work I do is the writing up of a discussion for homework and I never really concentrate on the homework. I often become very bored in the lessons because I think the discussions last too long and after a while of listening I tend to only half pay attention, then by the time I have got round to do the homework I only vaguely remember how to do it. I think it would be a good idea if we studied the different religions of different countries. I think this would be a bit more interesting than just working from the Bible all the time.

Teacher's Report

Ann . . . has not really taken to the idea of forming her own views and would much rather, apparently, that I tell her what she should think. I think it has been made clear enough by now that I won't!
What she needs to do, eventually, is to decide that a discussion is not an easy way out of work; it is in fact harder because one needs to speak, listen and make notes in order to remember what has happened. Too frequently, Ann does not do this because she chats to the person next to her and the effect has been shown once or twice when she has asked a question just after we had spent some time talking about it.

Here we approach the boundary between formative and summative assessment. It is when we step into the firmly summative and credentializing that the student's contribution to assessment becomes problematical. The point is, how much notice can be taken of his opinion when it comes to deciding whether he should pass or fail, or get this grade or that, or one label rather than another? Either his assessment agrees with the teacher's, in which case there is no problem, or it does not, in which case there is!

Barnard Gilmore (1973) reports four years of experience with a self-marking system in which students do usually rate themselves as their teacher would. However, this is accomplished by asking them merely to decide which of several categories established by the teacher they fall into and making clear that their self-marking will be 'corrected' for error. Unfortunately, guessing how other people would rate you, and knowing that it will make no practical difference if you guess wrong, is an activity that can be engaged in without any personal assessment of your achievements or any reflection on whether you value them more or less than those others would. In informal discussions, one might get the impression that many students will under-value themselves. But where grades are important, it is hardly surprising to find, as did Ronald Burke (1969), that students appear unable to assign their own grades 'realistically', almost always believing, or at least asserting, that they deserve a grade higher than the teacher thinks appropriate.

Nor is it surprising, as Ronald Burke goes on to demonstrate, that such students are considerably more 'realistic' when they are asked to assign grades to one another! Thomas K. Bloom (1974) recommends such 'peer-evaluation' as a source of insights to the teacher and as a means of involving students more actively in the learning process, not least by requiring them to think critically about the relative value of the various objectives their colleagues are achieving. Peer-evaluation is perhaps more productive as a 'source of insights to the teacher', however, when students are using their own criteria to assess one another. Eliot Eisner (1972, p. 234) recommends to art teachers the 'group critique' method of assessment. Each student displays one or more pieces of his work, describes it, and solicits reactions from classmates. Besides offering students the opportunity to explain their products and to see how others tackle similar problems, 'it provides the teacher with an opportunity to use student comments diagnostically. To what do students respond in the work of their peers: its technical quality, its ingenuity, its aesthetic character, its subject matter? By noticing what students see and react to first, the teacher is in a better position to understand what students *miss* seeing.' Here, students' assessments of others are being interpreted, reflexively, as assessments of themselves. Bernard Beck and Howard Becker (1969) recommend, as an alternative to examinations in sociology, that students present and discuss their research reports and theoretical essays in a 'symposium' — a form of public meeting that would enable the student to benefit professionally from the reactions of his colleagues, and the teacher to learn about the critical skills and criteria of his students.

Students can certainly help one another with formative assessment, if the social climate is right. Douglas Barnes (1976) quotes many classroom discussions in which one child's assessment and consequent response to what his colleague has said enables that colleague to sharpen up his own ideas. Here is a short exchange (with Barnes's commentary) which follows on from Steve's explanation that they have been able to suck milk up, through a straw because 'you make a vacuum with your . . . mouth, don't you?' (p. 40):

Dialogue	Commentary
S What about this glass of milk though, Glyn?	Steve seems to have been uneasy about Glyn's previous explanation, as is indicated by his placing of the word 'though'.
G Well that's 'cause you make a vacuum in your mouth. . .	Glyn's answer to Steve's challenge is no more than a repetition of his previous vague account.

Dialogue	Commentary
S When you drink the milk you see . . . you. . .	Steve seems dissatisfied, and sets off on a more explicit reply to his own question. When he hesitates he implicitly requires Glyn to complete the analysis by using the explanatory framework which he has set up.
G Right! . . . You you make a vacuum there, right?	Glyn's first 'Right' accepts the task. His second 'right' asks Steve whether his explanation so far is acceptable.
S Yes well you make a vacuum in the . . . er . . . transparent straw. . .	Steve does not find Glyn's use of 'there' explicit enough and (most usefully) insists that the vacuum is 'in the transparent straw'.
G Yes.	Glyn accepts the correction.
S Carry on.	Steve urges his friend to continue with the explanation.
G And the er air pressure outside forces it down, there's no pressure inside to force it back up again so. . .	Here Glyn achieves the essential explanatory point that it is the different pressures at the surface of the milk and inside the straw that make drinking possible.
S OK.	Steve accepts this version.

Self-assessments and assessments by other students, then, can produce valuable knowledge in or about the student. In some cases such assessment will be not only different from, but also more 'true' than what might arise from the teacher's attempt to gauge the qualities in question. Thus the individual student will know better than anyone else what are his own interests, distastes and satisfactions. Thus the classmates who've worked with the student in small groups are in a position to make better-formed judgements of his qualities as a collaborator than is the onlooking teacher. However, even teachers who would encourage and respond to such assessments in formative situations usually see no way of using them in summative situations. How to incorporate them in the student's grade or label, which averages out all the data available about him, while making clear how much has been contributed by what is 'only' student-opinion? While I would disagree, as indicated above, that student-opinion always means less than teacher-opinion, I would agree that they are different. Interesting distinctions of viewpoint are lost in melling them together. Self-assessments and peer-assessments can take a proper place alongside teacher-assessments, and be interpreted sensibly, only in a summative assessment system whose outcome is not a grade or label but a *profile* of the student to which all who are able to speak about him can contribute what they know — and in which conflicting assessments are highlighted rather than ironed out.

Convergent vs. Divergent Assessment

To label the distinction I wish to make in this section, I have borrowed the terminology from Liam Hudson (1966b). He popularized the terms 'convergent' and 'divergent' to distinguish between two styles of thinking and expression he found among English schoolboys. Briefly, the convergers excelled when rationally focusing on a clearly defined task with a single correct answer, but the divergers came into their own when the task was open-ended, with no single correct answer, allowing them full vent for fantasy, imagination and creativity. As a matter of fact, this distinction was established in a context of assessment. Hudson found convergers (generally science-specialists) doing better on 'intelligence' tests, while the divergers (generally arts-specialists) were more productive with 'creativity' test items like 'Write down as many uses as you can think of for, e.g., a house-brick, a water-barrel, a paper-clip, etc'. But we can use the terms to delimit a continuum that will enable us to think of any test or assessment situation (not just the kinds Liam Hudson was using) as being more or less likely than another to elicit and reward convergent qualities or divergent qualities in the student. At different times and for different purposes the teacher may wish to know of both kinds of qualities: whether he does get to know will depend on how he assesses.

In psychological testing, the archetypal convergent, or closed form of assessment, where each item has one correct answer, is the so-called 'objective test' — made up of multiple-choice questions of one kind or another. (The description 'objective' should not be allowed here to refer to anything but the decision as to whether or not the student has chosen the approved answer; the prior decision as to which questions were worth including in the test is as subjective as any we get in education.) By contrast, psychologists also use open-ended tests, especially in the study of personality, in which there is no correct answer and the interest lies in the *kind* of answers the student gives. These tests are often called 'projective' tests because the student is expected to project his own world-view into answering the questions. A typical projective test is the famous Rorsarch test where the student is presented with a series of suggestive 'ink-blots' and asked to describe what he sees in each. Another is the Thematic Apperception Test where the student is shown a series of pictures, usually involving one or more people in situations capable of diverse interpretations, and is invited to tell a story explaining what is happening. His answers — what he says about the ink-blots or the pictures — are presumed to tell the tester something about how he sees the world. Provided, that is, he hasn't learned about such tests through introductory psychology classes and taken care to present only what he sees as 'interesting' or approved-of responses! Unlike intelligence tests, which can only be faked 'downwards', it is possible for the student on personality tests to 'improve' the image he offers of himself, e.g. by bringing to mind, from fiction if necessary, some person he believes the tester would approve of and answering the questions not as he truly would but as he believes that other person would answer them (see Huff, 1961, Ch. 13).

Sometimes psychologists will abandon paper-and-pencil tests altogether in their search for divergent qualities or for information about how the student will cope in situations where there is no one correct response. They may indeed use what is sometimes called 'situational testing'. Thus, for example, potential business managers may find themselves facing an 'in-tray exercise' (see Lopez, 1966). Here the candidate or trainee may be presented with an 'in-tray' containing all the letters, memos, financial statements, committee agendas, etc., that might come to him in the course of a normal day; and he is expected to handle them by issuing instructions, dictating letters, making telephone calls, planning meetings, etc., just as he would in the real job situation. Anyone who has been through military 'officer selection' procedures will recall similar situational assessments — the candidate perhaps being given some task to perform, building a bridge maybe, with the help of some 'subordinates' one of whom, unknown to him, is a confederate of the assessor briefed to be clumsy, or slow on the uptake, or hostile, and generally ready to make things tough for the candidates (see Shouksmith, 1968, Ch. 6-8).

Such tests would be used in the hope that they would give a truer idea of how the candidate would act in real life than could possibly be gained from his answers to test questions, whether convergent or divergent. But there are psychologists who would be suspicious of the controlled divergence possible in test situations. They would regard 'real life' as the proper situational test and look to a person's life-history as the ultimate criterion of truth about him. Henry Murray (1938) was the first to explicitly recommend the life-history model to assessment psychologists; but many have followed, as the titles of just a few books give evidence: *The Study of Lives* (White, 1964); *The Course of Human Life* (Buhler and Massarik, 1968); *Assessment of Lives* (Dailey, 1971). The basic assumption is that identifying some kind of ground plan or 'plot' in a person's life so far, considering not only what has happened but also what it *means* to the person, will enable the assessor to make verifiable predictions about how that person will be likely to respond to new situations as they arise in the future. (This phenomenological approach to 'a life' is well supported by the sociological concepts of 'timetables' [Roth, 1963] and 'careers' [Goffman, 1967], which can apply to short periods, e.g. a stay in hospital or progress through parenthood, as well as long ones.) Such assessment would normally be conducted through interviews and discussion. However, documents like auto-biographies and letters can be richly informative (see Allport, 1942; and Abbs, 1975): a prime example would be the fascinating series of letters edited by Gordon Allport (1965) in which a woman's correspondence with two young friends over the last twelve years of her life must represent the projective 'test' *par excellence*.

Teachers too may look to the student's real life for clues as to his divergent qualities — even if the 'real life' is mainly defined in terms of educational activities, with the student's 'leisure life' being something the teacher only learns about through what the student chooses to report of it. Unfortunately, the teacher may not always be capable of appreciating the student's divergent qualities, his ability to identify new problems and generate unexpected or alternative solutions. Some teachers may feel so threatened by such 'waywardness' on the part of the students, especially if developed outside the comforting frame of an academic discipline, that they write the students off as 'bolshy', 'know-it-alls' or 'student rebels'. Such attitudes, accompanied by a tendency to under-rate the school performance of divergers as against convergers, were uncovered in the classic study of creativity by Getzels and Jackson (1962).

Be that as it may, some educational activities are more encouraging of divergent qualities than others, and therefore more prolific of life-situations or products in which such qualities can be discerned and assessed. Apart from the unprogrammed to-ing and fro-ing of class-room intercourse, the teacher has opportunity for divergent assessment whenever the learning activities allow for the student to at least partly determine his own objectives and/or his means of attaining them. Projects would seem to be a case in point, so long as they don't take the form of 'cookbook' investigations in which the student's role is simply to follow instructions. Again, work done in the community (see Ball and Ball, 1973) should give the teacher interesting insights into the students' individual ways of defining and coping with a situation. Edward Angus (1974) discusses 'experiential' assessment methods that can be used with students who are spending several weeks out of the classroom gaining experience 'in the field'. Role-playing and simula-tion games, e.g. the 'in-tray' exercise, are another open-ended learning activity in which there are no predeterminate right answers. (See Boocock and Schild, 1968; Tansey and Unwin, 1969; Taylor and Walford, 1973.) When students are launched into negotiating the siting of a new airport, simulating a local election, conducting an industrial dispute, surviving a period of unemployment (or the social aftermath of nuclear war), coping with vandalism in a country town, or running the nation's economy, they will project their own perspectives and diverse styles: the outcomes of the game will likely reflect *them* rather than their knowledge of some subject-matter definable in advance by the teacher. Not all educational games will aim to stimulate divergence, however. A teacher of organic chemistry (Pusey, 1974) describes the card games he developed for use with his degree students and whose purpose is to allow the students to rehearse their knowledge and understanding of, for instance, four kinds of spectra or reactions in aromatic chemistry, in contexts akin to those of games of Happy Families, Poker, Patience or Bingo. His chief intent is to encourage self-assessment of (convergently) 'regions of confusion, misunderstanding, or ignorance'. But even in such fairly constrained games, divergent qualities may expose them-selves to assessment. A one-time president of the Gulf Oil Company was said to enjoy a game of poker with his business associates, as was Bismarck a game of chess with the military leaders of nineteenth-century Europe, because of the opportunity it afforded him to predict their likely styles and strategies in real life conflict-situations. The teacher who is alive to divergent qualities in such assessment situations may gain many insights into what the student has learned from agencies other than himself — from other teachers, from outside reading, from family and friends, from television, and so on. (It might seem theoretically possible to assess what the student has learned from, say, television or social contacts, with a paper-and-pencil test — but only by treating them as a kind of inefficient substitute for book-learning.)

Now what do we find when we turn away from assessment carried out while students engage in life or learning and look at the assessment carried out in situations created by the teacher specifically for that purpose? Here, while divergent qualities may still emerge (e.g. in a medical student's approach to taking a history from a patient), the teacher is more likely to be watching out for some particular qualities and a degree of convergence will be required or, at least, rewarded. Even in arts subjects, where the student might be expected to get excited by his subject, a certain circumspection may be demanded by the situation. B. R. Lee's poem *A Bit of Advice* warns:

> . . . keep a stiff upper lip, speak through gritted teeth,
> sound critical, prosaic, clerkly, neat:
> wear your heart upon your sleeve — but be discreet.

The teacher is likely to have one or more possible 'right' answers somewhere in mind, or at least 'right' methods of presenting (and thereby redeeming) what would otherwise be a wrong answer. Joe Spriggs (1972) sees this as applying especially to exams, even in English literature:

> The exam will make you read Byron in a certain way, read certain things about Byron and spend many happy hours trying to remember the whole in a manageable form for me to test whether you *did* read Byron . . . or you did read the right criticism . . . or that you came to the *right* conclusions about Byron . . . or that you came to the wrong ones in the *right* kind of way.

Indeed, one of the inherent weaknesses of formal assessment is the difficulty the teacher tends to have in generating situations or questions that allow students to express their own kinds of understanding in their own ways. The teacher finds it much easier to think up the sort of questions that would enable *him* to display *his* kind of understanding. As long as the teacher honestly believes that his kind is the only kind worth having, he can justify asking students the sort of questions he would relish being asked himself. But as soon as he begins to admit that students may find other legitimate ways of construing reality, ways whose validity he may recognize once they are deployed but which he cannot anticipate, his faith in such convergent assessment can no longer be so easily maintained. If he still wishes to assess formally, that is by events specially engineered for assessment purposes, he may ask each of his students how he wishes to be assessed, inviting him, for instance, to nominate topics or issues he would be happy to address himself to. Not long ago, I heard a revealing remark from a colleague in a technology discipline which seems to type him as an assessor of convergent qualities. Having been asked to produce four years'-worth of assessment and examination questions (including specimen papers and fall-back papers in case of security leaks), he complained bitterly but in all seriousness: 'There's only a limited number of questions you can ask in my field!'

No such anxieties beset the professor of Greek often quoted by another colleague, John Ferguson, when year after year he set the same examination question: 'Hellas is one, but the cities are many. Discuss.' Even more divergently, Clifford Bebell (p. 37 in Wilhelms, 1970) recalls the history department of a leading U.S. college setting its students an all-day examination on the one question: 'Write a history of the world to date.' Whether students actually are rewarded for being divergent in response to such invitations can only be ascertained by looking at their scripts and seeing how their assessors have responded to them. The fact remains that many different but equally viable answers are possible. Such 'projective' questions give the student some opportunity to display what he has made of his learning — from *all* sources — rather than how much he has learned of what the teacher was trying to teach. (Recall William S. Learned's remarks quoted on p. 62.)

There are grave problems, however. I'll mention two of them: one pedagogic, the other administrative. First of all, is it fair to the student to offer him so broad a canvas? Many students would resent such an unstructured situation — almost equivalent to being asked 'What have you learned from this course?' They might ask why the assessor can't be a bit more specific about what sort of answer he wants. (They assume, you see, that he's looking for convergence.) Secondly, how do you compare the students' answers? They may choose to tackle quite different aspects in quite different ways. Is it sensible and fair to apply the same grading system to such diverse products?

One way of solving both these problems is to make the question more specific. Instead of asking, let's say, 'What aspects of the political system of modern Sweden seem to you most worthy of comment?', we might ask the student to: 'Comment on the political *stability* of modern Sweden.' We might be yet more specific and indicate what kind of comment we'd think appropriate by saying, '*Explain* the political stability of modern Sweden.' We might offer the student even more structure (and less room for divergence) by saying, 'Identify and discuss *three factors* that might help explain modern Sweden's political stability.' We might give the student an even heftier nudge in the direction we want, closing off alternative ways of viewing the issue, by asking, 'Identify and discuss three factors that might help explain the emergence of a stable political system in Sweden *despite the massive social and economic changes engendered by processes of modernization.*'

Notice that what we are doing in the above transformations is successively to restrict the student's scope for manoeuvre. We are removing from the student the responsibility to decide what is significant about the issue under discussion or in what terms it might most usefully be discussed. Thus we are now able to successfully establish whether the student can answer a question formulated by us, using criteria we have suggested; but in the very process have *lost* the means of testing whether he could have formulated such a question and decided on such criteria for himself. However, comparability of answers will have been greatly facilitated. We can now be sure, where we could not have been with the original question, that all students will tackle the same aspect of Swedish politics and in the same terms. Thus the students' efforts can be ranked with relation to one another and grades can be sensibly assigned. Furthermore, there is now a much better chance that different assessors would agree as to the rankings and even to the gradings.* This would appear to be fairer to each student because the marks for what he has done are more justifiable. But it is also *less* fair because, had we not offered the heavy prompting, some students would have been free to show that they could formulate the question without it

---

*The question in its final form is virtually the same as one that was given to students as an assignment on an Open University course. The notes for tutors on that course, telling them how to mark the assignment, went into considerably more detail about what to look for and what to reward in the answers. Once committed to assessing convergently, how does one justify telling markers more than one tells the student about what his answer is to contain?

(or even diverge to answer some equally cogent question of their own); similarly, some students would have revealed an inability to say anything much at all without being told quite firmly what to write about. In short, we may have swopped one sort of unfairness for another; and, in an attempt to ensure comparability and make the grading more accurate, we may have ended up comparing and grading less significant abilities in the student. Macnamara's Fallacy, perhaps — making the measurable important rather than the important measurable?

However, there is yet one more transformation to consider. We can scrap the essay format altogether and substitute a series of multiple-choice questions, e.g. the first might be:

Which three of the factors discussed in the teaching text and listed below might best help explain the emergence of a stable political system in Sweden despite the massive social and economic change engendered by processes of modernization?

A   Affluence

B   Gradual economic development

C   Traditional legitimacy

D   Civic culture

E   A homogeneous political culture

F   Equality

G   Congruent authority patterns

H   Elite consensus

I   The habituation of mechanisms of conflict resolution

J   Political institutionalization

The next question could then take the factors suggested above and, about each one in turn, ask 'If this was one of the factors you chose, which of the statements below best explains the contribution made by that factor?' The student would then tick off his answers and the marking would be so non-controversial it could be done by a machine. However, the suspicion would linger that the baby had disappeared down the same plug-hole as the bath-water. In psychometrics jargon, we may have gained reliability at the expense of validity. We've now lost not only the student's opportunity to reconceptualize the whole problem area (divergence), or even (moderate convergence) his opportunity to show that he can come up with pretty much the same conceptualization we hoped he would, but also we've passed up the chance to establish whether he can even put together a coherent argument. (And even if our psychometric colleagues can prove to us, as well they might, that, in general, students who do well / poorly on the multiple-choice test would be the same ones who would do well / poorly on the essay test, we'd still not be entirely happy. To know that this is true of the students merely *in general* implies that there are exceptions and therefore leaves us ignorant as to whether Joe Bloggs or Mary Smith would have done better or worse on the essay. And of course it can suggest nothing at all about the *kind* of essay argument they'd have presented.)

The 'objective test' with its multiple-choice questions is the ultimate in convergent assessment. One answer (sometimes more) is deemed 'best' by the assessor long before the student sees the test. The student can do nothing to dispute or re-define the question. He cannot tell the assessor that, although he understands what answer the assessor wishes him to choose, he actually prefers another for the following reason. Such a constraint penalizes the divergent student and those who see subtleties that escaped the constructor of the test; hence they find it *more* difficult to answer than would students of less probing mentality (see Hoffman, 1962). Actually, there's no reason why we should not combine multiple-choice and essay, inviting the student to add short notes explaining his choices. But most people who set objective tests would dispute the need for such a device.

Sally Laird (1972), a student writing very critically of the objective tests in English she had recently taken, gives several examples of contestable items. More centrally to our present argument, she offers her conclusion that 'this kind of testing quenches any possibility of originality or personal interpretation' and then rounds off satirically with a telling stab at the soft underbelly of bureaucratic assessment:

> The roles of examiner and candidate have become confused. It is now we, the candidates, and not the examiners who choose, from a series of answers, which one we consider the best — knowing, however, that the person who composed the answers has the ultimate decision about whether our 'marking' is right or wrong. But if this idea is taken to its logical conclusion, one could well foresee the examiners eventually writing the essays also, with the candidates simply ticking the 'correct' one.

Her point here is very well observed. With objective tests it is the assessor who is doing the thinking — deciding what is most worth asking about in the subject-area, and creating a sensible question out of it. Objective tests can be useful, in areas where there really are unarguably correct answers; but even there one might ask whether it might not be more revealing of important qualities to have the student formulate multiple-choice questions himself rather than merely choosing among alternative answers to someone else's. Formulating questions, whether multiple-choice or otherwise, is indeed a very taxing activity for the student, requiring him to operate at the highest levels of Bloom's taxonomy — especially if he has to justify his questions and the kinds of answer he would expect. (Conversely, how instructive it would be for assessors to attempt answers to their own questions and have them marked by colleagues.)

Enough said. My purpose in this section has been to warn that if we rely too heavily on highly structured, standardized assessment tasks in pursuit of comparability, measurability and fairness to 'students in general' we may learn more about the similarities among students (and help create them?) than about ways in which they differ. We may lose touch with the creative, perhaps idosyncratic qualities that are so productive of new, unanticipated answers and up-ended questions.

Idiographic vs. Nomothetic Assessment

These Greek labels have entered the vocabulary of assessment psychologists out of German philosophy. The first label has to do with 'writings about the individual'; the second concerns 'the making of general laws'. Thus idiographic assessment aims to find out about an individual and arrive at a meaningful understanding of his uniqueness — what he does, and knows, and is — what 'makes him tick'. Nomothetic assessment, on the other hand, while it collects data about individuals, does so with a view to comparing one with another, generalizing from those assessed to others who have not been assessed, and aiming to understand people in general. In terms of the previous paragraph, the one is more concerned with differences, the other with similarities among people. (See the discussion in Mittler, 1973, pp. 12-14.)

We all of us, at different times, react idiographically and nomothetically to our experiences — not just of people. Sometimes we may be preoccupied with the individual quality of that experience; at others we may be more interested in relating it to other experiences, looking for general laws and patterns. William James (1902, p. 10) distinguishes crisply between the two modes of thought:

> The first thing the intellect does with an object is to class it along
> with something else. But any object that is infinitely important to
> us and awakens our devotion feels to us also as if it must be *sui
> generis* and unique. Probably a crab would be filled with a sense of
> personal outrage if it could hear us class it without ado or apology
> as a crustacean, and thus dispose of it. 'I am no such thing,' it
> would say; '*I am myself, myself alone.*'

Do we similarly try to 'dispose of' people by classing them as 'slow
learners', 'behaviour problems' or 'typical C-streamers'? Or even,
apparently more favourably, as 'high fliers', 'no trouble', or 'typical A-
streamers'? Negatively or positively, we are here responding nomothetically, sorting people into pre-existing categories, implying that
there are plenty of people like them around already and that what they
have in common with those similarly labelled others is more significant
than any respects in which they may differ. Whether or not this is
tantamount to disposing of them depends on what we do next. Do we
act henceforth as if such a classification is not only sufficiently
descriptive of the person but is also good for always? Or do we delve
deeper into the individual in order to demonstrate how different he is
from others in that class, perhaps in doing so to demonstrate that he
belongs in a class of his own; and that, in any case, he can never be
described completely and finally because he is always changing?

Early in Chapter 3 I discussed the side-effects of prejudice, stereotyping
and the self-fulfilling prophecy — all of which conspire to prevent a
person's education taking the form it should. Later in that chapter I
discussed the over-use of credentials, and the corresponding lack of
interest in personal qualities an applicant may possess, in selection for
employment and other benefits in society — again leading to
inappropriate use of human beings. Such are the hazards of nomothetic
assessment.

The temptation to be nomothetic is clearly strongest when engaged in
summative assessment, which often requires students to be labelled like
Plato's 'children of gold, children of silver, and children of baser metals'
or like Olympic medalists (gold, silver, bronze), runners-up, and non-
qualifiers. Bureaucratic convenience fosters the illusion that two
students each with, say, second-class honours degrees in physics, have
more in common than either would have with colleagues who obtained
thirds or firsts; and that whatever it is they have in common it is sensibly
summed up in the common label. Furthermore, there is a common

predictive inference — not as strong as a scientific law though of the same ilk — that students of such-and-such a description can be expected by and large and in general, to be capable of developing in certain foreseeable ways, and being useful in certain definable ways, in the *future*.

This ideology underlies all mass-assessment systems — e.g. the college entrance exams in the U.S.A., the Baccalaureat in France, the CSE/GCE in England — where the outcome is ranking and labelling of individuals in comparison with others in terms of a few crudely delineated traits and abilities supposedly held in common. As a methodology in experimental or social psychology, from whence it derives, the nomothetic approach has considerable power. Provided the sample of people assessed and labelled is sufficiently representative, quite strong generalizations can emerge, and the behaviour of other similar groups of people can be reasonably well predicted. For example, we may be able to forecast with some confidence that 10% of black girl delinquents will become pregnant before leaving school; or that children whose parents separated will later be twice as likely as other children to find their own marriages breaking up; or that, of arts students entering the Open University without educational qualifications, around 20% will fail to complete their first course. Victoria Rippere (1974) offers a splendid illustration of how quite rough-and-ready assessment can serve the administrative purpose of dealing with 'people in general': 'Consider a lift operator in a big department store. Let us suppose the lift has a maximum capacity of 2000 pounds. Under ordinary conditions, the operator will be unable to weigh each passenger on a scale before deciding how many to admit for each trip. So he has to make crude estimates. The big fat lady counts for so much and the [skinny] type for so much, and so on. The next time any passenger rides, she may be "weighted" somewhat differently, and the operator's colleague on the Saturday shift may assign them each different weights, but as long as the lift doesn't break down through overloading, their rough estimates [serve the purpose].'

Such nomothetic predictions, akin to the actuarial approach of insurance companies, are very valuable as an administrative early-warning system, e.g. how many students shall the Open University cater for on second-level courses, allowing for drop-out? But we must not jump to the assumption that what is 'actuarially' true for the group will also be 'clinically' true for the individual. The fact that 20% of Open University entrants who have this one feature in common with this particular entrant will drop out, does not mean that *he* is only 80%

certain to complete his first course. Although we do not know which, he is either 100% certain to complete or 100% certain to drop out. Likewise, no individual delinquent can become 10% pregnant and no individual child of a broken marriage can have a marriage that is twice as broken as someone else's. To predict the individual's future, we need to know far more about his personal style and qualities than can be encapsulated in general comparisons with others (see Meehl, 1954). Adjectives like 'self-disciplined' or 'courageous', or 'creative', for example, are not of much help, since there may be as many types of self-discipline, courage and creativity as there are people possessing (or observing) such qualities.

This has always been bad news to psychology, of course, struggling to assert its status as a science dealing in general laws. Yet clinicians — practitioners like psychotherapists, physicians and teachers, hoping to bend their expertise to the betterment of unique individuals — have long known that success depends on tailoring the treatment to that very uniqueness (see Loe, 1975). As Gordon Allport (1965, p. 159) pointed out: 'A man who wishes to please his wife with a Christmas gift does less well if he relies on his knowledge of feminine psychology in general than if he knows the individual desires and tastes of his wife.' Beset by large numbers of clients or feelings of inability to cope with individual needs, doctors and teachers may often lapse into treating their clients as 'types' without really getting to know them as persons with unique needs. But they are usually sophisticated enough not to be surprised when the therapy or medication or teaching, which works with 'such cases' in general, fails to work with some people in particular. Recall Hilda Taba's experience (quoted on p. 38) with teachers who learned to individualize among children previously labelled, nomothetically, as 'slow learners'.

In short, then, formative assessment that is truly to be conducive to the educational growth of the individual, must always be idiographic above all else. Of course, it may also have nomothetic implications: teachers, doctors and psychotherapists all will hopefully learn from their experience. It seems reasonable to expect that they will extract principles that apply to more than one person. Gordon Allport (1937), an early campaigner for idiographic assessment, would have disputed this, by the way, insisting that constructs developed in understanding one person would, virtually by definition, be inapplicable to anyone else; though in his more recent works this attitude has softened. But if formative assessment fixates on the nomothetic (not even going so far as 'He may be a slow learner, but . . .') then the resulting teaching is likely to be inappropriate and may, through the self-fulfilling prophecy, make the learner other and lesser than he might have been.

Summative assessment, if it is meant simply to ensure that necessary administrative ends are served, e.g. filling so many university or college places, might just as well be nomothetic. But if it is meant to serve the best interests of individuals, e.g. selecting people who are truly going to find themselves in a course or career being offered, it had better pay some attention to the idiographic.

Choice of Assessment Methods

From the welter of assessment methods and approaches mentioned in the foregoing pages, how do we decide which to use when? Sometimes this decision will be taken 'in advance' — whether or not to set a test or carry out an interview, what kinds of question to ask. Sometimes it will be an 'on-the-spot' decision — whether or not to pay heed to a particular event (e.g. views expressed by a student during a discussion) as a source of assessment data. Either way, whether planning assessment events or admitting those that have 'just happened', what criteria can we apply?

First and foremost, we must apply criteria of *educational relevance*. For instance, does a particular assessment method seem to 'go with' the content and style of the teaching and learning experienced by our students? Thus, laboratory practicals would appear an inappropriate assessment method when a course had concentrated on classroom discussions about the social responsibilities of science; simulation games would not 'go with' a course that had been conducted entirely by means of lectures and written assignments; essay examinations might seem irrelevant in a course that had been structured around student-initiated projects.

In identifying assessment methods that are appropriate to the content and style of the teaching and learning, we have hopefully thereby identified methods that are relevant also to our educational objectives and assessment constructs. This will be so insofar as our content and style relates to those objectives and constructs. However, this relationship may be out of true. Our teaching may over-emphasize the reading and writing of French, though we are equally interested in our students being able to understand and produce spoken French; we may have drifted into descriptive approaches to biology when what we really want from our students is analysis; we may have found ourselves encouraging students to memorize the facts of history when actually our intention is that they should learn to think historically. In such cases, an assessment technique that honestly mirrored the content and style of the teaching might actually get students to display the *wrong* qualities.

So we must ask explicitly: Which assessment methods relate to our objectives and constructs? Which will produce indications of the student abilities or qualities we are interested in? In this chapter and previous ones I have time and again pointed out that different assessment methods call forth different kinds of quality from the student. Students' answers to multiple-choice questions give no more information about what qualities might emerge in essays or in simulation games than would measurements of their blood pressures inform us as to their ages and heights.

Remember also that, just as different assessment methods engage with different abilities and qualities, so too do different ways of using whatever method is chosen. For instance, the examiner in a test of driving competence may show his candidate some pictures of various road-signs and ask, 'What does each of these signs mean?' or, alternatively, he may say, 'Describe to me the sign for "No Entry", "Stop and Give Way", "T-Junction", etc.' Now these are not equivalent ways of getting information about the candidate's knowledge. In his first question the examiner is asking the candidate to *recognize* road signs; in his second he is asking him to *recall* them. Of course, it may or may not be the case that, in general, candidates who can do one are usually able to do the other also. But such nomothetic correlations would not help us in our idiographic concern with the specific candidate in question. *He* may be one of those who can't recall what the signs look like but can recognize them when he sees them. Whether or not he does see them, when he's out on the road, is a further issue that casts doubt on the relevance of asking either of these two questions. Perhaps the examiner should have relied on the practical test rather than interview as his assessment method.

This aspect of the 'educational relevance' criterion cannot be emphasized enough. Assessment methods must relate to important objectives. It is fatally easy to assess related but different objectives as well as or even instead of those you really care about — especially when those related objectives lend themselves more easily to measurement. Even 'intelligence' tests often appear to depend very heavily on abilities supposedly not under consideration, especially 'general knowledge'. Brian Simon (1971) analyses an extreme example, a pre-war verbal intelligence test for children of about eleven, whose questions they cannot answer at all unless they know:

> . . . the meaning of such words as 'spurious', 'antique', 'external', 'irregular', 'inexpensive', 'affectionate', 'moist'; that a sovereign is made of gold, while a florin is made of silver; that pearls, emeralds, sapphires, diamonds and rubies are precious stones, while gold is not; the relative functions of telephone and telegraph; the use of thermometer; the reasons for saving money; the purpose of charitable societies; what a cubic block is; what a code is; what a clerk's job is; that ledger-clerks work in banks; what an individual's 'mechanical bent' is; what a person's 'inclinations' are; that a shorthand-typist is expected to spell well; what 'the adjustment of an individual to his vocation' means; and finally, that a parlourmaid is not expected to do the sewing in a house! (p. 63)

Such a test is measuring the verbal and social experience of children as well as their 'intellect'. This is tantamount to measuring not so much their personal qualities as the socio-economic status of their parents. More modern tests, even those consisting merely of shapes and pictures and aiming to be 'culture-free', cannot escape the criticism that they are assessing experience and attainment as well as, and to some extent instead of, ability and potential (see McClelland, 1973).

Returning to more academic areas, James Eggleston and John Kerr (1969) give interesting examples of CSE history questions, supposedly testing the students' ability 'to make inferences from evidence' but which are actually 'comprehension' exercises, demanding no particular historical knowledge or expertise. They also (p. 103) quote a question designed to assess the students' ability to 'enter imaginatively into the past . . . and tell something of their thoughts and feelings':

> Imagine that you were a boy or girl in 1841, taking a train journey for the first time in your life, from Leicester to any of the towns which appear on this timetable. Remember that railway travel itself was only about fifteen years old at this time, and that this particular route had been open for even less time. Write a paragraph describing some of your thoughts, feelings and experiences. You need not try to include details if you are not sure of their accuracy. The important thing is to convey your state of mind. N.B. Do not write too much.

True, the question has a refreshing 'modern' air about it. So much more human than the 'list and discuss' questions of long tradition. (Though that final cooling N.B. rather spoils the image.) But how far is it likely to call forth from the candidate those qualities it purports to be testing? Arguably, it is testing rather the candidate's ability to pin down the kind of thoughts and feelings that will seem appropriate to the assessor and then serve them up in an acceptable formula. If this seems cynical, consider what might be the assessor's response to a student who writes a poem, perhaps using the journey as a metaphor, or who expresses a 'state of mind' coloured more by the fact that he is, let's say, leaving home for the first time and going away to school, than by the novelty of his conveyance and the exterior world? How many professional historians, anyway, even those whose 'ability to enter imaginatively into the past' is not in doubt, could turn out the kind of stuff demanded? And doesn't all the above discussion beg the whole question as to whether written exercises are the most appropriate assessment method for the objective, rather than, for example, simulation games, conversation, or drama?

The aspect of 'educational relevance' we've just been concerned with is whether or not a particular assessment method can be expected to tell us whether a student has certain qualities or can perform in a certain way now. A further aspect is raised if we question whether the assessment method will allow us to predict how the student will behave in other situations in the future. Thus, school-leaving examinations may be accepted, uncritically, as better predictors of success in higher education than would be interviews or collections of course work. However, the fact that a person can do something or other now is no guarantee that he will be able to, or will care to, do it in the future. Indeed, what the assessment method requires him to do now may have only a spurious similarity to what he will need to do later on; effective prediction would necessitate a switch to a more relevant assessment method. Thus, for instance, Whitehand (1966) casts doubt on the relevance of university final examinations for selecting students capable of going on to do research. Among geography students who had written a thesis as part of their degree studies, less than half of those who were awarded alpha for the thesis subsequently gained a first or upper second in finals. So, if the thesis reflects research ability at undergraduate level and if this is a reliable indication of research ability at post-graduate level, then the Geography Department might have done better to use a thesis rather than finals as the assessment method whereby it selected research students.

Using examination results as the grounds for predictions about individuals in a hazardous business, as the researches of Hoyt (1965),

Hudson (1966), Berg (1973), etc., mentioned earlier, confirm. But circumspection and a decent humility is recommended with all methods, even life-history assessment. As T. S. Eliot reminds us in *The Cocktail Party*:

> We die to each other daily.
> What we know of other people
> Is only our memory of the moments
> During which we knew them. And they have changed since then.
> To pretend that they and we are the same
> Is a useful social convention
> Which must sometimes be broken. We must also remember
> That at every meeting we are meeting a stranger.

The criteria of 'educational relevance' discussed above can be found, more formally stated, in the psychometric concept of *validity*. Various assessment methods or tests or even specific questions are sometimes said to exhibit varying amounts of validity according to how truly they do in fact call forth the qualities or abilities they are purporting to elicit. Many types of validity have been defined: face validity, concurrent validity, construct validity, predictive validity, and so on. But these are discussed at length in most standard texts on assessment and need not detain us here. Indeed, Victoria Rippere (1974) rightly takes to task a number of authors for carelessly attaching the concept of validity to the assessment method rather than to the assessor's *interpretations* of the resulting data, so perhaps all further mention of validity belongs in our next chapter.

Finally, although I put the educational criteria first, there are other criteria also contributing to the choice of assessment methods, sometimes more heavily. *Respectability* criteria, for instance: we may feel that other people (employers, other institutions, etc.) won't have a proper respect for our institution and its students unless we emphasize certain assessment methods (three-hour exams, chiefly) rather than others. Clearly such criteria may act to safeguard our students' interests and it may well be that those other people's preferences do embody a clear appraisal of the educational relevance of available assessment methods. But one can also see the imagined preferences of others being used as an excuse for the status quo — much as landladies might say, in refusing blacks, children, and dogs: 'I've got nothing against them myself, dear, it's what the neighbours would say!' Other people are, in fact, considerably more willing to countenance non-traditional forms of assessment than they are usually given credit for (see Cox and Collins,

1975). A closely related constraint is that of *inertia*: we've always assessed in such and such a way — why should we change? A very proper question, of course, so long as it is not asked in such a way as to preclude convincing answers. And, to complete the set, we must recognize criteria of *cost*. Some assessment methods are considerably more expensive than others in time, materials or personnel. Thus, assessment by examination takes up more student time than assessment by course work (which would go on anyway). Interviews and oral examinations take up more staff time than written examinations. The marking of essay examinations takes more staff time than the marking of objective tests, but the compilation of the objective test items may take more time than that of the essay questions. And so on.

There are no ground-rules for manipulating these criteria in the selection of assessment methods. But it should be clear that any assessment innovation that will cost more, challenge local traditions, or differ from what our institution's 'significant others' have been believed to expect, can only be justified by firmly establishing its greater *educational relevance*.

CHAPTER 6

HOW TO INTERPRET ?

Whether or not the teacher has thought much about what he is going to assess, or how, his students will say and do 'assessable' things. That is, they will say and do things that would enable him to get to know more about them — their capabilities and interests, and what they are ready to learn or aspire to. But the manner and extent to which he gets to know will depend on what meaning he attaches to those sayings and doings. How will he interpret what students say and do?

Selective Perceptions

Interpretation begins when the teacher notices something significant in what the student says or does. The very act of noticing, and thereby picking out some things as more significant than others, can be regarded as the initial act of interpretation. Regardless of what sort of meaning he is about to attach to the things he's picked out, the teacher is about to attach *more* meaning to them than to the others. Hence the possibility (which we'll need to consider again later) that other people might interpret the student's activities differently. As an example, consider this snatch of conversation (quoted by Joan Tough, 1973, p. 31) between a mother and her three-year-old son who has just spotted the picture on the back of his cereal packet:

Jimmie: What's that?
Mother: It's a submarine.
          Hey — mind your feet — sit properly.
Jimmie: What's it do?
Mother: Did you hear me — get your feet off the chair.
Jimmie: What's that thing do?
Mother: What thing — oh that — it's a submarine. Sit on that
          chair properly, or else go out to play.

Clearly, Jimmie's mother is attaching meaning to what he is doing with
his body but is ignoring his request for information. Another of Joan
Tough's recordings (p. 56) shows a teacher who is interpreting a child's
statement in terms of what it tells her about his grammatical 'weakness'
and attaching no meaning at all to the fact that he is trying to tell her
something important to him:

Tommy: My mum gived me a penny and I —
Miss H: Gave, Tommy, not gived.
          Start again — my mum gave a penny — say that.
Tommy: My mum — she gived.
Miss H: Tommy — gave —
Tommy: She gaved me a penny and —
Miss H: She *gave* you a penny did she? All right — you *are*
          lucky — run along now.

The teacher's perceptions may be equally selective in *formal* assessment
situations. Even when there is a 'product' to look at, only certain aspects
of it are likely to strike him. (Figure 6.1 opposite is a supposedly
fictional example of a product getting much the same kind of partial
assessment as Tommy's attempt to communicate.) Whatever he focuses
on, whether it be form or content, or particular aspects of either or both,
the teacher's perception will be selective; and his selection will be value-
laden, revealing what he regards as significant. Albert Bandura (1970,
p. 80) offers an illustration from psychotherapy where the therapist's
professional affiliation determines what he notices and attempts to treat
in his client's behaviour:

Psychoanalysts will uncover and resolve Oedipal conflicts;
Adlerians will discover inadequacy problems and alter the
resultant compensatory power striving; Rogerians will unearth

Figure 6.1
Letter to an English teacher
(From *Up the Down Staircase* by Bel Kaufman. Copyright © 1964 by Bel Kaufman. By permission of McIntosh & Otis, Inc.)

Dear Mr. Barringer,
Last Sunday I took the subway to
p your stop ∧ having looked it up on your
p Time Card ∧. I hope you don't mind
sp the presumtion ..... I walked back and
forth across the street from your house ∧.
back and forth ∧.. and I thought I saw p
p cliché you and my heart was throbbing with
omit this love I bear for you ∧.. p
no caps cliché I feel so deeply the Beauty and
p Truth of the poetry you read in class .. ∧ p
I alone ∧.. especially such lines like gr.
" She has a lovely face, the Lady of
sp Shalot ..... "
I think of you all the time .. ∧.. p
word? at night, darkling, I pray to be worthy
not clear of you and all that you stand for .....
I believe we understand each other and
awkward construction no one else ..... And if ever you need me
to die for you I will gladly do so .....
I hope you don't think me
sp presumtious but I have to speak out
p the truth .. ∧ ... the only truth .. ∧.. p
Sincerely yours,
Alice Blake

Alice—
Thank you for your note. Watch spelling and punctuation; you tend to use a series of dots to avoid it! Watch repetitions and clichés.
You might look up the spelling of the Lady in Tennyson's "Idylls of the King"—
P.B.

and reduce self-ideal discrepancies; Rankians will resolve separation anxieties; existentialists will actively promote awareness of self-consciousness.

Thus, we cannot discuss interpretation in terms of the assessor seeing everything the student says and does and then trying to make sense of it. He does not see everything. And what he does see is what he has already started to make sense of. The learning objectives he espouses, or the 'constructs' he is attuned to, or the framework of expectations he has built up, will help him make sense of what he sees; but they also help him do the seeing. How many of us would even notice anything calling for interpretation in the apparently inconsequential behaviour of the patient described by Thomas Reik (1948, p. 263)?

> After a few sentences about the uneventful day, the patient fell into a long silence. She assured me that nothing was in her thoughts. Silence from me. After many minutes she complained about a toothache. She told me she had been to the dentist yesterday. He had given her an injection and then had pulled out a wisdom tooth. The spot was hurting again. New and longer silence. She pointed to my bookcase in the corner and said, 'There's a book standing on its head.'

But Reik, listening with his 'third ear', was able simultaneously to select out and fit an hypothesis to the 'uneasy' silence, the 'symbolism' of injection, extraction and pain, and the 'foetal' reference to an upside-down book. Thus he immediately ventured his (correct) interpretation: 'Without the slightest hesitation and in a reproachful voice I said, "But why did you not tell me you had had an abortion?"'

Beyond Behaviour

To make sense of his patient's behaviour Reik went 'beyond the information given'. This is required of any assessor who wants to achieve more than a selective description of what the student has said and done. He must at least ask himself, and preferably the student also, what the behaviour *means* to the student. From the stands at a soccer match, a striker who, even though he knows the whistle has already blown for some infringement, carries on to side-step the goal-keeper and slam the ball between the posts, might have his behaviour interpreted as petulant, stubborn, time-wasting, and anti-social; but to him, deep in his game, it might well have the almost mystical interpretation of 'letting the ball know where the net is'. Christopher Cornford (1976) retells the story of a Viennese child prodigy, a girl of six, who, whenever she encountered a poem, picture, play or piece of music that was kitsch (i.e. facile, pretentious and over-sweet), would unerringly say 'kitsch!' After some persuasion from the psychology professors who were investigating her uncanny insight, she finally consented to explain how she did it: 'It's very simple, really: if I like it I say "kitsch!"'

Human behaviour is not always what it seems. The superficial level of interpretation that often suffices in everyday discourse will not be adequate in an educational context, any more than it would in a context of therapy. In such contexts the assessor is interested in diagnosis with a view to treatment. He wishes to extrapolate from what he has witnessed the student say and do, making inferences about how the student would behave in other circumstances. He needs to hypothesize about the likely causes and constraints underlying such behaviours. He needs to predict how the student's future capabilities and dispositions might be modified by the various possible teaching (or therapeutic) interventions he might make. Even if the assessor is interested simply in labelling or selecting students rather than in teaching them, he still needs to take into account the student's reasons and intentions — what goes on in his mind as well as what appears in his performance. Otherwise he could not communicate truthfully with whoever is to be the recipient of his assessment. Take the case of Mary, described by Joan Tough (1973, p. 11) — a three-year-old newly started at nursery school. She is not speaking at all, even when provoked by other children infringing her 'rights'. Why? What does it mean? What to do about it? Perhaps she is shy; understandable during her first few days. But the behaviour persists. Perhaps she is retarded. But her Mum says Mary can't stop talking at home. So a more refined diagnosis might be that she is shy with strangers and has difficulty making new relationships. So the question becomes how to help Mary settle in without continually demanding she should talk. Mary's behaviour is thus interpreted in terms of what action from the teacher it seems to call for. The action will test the interpretation.

Explanations and Implications

In a court of law, one of the most important functions of assessment (cross-examination) is to establish a witness's *state of mind* — his past intentions or his attitude to the matters at issue. Michael Balint (1964) is concerned with patients' states of mind: he advises doctors that they should spend more time just 'listening' if they are to reach the deeper level of diagnosis that assesses the neurotic as well as the physical signs presented by patients; he suggests (p. 121) that 'if you ask questions you get answers — and hardly anything else'. One of the hazards of educational assessment is that students can produce the 'right' answer for the 'wrong' reasons. And *vice versa*. Hence we are always liable to deceive ourselves if we base our interpretations entirely on what people say and do, without asking *why* they do it or what principles they are following.

Even in a mathematics test we might be unwise to judge the student on his answers alone. He may have grasped the complex mathematical ideas involved and have correctly set up the appropriate procedures and formulae — but yet have failed to come up with the correct answer because of 'silly' slips in mechanical arithmetic. To begin to see what was going on in his mind, and locate his error, we need to check over his 'working'. Glenn (1977, p. 101) notes a technique, suggested by Russian educators, of asking the pupil to think aloud as he solves a problem. Getting the right answer for the wrong reason is also possible. A recurring anxiety among devisers of multiple-choice questions, for example, is that they may have included 'give-away' clues that would enable a student to pick out the correct answer even if he were ignorant of the subject matter. An alternative answer that is much longer than the others might be such a 'give-away'.

Whatever the form of the questioning, a moment's reflection suggests several other ways in which a student's 'correct' answer may be misleading:

1.   He may simply be recalling the answer from having seen the problem tackled before;

2.   He may be copying the answer from a book without understanding it;

3.   He may be copying from a colleague;

4.   He may be guessing, wildly or intelligently;

5.   He may mean something different from what his answer appears to say;

6.   He may believe something different from what he chooses to convey;

7.   He may despise the answer he chooses to give; and so on.

John Wilson (1972, p. 12) gives a particularly elegant example of being right / wrong for the wrong / right reasons:

The child that puts down *animale* as the ablative singular of *animal*, on the grounds that ablative singulars of most third declension Latin nouns end in *-e*, knows more Latin than the child who thinks that they all end in *-i* and therefore puts down *animali*: even though *animali* is right and *animale* is wrong (the word is an exception to the general rule).

The practical message in all of this is that if we need to know what the student *is*, or even knows, we must look beyond what he *does*. And we do need to know what he is if we are at all to adapt our teaching to his needs. As the Romans said, *Si duo idem faciunt, non est idem* — if two people do the same thing, it is not the same thing. Yet much of assessment, and not just in public examinations, is concerned only to discover whether students can do some such 'same thing'. Not 'What can the student do?', let alone 'What does it mean to him?', but only 'Which of the things already anticipated by the assessor can he do?' Hence the danger of entering an assessment situation with too specific and exclusive a set of learning objectives or 'constructs' in mind. On seeing them either exemplified or not in the student's behaviour we may be too busy to ask the interpretive questions 'Why?' or 'Why not?', let alone to notice what *else* might be there as well or instead. Thus Johnny might be recorded as being a 'slow reader' — by a teacher who hadn't noticed that Johnny reads reflectively, trying to relate his reading to his life, and despite his low reading speed, reads *more* books than most of his faster-reading peers.

However deep he goes in his assessment, the assessor can be expected to interpret differently according to whether he is a Teacher or a Selector. The selector will interpret what he knows of the student in terms of how well that student can be expected to fit in with some situation external to him. How well might he meet the requirements of a certain job or social situation? How well might he respond to the kind of training or further education that is available? The selector is interpreting in terms of 'horses for courses'. The teacher, by contrast, is concerned with 'courses for horses'. Rather than asking how well the student can be expected to fit in with the external situation, he must ask how well the external situation (specifically, his teaching efforts) can be made to fit in with the student.

Thus the teacher's interpretation of what he knows and can surmise about the student will not restrict itself to how the student is now. It will be concerned also with the possible causes of his 'strengths and weaknesses' and with those dynamic features of his 'learning style' that could contribute to his further development. Such interpretation clearly would not be possible unless some attempt were made to assess processes as well as products. For instance, in the case of some particular area of difficulty in an individual student's learning, the teacher might infer that the student:

1. lacks some essential prerequisite concepts or skills; or
2. possesses knowledge or skills which conflict with those he is now learning; or
3. doesn't appreciate the need to develop the new knowledge or skill; or
4. doesn't care enough to involve himself wholeheartedly in the learning; or
5. doesn't believe himself capable; and so on.

In trying to overcome such difficulties, the teacher will need to build on what he knows, or believes he knows, of the student's strengths, e.g.:

1. What special interests does he have?
2. Does he learn best in groups or on his own?
3. Does he prefer to begin on a problem by ranging over it widely or by plodding through step by step?
4. Is he a converger or a diverger?
5. Does he learn best through verbal explanations (written or spoken?), visual representations, or physical manipulation? And so on.

The extent to which, in his interpretations of what the student says and does, the teacher identifies individual strengths and weaknesses determines how far his teaching can be individualized. Without it, the student can only 'fit in', or not, with some catch-all teaching strategy directed at 'students in general'. How to achieve such depth of interpretation is not easily specified. 'Only love can reach and hold them' said Rilke of the appreciation of works of art; and something akin may be demanded of the teacher who would appreciate those who are his students.

So if there is any such thing we can properly call the 'raw data' of assessment — what the student actually says and does — it does not remain 'raw' for long. The assessor begins to process it, attaching meaning, interpreting. One approach, as we've seen, is to attempt to *explain* the data — attributing causes, speculating about implications. Another approach is to make *comparisons*. The assessor may compare what he sees as the student's present state with other possible states. Such comparisons may lead him, though not necessarily, to ranking the student 'better' or 'worse' on that account. That is, comparison may (but only 'may') lead to the aspect of interpretation that is commonly held synonymous with assessment — judging.

Comparisons and Judgements

Your student has said or done something. You take this as evidence of some trait or capability or disposition. But to decide what the evidence implies, you may need to compare it with something else. Let's say you have given a child a spelling test: suppose he has correctly spelled 70% of the words. In interpreting this performance you may, for example, check to see what distinguishes the words he can spell from those he can't and discuss the latter with him, looking for causes and remedies for his difficulties. But you may also want to compare his spelling on this test with his past performance: how accurate is his spelling usually? has he had trouble with these particular words before? can he now spell words that previously he could not? has he started making any new systematic errors? Alternatively, you may compare his performance with some target, some ideal criterion of success, e.g. that he should have spelled correctly at least certain immediately relevant words, or that he should have spelled well enough to at least attain a predetermined 'pass-mark'. Or yet again, you might compare his spelling with that of other children: maybe with the other children in his class, maybe with other children you have taught in the past; maybe, using national, standardized tests, with children of similar age throughout the country.

On account of these comparisons you might interpret your student's spelling as improving or deteriorating (or a bit of both). You might judge him to be better or worse than he was; better or worse than the criterion performance you'd like him to reach; better or worse than the norm for his class, or for such classes in the past, or children of his age in general. You might decide he was better on one or more of these comparisons; worse on the other(s). You might decide he was not sufficiently better or worse to call for any specific commendation or remedial action; or you might not.

Self-referenced, Criterion-referenced and Norm-referenced Assessment

The big debate in the literature (e.g. Glaser, 1963; Popham and Husek, 1969; Glaser and Nitko, 1970; Block, 1971) seems to be between 'criterion-referenced' assessment on the one hand and 'norm-referenced' assessment on the other. Bluntly, that is, do we judge the student according to:

1. how well he has done by comparison with some predetermined criterion; or
2. how well he has done compared with the norm established by his colleagues?

This polarization of the debate should not blind us, however, to the other possibility we have discussed; that of judging:

3. how well he has done by comparison with *himself*.

Much informal assessment is self-referenced. If you're teaching Katy to ride a bicycle, you're pleased to see that she can now ride one-handed whereas yesterday she needed both hands to control her wobbling. You do not acclaim her, however, for having now attained a 'criterion level of mastery' in bicycle-riding. Still less does it occur to you to temper your pleasure in her new attainment according to how well other kids in the street ride. Instead, it takes its meaning from her personal progress. You praise her, or are pleased for her, not because she has beaten a target or done better than someone else, but simply because she has improved.

In more formal assessment situations, teachers are usually expected to base their judgements on criteria or norms. Thus, when it comes to handing out labels, a student mustn't be given 'excellent' or 'A' simply for having enormously improved. He must also have reached some criterion of mastery or at least done better than most of his peers. This troubles many teachers. They point to the injustice of giving greater rewards to a student who has, let's say, increased his performance from 90% to 95% (or even dropped from 95% to 90%), than to one who has increased from, let's say, 20% to 80%. Putting it another way, suppose students X, Y and Z had got the following grades on five consecutive tests during a term:

	Test 1	Test 2	Test 3	Test 4	Test 5
X	E	D	C	B	A
Y	C	C	C	C	C
Z	A	B	C	D	E

On the face of things, perhaps all should get an overall C. But many teachers would want 'in all fairness' to give a higher overall grade to Student X than to Student Y and certainly higher than to Student Z who, although he has the same individual grades as X, is deteriorating as X improves. Hence the often covert practice of giving marks for 'effort' or 'improvement'. This can be seen in essay-marking in school, where a teacher gives a particular student 'B' for a piece of work that might have earned only 'C' for another student. Conversely, just as he might encourage the 'trier' by marking up, so he might try to shame a 'slacker' by marking down. An ingenious and half-serious 'handicapping formula' is offered by Hinely (1968) which enables a 'raw' test score to be increased in inverse proportion to his I.Q., current grade-point-average, and last test score. Such practices are understandable, of course, in formative assessment but they do court the danger, if overdone, of *misleading* the student as to his likely standing in any less self-referenced summative assessments that are to ensue. There will be none of it, for instance, in externally marked examinations where the assessors know nothing of that 'self' except what emerges in the candidate's paper. However, such 'effort' or 'personal improvement' factors can often be seen influencing decisions in university examining boards — especially when a candidate is hovering on the border-line between one class of degree and the next.

Leo Haak (1960) outlines a method for systematically adjusting overall summative grades in the light of an 'improvement factor'. In essence, he proposes a final test comprised of a selection of the questions students have found most difficult in earlier tests in the course and using each student's 'improvement as a percentage of possible improvement' (which could be negative!) as one factor in deciding his overall grade. This has the advantage over a simple pre-test/post-test method in that students can't risk doing worse than their best at the start of the course in order to enhance their 'improvement factor', because the earlier tests *also count* towards the final grade. That very safeguard, however, limits the influence that the 'improvement factor' can be allowed to wield.

But individual progress is sometimes not enough. If we want a leg amputated, or need to be flown across the Altantic, or desire a new pump fitted in the central heating system, we'd like to feel that the surgeon/pilot/plumber has reached a reasonable standard of competence. To know merely that he or she has improved greatly might not be sufficiently reassuring. In such cases we take it for granted that the practitioners have been licensed on the basis of a criterion-referenced assessment of their skills or knowledge. Did they measure up to what is expected of a newly-qualified surgeon, pilot, or plumber? Such criterion-referencing underlies all talk of 'keeping up standards'. The interest lies in whether the student has at least the minimum essentials to be recognized as a qualified historian, house-painter, lawyer, trombonist, or whatever. Criterion-referencing is also vital to any sequential teaching where it is essential to check that the student has achieved some prerequisite skill before going on to the next stage, e.g. a child learning to read a clock must first attain the criterion ability to say the number represented by each of the numerals 1-12. An early and macabre example of criterion-referenced assessment was unearthed by Stephen Wiseman (1961, p. 105) concerning the Scottish rebel Lord Patrick Stewart, who was beheaded in 1615:

> The clergyman attendant upon him during his imprisonment found him so ignorant that 'he could scarce rehearse the Lord's Prayer', and they asked for a stay of execution for a few days 'till he were better informed'. The traditional Scottish reverence for learning — and examinations — seems to have been well established even at this period: the request was granted.

Criterion-referenced assessment became popular along with the programmed learning movement. The writer of a programme would also write a 'criterion test' related to the objectives of his teaching. He hoped to teach so well that practically all students would answer all the questions correctly. Indeed the conscientious programmer would try out and revise his programme on consecutive groups of students until he could be certain of virtual mastery from similar students in future. He would have to resist the pressure from psychometricians who would have had him insert some extra-hard questions and cut out the easy ones — 'in order to spread the students out a bit and show that some have achieved more than others'. He would reply, 'No, my intention is not to show whether some have learned more than others but to show whether or not they have learned well enough to have attained the objectives. If all score 100% I shall be pleased.' In short, the criterion-referencing assessor would be reasonably pleased with a score-distribution like Y below in Figure 6.2 but unhappy about X. Conversely, the norm-referencer would construct a test that would give him something like X below, even if this meant discarding all questions that 80% or more of students were able to answer correctly and retaining as his ideal questions the ones that are failed by about half the students.

Because the norm-referencer is ignoring questions that too many students would get right, he ends up unable to tell you what subject-

Figure 6.2

Norm-referenced (X) and Criterion-referenced (Y) Score Distributions

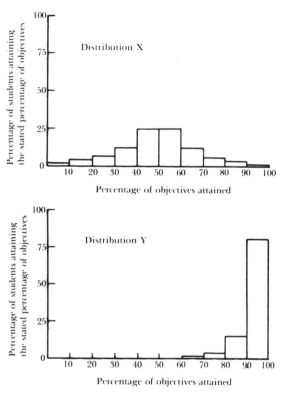

Percentage of objectives attained

matter expertise a particular student has — whether or not he has attained this or that objective. What he is able to tell you is whether that student is more or less expert than each other student. With norm-referenced interpretation of performance, a student's standing depends on how well he does in relation to how well *other* students do. 'Grading on the curve', or awarding grades in more-or-less predetermined proportions (see p. 52), means that a given performance will earn the student a better grade if he's in with a poor group than it would if he were in with a good group. Thus criteria, standards, may begin to slip — up or down. Lewis Carroll may or may not have been onto this anomaly:

'. . . how can you possibly award prizes when everybody missed the target?' said Alice. 'Well,' said the Queen, 'some missed by more than others and we have a fine normal distribution of misses, which means we can forget about the target.'

What happens when we forget about the target, about aiming to have all students reach certain standards in a variety of areas, and concentrate instead on ranking them in relation to one another? For one thing we may be reducing the incentive to teach: after all, standardized tests of ability or aptitude (e.g. 'intelligence' tests) are already available for 'discriminating' among students and might well rank them in pretty much the same order as the tests we'd construct to facilitate norm-referencing. Thus, public examinations may risk doubly disadvantaging children from less favoured educational backgrounds. Firstly, such students fail to get credit for improvement unless they improve sufficiently to reach a standard of attainment set perhaps by students from more 'cultured' socio-economic classes or schools with better training, who, in effect, were 'half-way up the mountain' when the course began and so, although they ended up a little nearer the summit, may actually have made *poorer* progress than their less accomplished colleagues who started from the bottom. Who would then be the 'slow learners'? Even with Mode 3 CSE, when a school has developed its own curriculum and is doing its own marking, 'moderation' procedures are used to adjust that marking to standards in other schools. How far does such apparent 'fairness' fail to give credit where credit is due? The second potential disadvantage is that teachers, knowing the dice are already so heavily loaded against late-developers and that, in any case, if the teaching and learning were to get so effective that hordes of extra people began reaching some previous pass standard then the standard would be raised again beyond their reach, have less incentive to teach as well as they know how. Fairer perhaps not to push the late-starters too much or perhaps to suggest they climb smaller mountains with gentler slopes — CSE rather than GCE, domestic science rather than chemistry, college rather than university, general degree rather than honours, etc.

Self-, or at least criterion-referenced interpretation is not too difficult to justify with formative assessment. E. L. Thorndike (in Volume 1 of *Educational Psychology*, 1913) stated the case very succinctly in terms of motivation:

> Rivalry with one's own past and with a 'bogy', or accepted standard, is entirely feasible, once we have absolute scales for educational achievement comparable to the scales for speed at which one can run and the height to which one can jump. Such scales are being constructed. The strength of such impersonal

rivalry as motive, while not as great for the two or three who would compete to lead the class . . . is far greater for the rest of the group. To be seventeenth instead of eighteenth, or twenty-third instead of twenty-fifth, does not approach in moving force the zeal to beat one's own record, to see one's practice curve rise week by week, and to get up to the standard which permits one to advance to a new feat.

I'm not sure what 'absolute scales' he thought were lacking or whether their construction was ever finished. Indeed it is not clear why 'scales' are necessary for standards to be applicable. Paul Goodman (1971, p. 107) suggests that we use normative assessment because we are no longer as confident about reasonable criteria as were, say, the teachers in mediaeval universities deciding whether or not to accept a student as a peer: 'My philosophical impression is that the mediaevals thought they knew what a good job of work was and that we are competitive because we do not know. But the more status is achieved by largely irrelevant competitive evaluation, the less will we ever know.' One is reminded of Bertrand Russell's dictum that man describes the world in mathematical terms because he is not clever enough to describe it in more profound ways.

But many teachers who readily practice self-referenced or criterion-referenced assessment in helping 'form' the student are much less happy when it comes to 'summing' him. They may subscribe to the ideal of absolute academic standards in their discipline. They may feel that 'good work' can generally be recognized — 'the first class mind proclaims itself'. In theory, they might be prepared for a situation where all of their students failed to reach a passable standard or where, in a specially good year, all gained distinctions. But, in practice, one sees teachers lose their nerve if 'too many' students are failing to meet the pass standard, or are reaching the distinction level. Competitive considerations begin to re-assert themselves and the student's chance of getting a distinction is less if students generally do well that year — and his chance of failing is greater — than in a 'poor' year.

I recently reviewed an Open University course in which the drift of teacher-intention from self-referenced, through criterion-referenced, to norm-referenced assessment is clearly evident in a succession of course documents written by different hands. The course (described by Duchastel, 1976) is structured around a series of projects whose aim is to develop the student's personal awareness and capacity to relate creatively to his environment. In the Guide, at the beginning of the course, the student is told:

> Assessment is likely to be more on the basis of how much you seem to have learned and how much you have tried to exercise your imagination, than on how well-finished the end-product is. . . .

> An important aspect of assessment for this course is self-assessment . . . send in your own comments on your work . . . the finished product is far less important than what you learn through producing it.

Clearly, self-referenced assessment is intended so far. The student is led to expect that his performance will be interpreted in terms of how much he has learned. He is also led to expect an assessment emphasis on process rather than product. He is even told that *self*-assessment is important — though he is not told whether or not it will actually *count*. And when he is told to 'send in' his self-assessment comments (send in to the tutor that is — remember that this is a 'distance' assessment operation) one wonders whether his self-assessments also are to be assessed.

In the next document, however, Notes on Projects, the emphasis has shifted to the criterion-referenced:

> Assessment of your work will be based on . . .

> (a)   how well you have understood the unit through learning-by-doing,

> (b)   how well you used your imagination in the doing.

Finally, in the Student-Tutor Notes on the first three units and assignment, comes the normative, comparative crunch:

> What about assessment? What criteria will be used by the tutors who look at and comment on your project work? . . . it seems certain that, whenever a sample group of [assignments] is brought together and looked at *comparatively* it will turn out that some students have given a greater input of *enthusiasm* and thoroughness than others; some contributions will seem more *authentic* and *closely observed* than others; some will seem more *acute in analysis;* some more *compellingly and imaginatively presented.*

Now this is a courageous, pioneering course which has my deepest educational respect. All the more poignant, then, that its declared emphasis on process and on personal growth towards creativity, should tacitly concede to the same product-based, norm-referenced assessment as other conventional, didactic Open University courses. Scarcely surprising though: tutors may never meet their students and so have little opportunity to observe them 'in process'; but nevertheless those tutors have to come up with grades that will allow this course to contribute just like any other to the student's eventual degree classification, and those grades must be 'seen to be fair' (especially to students who took other courses). Thus can the assessment tail acquire power to wag the educational dog.

You will often see references to criterion-referenced *tests* and norm-referenced *tests*. There is no such thing. Not if we mean by it that we should be able to look at a question-paper, or hear a description of a situational test, and say whether norms or criteria are being applied. The results of any test or observation can usually be interpreted either way. To shift the adjective on to the test, and away from the assessor's interpretations based on the results of the test, looks like an attempt (unconscious perhaps) to reify the procedure he has chosen to adopt and disguise its subjective basis. A similar confusion is perpetrated by those who talk of the validity or reliability of a test rather than of the interpretations made of students' responses to it.

Moreover, norm-referencing and criterion-referencing have more in common than is usually recognized. Consider a test whose results we are to interpret by comparison with criteria. To do so we must already have decided on a standard of performance and we will regard students who attain it as being significantly different from those who do not. For example, we may award them a degree, accept them as 'qualified', decide they are ready to move on to the next stage of learning without further revision, and so on. The question is: How do we establish the criterion level? What is to count as a satisfactory standard? Naturally, we can't wait to see how well our students actually do and base our criterion on the average performance of the present group: this would be to go over into blatant norm-referencing. So suppose we base our criterion on what seems *reasonable* in the light of our past experience? Naturally, if the criterion is to be reasonable, this experience must be of similar groups of students in the past. Knowing what has been achieved in the past will help us avoid setting the criteria inordinately high or low. But isn't this very close to norm-referencing? It would be even closer if we were to base the criterion not just on the average performance of previous students we've known but on that of previous students in general. In one case, our criteria would be related to the norms established by the sample of students we had met previously, in the other case it would be related to national or even international norms.

Most informal assessment approximates to the former type if it is criterion-referenced: that is, the teacher's expectations of this year's class are likely to be heavily influenced by the performances of previous classes. On the other hand, where formal assessment is criterion-referenced, especially if it is also summative, it is likely to be of the latter type, purporting to base its criteria on national or even (say, in the licensing of medical practitioners) international norms. Thus, when using standardized tests to estimate the 'intelligence' of a group of children we are actually carrying out criterion-referenced assessment since a child's IQ will depend not at all on the performance of his colleagues but simply on how his own performance compares with the criteria established by the wider population of children on whom the test has been validated. But though the assessment is criterion-referenced for the sample, it is not so for the population: the test is engineered so that the scores obtained by all children would approximate the so-called 'normal distribution' or bell-shaped curve (see Figure 3.1, p. 53) with most children getting middling scores and fewer and fewer getting higher or lower scores.

So, much assessment that appears to be criterion-referenced is, in a sense, norm-referenced. The difference is that the student's performance is judged and labelled by comparison with the norms established by *other* students elsewhere rather than those established by his immediate fellow-students. As I've mentioned earlier, many university teachers who subscribe to what they believe to be the former set of norms would tend to take fright and drift towards the latter if they felt vulnerable to the charge that they were crediting too many or too few students with having reached the criteria.

It is a common misconception that while norm-referenced assessment looks for a spread of attainment in students, criterion-referenced assessment sorts students into two categories only — those who reach the criterion and those who don't. This need not be true at all. Only when the criterion performance is grossly defined, in such a way that there can be no doubt as to whether or not it has been exhibited by the student, are such binary decisions possible. Has the student spelled 'Mediterranean' correctly, or not? Has he ridden his bicycle round the block without falling off? Has he managed to give the ablative singular of *animal*? But the criterion performance (and the learning objective that lies behind it) may not lend itself to such crude analysis. Think back to Chapter 4 where we considered such objectives as 'be able to decide on a course of action based on his own moral principles' or 'to make and justify a personal statement as to Lawrence's meanings' or 'to isolate and define the variables underlying similarities occurring in a variety of situations'. I spoke of the 'infinite improvability' of such objectives. How can one ever say one has attained them? Rather one would expect to go on 'improving' at such performances all one's thinking life. Hence any test attempting to elicit a criterion performance on such an objective would have to decide what was to count as an *acceptable* performance — not simply whether or not the objective had been attained. Furthermore, such a test would be likely to elicit a *range* of performance. Some students would fail to achieve the criterion level, to varying degrees. Others would just reach it, and some would surpass it, again to varying degrees.

Even with the supposedly cruder criteria mentioned earlier, some students may achieve them in ways that could be interpreted as a 'better' or 'worse' performance than that of others. For example, some students may have cycled round the block with less wobbling than others, or have knocked down fewer pedestrians on the way. Students may have spelled 'Mediterranean' correctly and given *animali*, but have succeeded with more such tasks on the whole test than did some of their colleagues and with fewer than others. In other words, if the test comprises a complex criterion performance which can be attained to varying degrees, or a number of cruder performances which can be seen to be attained or not, some students will do better than others and, unless the criterion level is set very high, better than that too.

From the diagnostic, or teaching point of view, it may be crucial to know not just whether or not a student reached the criterion level but also how far he exceeded it or fell short. So, too, from a selection point of view, it would be a waste of information not to notice whether the student just qualifies or surpasses the minimum essentials. Though we are assessing by comparison with criteria and not by comparison with other students' performances, we thus may look for more than the yes-no interpretation often associated with criterion-referencing. We may, if we like, think of multiple-criteria: 'Achieve this for a D, that for a C, such-and-such for a B, and so on.' We may, in effect, be ranking students according to the criteria they achieve. The essential difference between this kind of spreading out of students and that encountered in norm-based assessment is that in one case the value we put on a student's performance depends on how it compares with a predefined standard while in the other case the value we attach depends on the performance of his fellow-students. Suppose, for example, a group of candidates competing for a limited number of places on a college course, or in a firm's training scheme, are invited to take an entrance test. On the basis of the test, the candidates are ranked in order. If all the candidates reach the minimum acceptable level, and places are limited, then the interpretation of their results will be norm-referenced as well as criterion-referenced, since whether a student is put in the 'accept' category or the 'reject' category will depend on his performance not only in relation to the criterion but also in relation to that of other candidates. If, on the other hand, the number of candidates reaching the criterion level of acceptability is equal to the number of places available, then the interpretation is solely criterion-referenced. (The fact that some of the students reaching the criterion did better than the others is irrelevant to the immediate decision.) The same should apply if fewer students meet the criterion than there are places available; except that, in the real world, if the short-fall is severe and the college or firm desperate for recruits, norm-referencing is likely to be reverted to, with the 'best of the worst' being given places even though they've failed to reach the criterion. Euphemistically, the entrance standard has been 'adjusted'.

An example of how criteria can be introduced into norm-referenced assessment arises with what John Pearce (1972, p. 161) calls 'critical elements'. That is, it could be arranged that a student's overall rank on an examination would be reduced, even to the failure level, if he performed unsatisfactorily on some critical element like, say, the oral test in a language or the practicals in science and craft subjects. His inability to meet the criteria would thus hinder him in the norm-referenced competition: doing supremely well in other aspects would not allow him to fully compensate.

Validity and Reliability in Interpretation

The wise assessor will always be sceptical as to how far he can depend on his interpretations of the 'raw data' of assessment. How *true* are they? Is he justified in 'making' what he does of the things students say and do? The further he goes 'beyond the information given' the more he risks acting inappropriately towards the student.

As I have already indicated, the assessor is rarely concerned simply with the specific thing said or done by the student — whether this be a 'revealing' remark in conversation, or a 'sound' approach to a particular experiment, or a 'brilliant' Ph.D. thesis. Rather this is taken as evidence of some ability or disposition in the student. On account of the hypothesized ability or disposition the assessor conceives expectations about how the student might behave in *other* situations, now and in the future. (Or else his reports provoke such expectations in others.)

When the ability is fairly precisely defined (e.g. 'the student can correctly calculate the square root of any 3-digit whole number') and the 'other' situation is very similar, he can probably depend on his interpretation. The student who has just correctly calculated such a square root can probably do it again. However, the 'truth' of the assessor's hypothesis about the student's ability might not survive if much time elapsed between the two performances. Nor could the truth be 'extended' to cover very different situations, e.g. where the student is asked to calculate the square root of *any* number, still less to calculate the cube root.

If the assessor's hypotheses about the student's abilities and dispositions have developed through observations of him in a *variety* of different situations they will be more robustly dependable. Even so, a new context may reveal inadequacies in the assessor's hypothesis or even overturn it altogether. In discussing the assessment of trainee-teachers' practical teaching performance, Professor McFarland (1973, p. 93) tells why fine grading is gradually being abandoned in favour of a pass-fail categorization and how even the fail category might well be eliminated because of evidence that:

> students may do badly in one situation and surprisingly well in another, and *vice versa*. One has known a headmaster, supported by tutors, judge a student to be a definite failure. In less than a year, another headmaster, having admitted the student to teach in his school in a special capacity, clamours for him to be re-examined and passed because he is proving so acceptable. . . . Another gains a teaching 'distinction' and then fares badly in a first appointment which proves uncongenial.

So, the assessor's interpretation may not hold up because the circumstances are different from those in which he developed his hypothesis about the student. This possibility is augmented by the passing of time. That the student can be credited with the present ability to solve simultaneous equations, converse in Urdu, and design experiments, or with the present dispositions towards honesty, industry and creativity, is no guarantee that the same will be true of him next month even, let alone next year or a decade hence. Predicting how a person will turn out in the future, on the basis of what we think we know about him now, is hazardous. Even if he retains the ability, he may no longer have the disposition. As the gnarled old African farmer said to the visiting expert from UNESCO who was trying to persuade him to learn more modern and effective farming techniques: 'Listen, son, I already know how to farm twice as well as I'm doing at present.'

There is another common reason why the assessor's interpretation of the student's behaviour may fail to explain what he does in other situations. It may never have been true in the first place. In previous chapters we have touched on many cases where assessors have been misled as to what ability or disposition they were seing evidence of. Thus, for instance, it is not valid to infer from a student's untidy desk or disordered appearance that he has an untidy, disordered mind. Even formal tests do not always test what some teachers think they test. A student's high score may be taken as evidence of the ability to think critically when all he was exercising was his general knowledge. His performance in comprehending a piece of prose about an historical event may be misconstrued as evidence of ability to enter imaginatively into the past. His high marks on final examinations may be taken as predictive of his likely future success as a research student (even though he has not shown particular ability at thesis writing). Because the students didn't cheat on the 'let me help you' test, the teacher labels them 'honest'; but some of them didn't cheat because they guessed what was going on, some because they thought they might be found out, some because they weren't tempted, some because they believe in obeying authority, etc.: consequently, children with such diverse motivations may, in another situation, confound the assessor by behaving quite differently from one another.

So far, what we have been raising questions about is the *validity* of interpretation. Is my assessment of the student's behaviour true? Have I really seen evidence of what I think I have; or is it of something else instead? Would I see similar evidence if I observed the student in another (how similar) place or time? How confidently can I generalize from what I have seen? Can I predict anything of the student's future? Can I at least predict which educational 'treatment' he is likely to respond to best? How far can I trust my own judgement? The fact that such questions are usually either shelved (in the case of formal, summative assessment) or else answered intuitively (in the case of much everyday, informal assessment) does not detract from their importance.

But we might also recognize questions about what is called the *reliability* of assessment. 'Reliability' is a rather confusing term here and some writers have tried to substitute 'consistency'. Anyway, the basic 'reliability' question is: Would *other* assessors agree with my interpretation of the student's behaviour? But a disturbing variant is: Would *I* myself interpret his behaviour in such a way if I saw it again?

There is an assumption, rampant in talk of 'academic standards', that all 'qualified' assessors feel, understand and judge in much the same way when confronted with the work of a particular student. It is presumed that they would notice and value the same skills and qualities and would broadly agree in their assessments. Abundant evidence attests to the falsity of such assumptions (see Beard in CVC, 1969). Indeed, we might well substitute the verb *vident* for *faciunt* in the 'anti-behaviourist' Roman saying mentioned earlier, making it: *Si duo idem vident, non est idem* — if two people see the same thing, it is not the same thing.

The unreliability of assessment first became an 'issue' when it was noticed that the mark awarded a student essay depended on who marked it. The earliest investigation I have come across was carried out in 1889 by an Oxford Professor of Political Economy, F. Y. Edgeworth, who published a piece of Latin prose in the *Journal of Education* together with a request that 'qualified' judges mark the paper as if it were written by a candidate for the India Civil Service. As a result, 'twenty-eight highly competent examiners were so kind' as to produce the following set of marks (out of 100):

45 59 67 67.5 70 70 72.5 75 75 75   75 75   75   77

80 80 80 80   80 82 82   85 85 87.5 88 90 100 100

Edgeworth followed up with a study of examination marking, especially that for selection to the India Civil Service. His report (Edgeworth, 1890) concludes:

> I find the element of chance in these public examinations to be such that only a fraction — from a third to two-thirds — of the successful candidates can be regarded as quite safe, above the danger of coming out unsuccessful if a different set of equally competent judges had happened to be appointed.

Every now and again, in subsequent years, someone or other has worried in print about such inter-marker inconsistencies. Ben Wood (1921) tells how one of the six college professors grading a set of history papers in the summer of 1920 wrote out for his own satisfaction what he considered to be a model paper for the set of questions. By some mischance this paper got amongst those being marked by one of his colleagues who unsuspectingly graded it but deemed it unworthy of a pass mark. According to standard precautions, the model was accordingly marked by other readers to double-check its grade and was given marks ranging from 40 to 90. A similar horror-story was told by Paul Diederich (1957) reporting how 53 'experts' were given 300 short essays by first-year students in three colleges and each was asked to sort them out into 9 categories of merit with at least 12 essays in the smallest category. The result? No essay was given less than 5 grades (out of the possible 9), and 34% of the essays received all 9 grades!

But the classic revelations about inter-marker unreliability were those of Hartog and Rhodes (1935, 1936). These investigators persuaded experienced examiners to re-mark students' scripts from School Certificate and other examinations. With School Certificate history, for example, fifteen scripts, each containing answers to six questions and each with the same 'middling' mark, were selected and, after having all marks made by the original examiner removed, were circulated to fifteen other examiners. The new examiners were each asked to give each script a numerical mark and then classify it as Fail, Pass, or Credit. So, each of the fifteen scripts was given fifteen ratings. Needless to say, the examiners disagreed, often widely, over the numerical mark deserved by a particular script. Even more significantly, they disagreed as to whether a particular script was better or worse than others and in not one single case did they all agree on the appropriate classification. As can be seen from the following figures, more than half the candidates failed *and* passed *and* gained a credit:

Figure 6.3

15 Students	Classification awarded by 15 examiners		
	Fail	Pass	Credit
A	4	5	6
B	3	7	5
C	3	8	4
D	5	8	2
E	4	9	2
F	4	9	2
G	1	5	9
H	3	11	1
I	9	6	0
J	6	9	0
K	10	5	0
L	10	5	0
M	0	5	10
N	0	4	11
O	0	2	13

A year later, Hartog and Rhodes unexpectedly asked the same examiners to mark and classify the same scripts again. The new markings differed considerably. In eighty-three cases, an examiner reclassified a student from Fail to Pass or Pass to Credit, or *vice versa*. In nine cases, the student was shifted by two categories. Parallel multiple-marking exercises with scripts in Latin, French, English and chemistry confirmed the pattern: how a student's examination work was assessed proved heavily dependent on *who* marked it and *when*.

In subsequent years, much has been done to damp down the effects of such inconsistencies. In the U.S.A., especially below college level and even there to a large extent, the issue has been fudged by widespread reliance on the 'new-type' or objective tests. These call for no judgement on the part of the marker (who could be an unskilled worker or even a machine), and ensure that a given student's answer sheet would get the same score no matter when or by whom it was marked. One is merely left asking how far the kind of the student understanding that must be demonstrable through answers that can be indisputably labelled right or wrong is the kind most worth finding out about.

In Britain, the tendency has been rather to stick to fairly divergent assessment vehicles (like the essay), because they are seen as more educationally valid, but to attempt some control over marking. Hence the schemes for multiple-marking by examiners of sample essays in order to agree on common standards. Hence the reliance, in university finals for example, on averaging the student's grades over several examination papers marked by separate examiners. Hence the attempts to produce 'analytic mark schemes' by means of which the examiners are directed to award the student so many marks for this point and deduct so many for that, to such an extent that, ideally, all would give the same total score to a piece of work. The fact that examiners, in my experience, having totted up their marks according to the scheme, are then quite likely to go back and 'adjust' them all because the total somehow seems more or less than the student deserves, does not soil the nobility of the intention. The genuine dilemma facing examiners who are trying to steer a defensible course between the nomothetic demands of the mark scheme and the idiographic uniqueness of the student's response is well captured by Frances Stevens (1970, p. 124) in the context of a GCE 'A'-level question on *Paradise Lost*:

> . . . Is the well trained candidate who can smoothly adapt a carefully prepared essay to the slightly different requirements of the set question to be preferred to one who treats the situation as one embodying a unique problem, and tries to struggle through to

some kind of authentic though inarticulate and badly ordered statement? Are all 'points' of equal value; would, for instance, an answer which managed to include eight or nine acceptable details relevant to the impression of Satan as an angel in defeat automatically score more than one which showed that the writer had suddenly been caught by the undefined horror of the confrontation with Sin and Death at the gates of Hell and had spent all his time elaborating his feeling for that one situation?

Behind the urge for consensus judgement among assessors — the 'ideal mark' as Hartog and Rhodes called it — lies the 'true value' concept of assessment. See Guilford (1965, pp. 438—68) or Bock and Wood (1971, pp. 197—99) for a technical explanation or, as William Cowper put it:

> And diff'ring judgements serve but to declare
> That truth lies somewhere, if we knew but where.

The 'true value' theory, derived from the physical sciences, assumes that all observable or measurable quantities have a true value even though it cannot be obtained. So, the value we actually attach to the thing observed is made up of the true value plus an *error*. This notion prompts the idea that the *average* of a number of raw observations is likely to be 'truer' than any one of them — because positive and negative errors in the measured value have an opportunity to cancel each other out. Hoste and Bloomfield (1975) are clearly not strangers to this way of thought: 'The number of times pupils are above average in *joie-de-vivre* or emotional state is likely to be balanced by the number of times they are below average. The result is likely to be nearer their "true" performance (i.e. more reliable) than that produced by an examination at one point in time.' What tends to get overlooked by the true-valuers is that, while the average may be truer of the student than is any single one of his separate performances, it may well not be truer than the *set* of separate performances considered in context and as a succession. The fact that a group of examiners differ greatly in how they value candidate A but are nearly unanimous about candidate B may help sensitize us to important differences between the two that would not emerge were each set of valuations to be averaged, quite possibly producing similar overall scores for both.

Students, of course, may share the true value theory. Clearly, they are justified in feeling uneasy about unreliability in assessment, especially when careers are at stake. They may be able to accept the kind of unreliability that Hoste and Bloomfield allude to above — that is, that their score may depend on an 'untypical' performance on a particular day.

They may even accept, as the 'luck of the draw', the unreliability attaching to the fact that they might score better on one set of questions than on some alternative set supposedly tapping the same underlying objectives. But, given the performance they do turn in on a particular day in relation to a given set of questions, they may not take so kindly to the idea that its 'value' depends on which of many supposedly equally-qualified judges actually assesses it. Even with informal, formative assessment, where the student may well prefer a teacher's subjective, human response to his work than an objective, computer-style error-analysis, he may still expect the teacher to be commenting from within a fairly narrow frame of appraisal shared by his 'community of scholars' or 'guild of craftsmen'.

However, unless they are encouraged and content to perform routine tasks that lend themselves to routine analysis, they will be disappointed. If the assessment 'event' is at all rich — where more than one trait or quality is being deployed, or where 'infinitely improveable' abilities are being practised, or where the student is doing anything at all that might be considered expressive or creative — assessors will disagree. Especially so, perhaps, in the case of unrecordable 'process' events. They will disagree as to which traits, qualities, abilities, etc., are in evidence. They will disagree as to the extent to which they are evidence. They will disagree not only as to what they see but also as to what meaning and value to attach to it. As Ralph Bennett (1974, p. 2) puts it: '. . . at the crucial moment of an examiners' meeting decisions turn upon one man's *impression* that a particular answer deserves alpha and another's that it is worth no more than beta.' Frances Stevens (1970, p. 64) saw evidence of just this when she reviewed a GCE 'A'-level English answer that happened to have been assessed by two different examiners:

> The first commends the initial paragraph, quoted below, with the words 'good opening':
>
> *The school of Metaphysical poets sprang up closely after the period of the flowering of drama, following the decline of the theatre of Shakespeare, Marlowe, and Jonson. We know that Donne was 'a great frequenter of plays in his youth'; and the drama had a profound effect on his work. This, together with the fact that Donne was a revolutionary, reacting violently against the formal conventionalism which preceded him, shows why the dramatic element is so important in his poetry.*
>
> Against this remark the second examiner writes 'NO', and he strikes out the whole paragraph with the word 'irrelevant'. He

reduces the first examiner's mark of 16 (an 'A' mark) to 7 (a failure mark). This exercise prompts many reflections, the most important at this point being that if the sophisticated cannot agree about what the question demands, it is hard on the candidate.

Examiners may simply have different orientations towards the subject. Husbands (1976) suggests, in mild parody, how the 'ideological bias' of an examiner may affect his marking:

It could be that the free-enterprise economist, for example, having read a rather mundane effort that was nonetheless written from his own standpoint, says, 'What a pedestrian attempt! Forty-five, I suppose. But at least he doesn't drop a lot of leftist slogans. Okay, fifty-two.' Or the Marxist sociologist may read a strongly pro-functionalist effort and conclude 'Quite well argued. Sixty-two, maybe. But he refuses to get to grips with the real issues. Fifty-seven.'

Then again, when assessors have several pieces of a student's work to look at, or several assessment 'incidents' to recall, they may differ in the extent to which they allow their *overall* judgement to be influenced equally by each. Some would follow the advice passed on by Samuel Butler in *The Way of All Flesh*:

'I tell you, Edward,' said my father with some severity, 'we must judge men not so much by what they do, as by what they make us feel that they have it in them to do. . . . It is not by what a man has actually put upon the canvas of his life that I will judge him, but by what he makes me feel that he felt and aimed at.'

Thus they might give less weight to data that seemed to them less typical of the student's 'intrinsic quality' — which they have decided upon by 'reading more into' some other data than fellow assessors might do. Jennifer Platt (1972, p. 31) suggests that the practice among many of her fellow-examiners of marking a student higher or lower than the average of his separate answers is no more defensible than doing so because one knows the candidate, especially since based on less adequate evidence. (Marking *up*, however, could be seen as an examinations-equivalent of the 'best work only to count' policy in continuous assessment.) The dilemma would not arise at all, of course, were it the practice to report the variability of a student's work *as it is* (e.g. in a profile) rather than to try to average it out in an overall grade.

Disagreements among assessors can never be entirely resolved, though they may be glossed over or tactfully ignored by discussion; because there are so many different ways of demonstrating depth of knowledge and understanding in an area that assessors will inevitably, and legitimately, and with justification from within what is still believed to be a fundamentally shared frame of reference, *differ in which they prefer.*

Artists, of course, are quite resigned to the products of their imagination being interpreted differently by different assessors. Nevill Coghill (1948, p. 86) reports a conversation about a production of *Sweeney Agonistes* with its author T. S. Eliot who seems calmly unconcerned that his work can mean different things to different people:

Myself: I had no idea the play meant what [*the producer*] made of it. . . that everyone is a Crippen. I was astonished.

Mr. Eliot. So was I.

Myself: Then you had meant something very different when you wrote it?

Mr. Eliot: Very different indeed.

Myself: Yet you accept Mr. Doone's production?

Mr. Eliot: Certainly.

Myself: But . . . but . . . can the play mean something you didn't intend it to mean, you didn't know it meant?

Mr. Eliot: *Obviously it does.*

Myself: But can it then also mean what you *did* intend?

Mr. Eliot: I hope so . . . yes, I think so.

Myself: But if the two meanings are contradictory, is not one right and the other wrong? Must not the author be right?

Mr. Eliot: Not necessarily, do you think? Why is either wrong?

The more a student's performance approximates a 'work of the imagination', the less 'reliable' is assessment — unless assessors agree to ignore the contentious aspects and concentrate on the measurable. And the more we look for high quality in students, the more divergent and open to exercise of the imagination are our assessment methods likely to be. In this respect, reliability and validity may be opposed. Look back for instance at the series of questions (pp. 155-156) on Sweden's political system. The more structured the question, perhaps, the *less* evidence will be forthcoming from which to make valid assessments of the qualities we really wish to know about in students, but the *more* likely we are to get agreement from other experts as to which qualities are in evidence; and *vice versa* as the question becomes less structured and more open.

Yet there is no absolute refuge from differential marking even in assessment tasks that seem structured and convergent. In tests of arithmetic, for instance, assessors will differ as to how much credit should be given for partly correct working or deducted for sloppy layout. Even in examinations where examiners meet to discuss a mark scheme that allocates points almost exclusively for factual recall, diversity can emerge. J. J. Head (1967) levelled such an accusation against GCE 'O'-level biology examinations where students might be asked, for example, to 'Name three conditions necessary for the germination of seeds', resulting in examiners differing as to whether or not to give credit for answers like 'moisture', 'wetness', 'dampness', or other alternatives not discussed at their marking meeting but which crop up instead of the expected answer 'water'.

I can't believe that 'fairness' in assessment should be reduced to ensuring that assessors agree. The price, in terms of educational relevance, is too high. Better, I believe, to stick with divergent assessment tasks that produce divergent responses from both students and assessors and from which both are likely to learn. Even in, say, medical certification, one would prefer one's doctor to have shown himself capable of (divergently) thinking out a sensible diagnosis and treatment on his own rather than merely of (covergently) choosing the best of five alternatives suggested to him by his assessors. Of course, with formal, summative assessment, the student may properly resent the risk of having his 'divergent' work fall foul of an assessor who happens to be less sympathetic to his style than others would be. Ideally, as may happen in school-based assessment, the student's work should have more than one assessor. Where only one assessor is practicable, or only one for each aspect of a student's work (e.g. his performance in different subjects), fairness might best be achieved by calling for the assessor to spell out just what he sees in the student's work and how he justifies his response to it. (I suspect this gentle suggestion has truly revolutionary implications.) The greatest unfairness is perhaps to quantify and average out the assessors' interpretations of a student's work in order to label him with that educational enigma — the 'all-talking, all-singing, all-dancing' uni-dimensional grade.

CHAPTER 7

HOW TO RESPOND ?

Our cycle of assessment is almost complete. Early or late we have decided on what we are assessing in the student's repertoire. We have planned and implemented a particular assessment technique, or at least recognized as appropriate some assessment 'incident' that has emerged without our planning it as such. At all events, the student has done or said something significant and we have interpreted it, coming to some conclusion, however tentative, as to what it tells us about him. Hence to the ultimate question in the assessment cycle: What to *do* about it? How are we to *respond* to what the student has shown us of himself?

Teaching and Reporting

How we respond can be seen in terms of which of the purposes described in Chapter 2 we are pursuing. Essentially, the assessor can respond as an interacting change-agent or as a disinterested reporter. When practising formative assessment, the former is likely; with summative assessment, the latter. In other words, the assessor may respond as a teacher, using the knowledge gained to interact with the student in helping him grow; or he may respond as a reporter, classifying, labelling, or describing the student for the benefit of others who have an interest in the student. At different times, of course, the same assessor may respond in either or both ways to a student's work.

As a learner, however, (rather than as a 'candidate'), the student is entitled to expect his teacher to respond with help and encouragement rather than with definitive reports and labels. As Ralph Tyler remarks (in Tyler and Wolf, 1974, p. 5), if we're learning golf we wouldn't expect our coach, after a few practice sessions, to say, ' "You are getting a D in your work. I may have to fail you if you don't improve". Instead, we expect him to say, "You are making progress on your drive, but you need to bring your full body into the swing. A little later I'll give you further practice on your putting to increase accuracy and decrease power".'

To offer a tentative *report* to a student may be intended and accepted as a teaching-type response. That is, the teacher may *initiate* his teaching by telling the student how he sees him *at present*. He may list what he believes to be the student's strengths and weaknesses. Even the golf coach in the previous paragraph is telling his student, in effect, that his swing is weak while his putting is over-powered and inaccurate. This 'feedback' he may see as essential if the student is to help himself. But he may also be able to justify predicting to the student that on his present showing, he would fail, or barely succeed, or succeed with honours in achieving some extrinsic reward he is interested in — gaining entry to a particular club, qualifying for the team, becoming certified as a coach himself, or whatever. This he would justify on motivational grounds, arguing that the student needs feedback about what is good and bad in his performance to help him improve, and this 'extrapolatory' feedback may, in addition, impress on him *how far* he needs to improve to attain the criterion level he aspires to. But to be regarded as teaching-type responses rather than as classificatory, labelling responses, such descriptions and extrapolations must imply to the student that his teacher can help him *grow out of them*. They must then be followed by teaching, or at least subsequent assessment, that is clearly based on this implication.

However, telling the student his weaknesses, whatever the intent, may not be an effective teaching response. Nor may extrapolating his grade or eventual label from present standards. While some students would thus be helped and encouraged to co-operate in self-improvement, for others it would be counter-productive, encouraging them only in a negative and pessimistic view of themselves. Different students will be differently receptive to the teacher's message that they can 'grow out of' the assessment. If they don't receive it, or don't believe it, then students 'labelled', for example, as poor spellers or poor readers, may settle into acting in ways consistent with this concept of themselves (see Lecky, 1945) and what was not meant as a prophecy nevertheless fulfils itself. The teacher needs to be very sensitive to the differential effects of such feedback on different individuals if he is not to function, willy-nilly, as a labeller for some of them. Sometimes he will decide not to spell out the weaknesses but to concentrate attention on the strengths — see Charity James (1968) for a fuller exposition of the 'relative strengths' approach to teaching. Or he may draw attention to weaknesses only in his vigorous action to eradicate them.

The Teaching Response

So we come to the more explicit teaching responses. Here the teacher is obviously saying or doing something, as a result of his assessment, that is directly meant to help the student 'grow'. (Simply 'telling the student' is less explicit because it merely suggests where and to what extent growth is needed; the student might then be expected to teach himself for all one might know.) The teacher may respond by suggesting what the student might do next, by arranging a sequence of learning activities for him, by offering new stimulation, possibly simply by letting the student see that his contribution is worthy of consideration and replying to it with interest. The teacher may respond with formative intent when face-to-face with the student, but he may also do so 'at a distance', on the telephone for instance or, more commonly, in his written responses to the student's work.

In face-to-face situations, teaching-type responses are made in the light of on-going, usually informal, assessment. The categories developed by Ned Flanders (1970) for his 'interaction analysis' provide the basis of a typology for such responses. Flanders developed his system in order to interpret what teachers and students say to each other in classroom interactions. Observers are given ten categories among which to classify the communication that is taking place during any three-second period and are trained to a high level of agreement with other observers. Of the ten categories, one represents silence or confusion, two represent student-talk and seven represent teacher-talk. This division perhaps reflects Flanders's famous 'rule of two-thirds': that for roughly two-thirds of the time in classroom, someone is talking; for two-thirds of that time it is the teacher; and two-thirds of his talk takes the form of lecturing (Category 5 below). Here are the seven 'teacher-talk' categories:

1. *Accepts feelings expressed by students*
Accepting and clarifying the feelings (positive or negative) in a non-threatening way. Can include predicting and recalling feelings.

2. *Praises or encourages student*
Jokes that release tension, as long as they are not at the expense of another individual, are included; as are expressions like 'Go on', 'Yes', 'Uh-huh', and nods of the head.

3. *Accepts student's ideas*
Accepting the student's ideas by, e.g. using them, clarifying them, giving examples, building on them, relating them to others. As more of the teacher's own ideas come into play, Category 5 becomes a more appropriate classification.

4. *Asks questions*
Asking a question about content or procedure, expecting student to answer.

5. *Lectures*
Giving facts, opinions, speculations about content or procedures; expressing his own ideas; telling stories; asking rhetorical questions.

6. *Gives directions*
Directing, commanding, ordering, telling students what to do.

7. *Criticizes students or justifies own authority*
Disciplinary statements intended to make students 'behave', including scolding the student; explaining teacher's own actions; or justifying his decisions.

Clearly these categories are rather wide. Even so, it is obvious that Categories 1-3 and possibly 7 are dependent on some prior assessment-interpretation of what students are saying or doing, whereas Categories 4-6 can be responsive but need not be so. That is, one could ask questions, give facts and opinions, and give directions in the light of something a student has just said or done; but one could also be doing so without any knowledge of student behaviour or even (e.g. when writing a textbook) with no students present.

If we are looking for indications as to how the teacher responds as a teacher to his assessment-interpretations, Categories 1 and 3 seem particularly worthy of deeper analysis. In Category 3, for instance, the teacher may respond by repeating the student's idea; by summarizing it; by rephrasing it in terms of a technical vocabulary he is trying to teach the student; by relating it to another idea, perhaps to an earlier idea from the same student or another, or to an idea of his own; by analysing it, looking for implications; by offering examples and non-examples; by applying it to reach an inference or build up to the next stage in a line of argument. Yet Category 3 merges into Category 5 as the teacher brings more of his own ideas into play. Running through 5 will be many strands of communication such as defining, explaining, classifying, evaluating, and so on. Meux and Smith (1964) teased out eleven such categories from episodes of teacher discourse.

Too little is known about how teachers actually sequence the minutiae of their teaching — especially in one-to-one situations. Most studies have concentrated on class teaching. The useful concept of *diagnostic appraisal* — assessment with a view to responding to student needs — is one that only really rings true in relation to one student at a time. The diagnostic build-up to the teaching response can be well defined, as in the example below (from Schneider *et al*, 1973, pp. 193-4), where the assessment activities of a teacher and a veterinary surgeon are contrasted, but the response (the 'prescribing') remains enigmatic ('instructs, guides, facilitates, provides feedback, teaches'):

Activity	Teacher	Veterinarian
Diagnostic observation	Third grade student seems reluctant to read; cannot sound and understand many words and phrases encountered in reading text and library books; observes student reading in other subject matter areas.	The dog in this case has a very good appetite, drinks lots of water and passes quite a bit of urine (all of these are different behaviour patterns noted by owner), and loses weight gradually.
Gathering data	Discusses problem with child; determines specific reading skills needed; formally and informally assesses word vocabulary, phonetic usage, and comprehension; consults results of informal and formal achievement tests. Determines lack of ability to use phonetic reading skills.	Considers malabsorption and age of animal; tries to pin down most likely differentials (causes that could be attributed to the symptoms). Determines the specific gravity of the urine, and blood sugar and glucose tolerance levels; measures insulin level. Determines an insulin deficiency— regulatory mechanisms not working.

Activity	Teacher	Veterinarian
Making decisions	Arranges data on phonetic skill related to word recognition needs, social interest, and motivation of student and determines consonant blends and vowel constructions. Reviews instructional materials and methods that could be used. Reflects on availability, priority, and sequence for alternate instructional approaches.	Arranges data and tests and determines insulin deficiency, a specific form of diabetes (clinical). Reviews treatment procedures (in this case, increasing insulin levels) through injections or oral prescriptions.
Prescribing	Obtains instructional materials; instructs, guides, facilitates, provides feedback, teaches.	Specifies and administers insulin, adjusts dosage on the basis of body weight and amount of calorie intake.

No doubt Category 3 responses will be well-represented in one-to-one teaching because the teacher is free to concentrate on his student's individuality, undistracted by having to keep the rest of the class interested. Category 5 responses will also be present, but an analysis of tutorial dialogues should reveal that straight exposition from the teacher gives way to Category 4 (questioning) as a means of getting the teacher's ideas into play. Questions play a prominent part even in class teaching as a spur to the students' active involvement. The technique of leading the student from what he knows to what the teacher wants him to recall or reason out is often graced with the epithet 'Socratic'. (Though on inspection, the actual Socratic dialogues appear to be short statements from Socrates to which his student can but reply yes or no!) Here is a rather less didactic example — an extract from a discussion with students arising out of an air pressure experiment, in which the teacher's questions are directed at helping the students analyse and re-structure their experience (Barnes, 1976, p. 72):

B.:   Well . . . Theresa blew down it and it bubbled, and then she took em . . . her mouth away, and it all came up because of the air pressure.

Teacher: Which air pressure?

B.:   The . . . er . . . inside the bottle.

Teacher: Alright! Now why didn't it come up before then? Before we blew the air in why didn't it come up?

C.:   Sir, 'cos . . . em . . . 'cos there wasn't enough air . . . air pressure.

T.:   There wasn't enough air in, but when you blew into it . . . there was more air and it came up.

Teacher: And it forced it . . . Why did it stop? At what point did it stop? It's not going now . . . why isn't it going now?

T.:   'Cos there's no air left in.

Teacher: Well there's still the air left in; but what can you tell me about the air out here and the air in here?

C.:   Sir, the air outside is stronger than the air in the bottle.

Some teachers are so wedded to the questioning technique that if they themselves are asked a question by a student (though not by a colleague, of course) they are likely to reply with another question. Michael Crichton (1970, pp. 184-85) tells how, in medical education, a student who asks a question of a teacher 'will most often get a question back, as in "Sir, what does the serum calcium do in Chicken Little disease?" "Well, what do the plasma proteins do in Ridinghood's Macroglobulinemia?" If the student fails to see the light, he will get another hint, also in the form of a question: "Well, then, what about the serum phosphate in Heavyweight's Syndrome?"' Such a teacher is not trying to be awkward in refusing straight answers; he is hoping to make the student work for an answer that will then become his own, and his to remember. In short, he responds with questions in order to *teach*. Even the teacher whose students are moving into content areas in which he is not himself an expert will be able to teach them if he probes diagnostically with questions along the lines of 'What do you mean? How do you know? What other evidence exists? How else could you analyse this? What sources of bias are there? How would you relate this to . . .?', and so on.

Responding at a distance

Where we *can* see in detail how teachers respond with teaching to the diagnosed needs of their students is in the recorded remarks they leave on students' written work. Where the teacher is expecting face-to-face contact with the student in the near future, these remarks may be minimal, e.g. the classic storm-warning 'Please see me'. In other cases we may get real evidence of the teacher trying to write down a response that will help the student think again about what he has done and guide him as to how he might do such things better another time.

Open University assignments offer a rich field for investigation of such tutorial response. The written exercises which students complete every two or three weeks are 'marked', not by the central course team who produced the teaching materials from which students have learned, but by a vast army of part-time tutors — more than 5,000 in 1976. It is heavily impressed upon these tutors, each of whom will be responsible for the work of 20 or so students, that each should think of himself 'pre-eminently as a teacher, with the tutorial function taking precedence over the assessor function' (Open University, 1973, p. 7). Furthermore, since students are not required to meet with their tutor, and less than half take the limited opportunity to do so, he must be able to teach *in* *writing*. (In principle, communication by telephone is also possible; but, in practice, it is rare, and cannot be relied upon as an alternative to writing.) In fact he is expected to teach ('reply' as the official guide puts it) to the individual's assessed needs in a way that the course team, writing for 'students in general', could not.

A tutor's comments or 'replies' fall into two broad categories. First are the comments which the tutor writes in the margin, paragraph by paragraph, as the student develops his argument. Secondly, there are the comments he makes on the assignment as a whole, perhaps even relating the present effort to the student's progress so far. The former comments, had they been made face-to-face in a tutorial, would be clearly seen as 'formative'; the latter are more 'summative' in intent.

Some scripts get returned to students with scarcely any marginal responses other than ambiguous ticks or query-marks or the occasional word in the script underlined or circled. Such responses are too cryptic to be useful. They could be illuminated by the tutor's summative comment; but if that takes such a form as 'This is quite a fair piece and you make a number of points well. But some are rather less well illustrated than others and the argument is sometimes weak or not fully expressed', then the student is denied the vital feedback that would tell him precisely *where* and *how* he has illustrated less well, argued weakly, expressed less than fully, let alone *what* he might have done to avoid this charge. Remember, there is normally no face-to-face contact to fill the vacuum. The tone of response is also important. The following marginal responses might well threaten the teacher-student relationship:

'This just won't do'

'Style!'

'Disorganized and inchoate'

'Your spelling is atrocious'

'You appear to be unable to distinguish between that which is given and that to be proved'

But guidance can be offered without sounding either condescending or threatening. The following responses, culled from margins, have the flavour of dialogue in which the tutors are seeking clarification, evidence, or amplification; or are drawing their students' attention to errors and anomalies; or are trying to stretch their thinking:

'The meaning is not very clear here. I find what it appears to mean very unlikely. Can you quote the figures?'

'This middle sentence is not related clearly enough to the other two.'

'What do you understand by "Revolution" in the phrase "Industrial Revolution"?'

'Important point but needs broadening out from specific example — also did any benefits accrue for schools and children?'

'If you had given the electronic structures of neon and sodium it would have helped show the essential difference between them.'

'Your answer is OK as far as it goes but you do not explain why the drop in IE is so large; look again at Figure 7 of Unit 7 and ask yourself what is so special about the electronic structure of neon and how does it differ from that of sodium.'

'Some parties would reverse the priorities (perhaps) i.e. the publicity would be more important than the end result.'

'Yes; it is very difficult to assess the effectiveness of the Labour Party, either nationally or locally in this role. I would have welcomed an example on a local issue known to you.'

These comments can be studied in the context of the actual assignments in Open University (1973) and more extended examples are to be found in Kennedy (1974). One can see reflected in such responses all of Flanders's categories (except 7); Category 4 (questions) is much in evidence. Here is a particularly handsome example, from a mathematics assignment in which the tutor's questions lead the student towards answering his problem which is to determine, given that set (i), $\{\wedge, \vee, \sim\}$, is an adequate set of connectives, whether set (ii), $\{\square, \sim\}$, is an adequate set:

> What does {∧, ∨, ∼} being an adequate set of connectives mean?
> All connectives can be written in terms of {∧, ∨, ∼}. How do we
> show that {□, ∼} is an adequate set? By showing all connectives
> can be written in terms of {□, ∼ }. Knowing set (i), how do we
> show set (ii)? In other words, how can we replace set (i) by set (ii)?
> How do they differ?

Besides the marginal comments, tutors make overall, 'summative'
comments which may nevertheless have teaching overtones, especially
when the student relates them back to the previous marginalia. Final
comments like 'Make your answers more positive, analytical and
critical' or 'Your approach ought to be more appreciative of artistic
subtlety' serve no teaching function unless they refer to weaknesses
identified, and alternative approaches discussed earlier in the script.
Here, on the other hand, is an example of an overall response which
conveys an appraisal of the work as a whole and its major parts but yet
manages to make a number of positive teaching points on which the
student might be expected to build*:

> The second part of this paper is better than the first. From the
> 'pupils' experience' section, you begin to be more specific in
> making your points. A basic omission in the earlier part was that
> you did not fasten down sufficiently on to what assumptions
> schools could be said to make (pp. 2-4). You rightly quote open
> and closed pedagogy and refer to space and time, but the assump-
> tions needed to be spelt out more. And assumptions from
> children's ages, sex and social background? You refer to
> intellectual ability, but this point could have been extended — tri-
> partitism, streaming. These involve assumptions about children,
> knowledge, work, society, and all impinge upon a teacher's
> pedagogy, all entail consequences for children. The paper is
> above average in its engagement with the question, in the
> intensity of its approach, but it does not bring out the wide range
> of assumptions in schools nor the deep nature of some of them. I
> liked your reference to staff meetings, by the way, and your
> account of the prize-day was both apt and evocative!

The kind of responding at a distance we've been talking about here is

---

*The similarity between this kind of response and the written review of a book should be
obvious. The parallels between assessment and literary criticism are even more apparent
in the examples quoted in *Assessing Compositions*, a publication of the London Association for the Teaching of English (LATE, 1965).

not so different in kind from that practised by many school and college teachers in 'marking' student's work. But, at its best, it probably goes further. It has to be more considered and articulate because it must carry all the weight of the teaching that other teachers are able to share between written comments and spoken amplification. Also, as Sylvia Rhys (1975) points out, the tutor 'is peering into an uncertain future, the time when the writer of the essay will react to his comment', and so he must be ultra-sensitive to the variety of misunderstandings which his messages may engender.

Furthermore, his interpretation of student needs must be subtle enough to detect that different students need a different response, even in what might appear to be the 'same' situation; as Sylvia Rhys makes clear with an example:

A tutor is marking answers to a question set part way through a foundation course and thinks it is a particularly difficult question for students to tackle at this stage in their academic careers. . . . His opinion of this question, plus his knowledge of the students whose essays he is marking, affects his role as teacher. He reads two essays and considers the writers have not fully grasped how to interpret the question. In the case of the first student, who has already shown he can produce a competent assignment, the tutor considers it worthwhile to go to greater lengths than usual to discuss how the question might be interpreted, and suggests two or three alternative ways of handling it. The tutor knows the second student has been experiencing difficulty in learning to express himself clearly, and decides that at this stage in the course he should concentrate on encouraging any signs of improvement in the student's presentation; he cuts down to the most important essentials his comments on interpreting the question, for he thinks that too many additions to the script might confuse and discourage this particular individual.

Do students read their tutors' carefully-wrought responses? Do they pay attention to them? How do they use them? Do the comments actually help them improve? The evidence is partial and anecdotal but many tutors and students certainly believe that thoughtful comments do improve learning (see Mackenzie, 1976). Bernard Harrison (1974) quotes at length a letter from a student commenting on the comments he made on her essay about *Mansfield Park*; in it she explores the lines of alternative thinking his responses have started in her mind but, at the same time, does not lose the opportunity to put him right over an unfounded comment! Letters and notes attached to subsequent assignments, commenting on comments previously received, are commonly reported by tutors as a sign of student-appreciation (Lewis and Tomlinson, 1977). But, as Kenneth Mackenzie (1976) remarks, 'most correspondence tuition must at present be (why not?) an act of faith. Much remains to be known, in any detail, about the average student's use of his tutor's comments.' The same could be said, in general, of *all* students and *all* teachers in *all* teaching situations. Equally little is known about how teachers *learn* to make effective teaching responses on the basis of their assessment of students. Certainly they are not usually taught how as part of their professional training.

The Reporting Response

As a teacher, the assessor might logically confine himself to teaching responses. But, in practice, more may be expected of him. He may be expected to *teach and tell* — to report what he thinks of his student's work. Some assessors (external examiners, for instance) may not be expected to teach at all; simply to interpret the student's achievements and communicate their interpretations to others.

If the teaching response essentially concerns the student as he might become, the reporting response concerns the student as he is now — or as he appears to be now, with no suggestion that change may be imminent. The one response tends to be dynamic, anticipating development, the other to be static, assuming equilibrium. The one tends to be formative, the other to be summative. On some occasions, the assessor may report his assessment directly to the student; on others he will report to the student's parents or to other teachers or prospective employers. If he reports to the student as a prelude to teaching him, he must, as I said earlier, take great pains to ensure that the reporting response does not subvert the teaching response. In addition, we might note that the teacher may 'report' to himself — by keeping a cumulative record of the student's progress which guides him in his teaching (see Foster, 1971; Dean, 1972).

The reporting response may relate to a particular assignment or to an incident observed by the teacher; it may relate to a course; it may relate to a complete programme of studies. The wider the span of student activity to which the report relates, the more it may seem that it is the student himself rather than his work that is being reported on — whether described, explained, evaluated, or whatever.

What forms may the reporting response take? Significantly, while little has been written about how to translate one's assessment interpretations into teaching responses, the shelves of our libraries (e.g. Dewey reference 371.26/7; Library of Congress, LB3051) groan with the weight of advice on how to represent these interpretations with marks, scores, ranks, grades, classificatory labels, and the like. The reporting response has a long and varied history (see Cureton, 1971; and Small, 1973).

Perhaps the basic question underlying a century or more of trying first-this-method-then-that is: *How many* symbols do we need to report something worthwhile about the student? Some say we need all the letters of the alphabet so that we can represent the student's work (idiographically) in prose. Others say two symbols are enough: P for pass and F for fail. The conflict is seen in many an educational institution that uses only the grades A, B, C, D and E. More than likely there will be one faction of the staff pressing to expand the range of grades by attaching pluses and minuses to each letter while another faction presses to reduce the options to P and F.

Numbers and Letters

Between the two extremes are those assessors who respond to the student's work with one of a range of numerical marks and those who respond with one of about five letters of the alphabet. The numerical markers usually give a percentage mark, implying that it is possible to distinguish between as many as one-hundred-and-one levels of student performance (i.e. 0% to 100%) on some common task. The meaning of such a percentage response may be far from clear to the recipient. Presumably a mark of 100% does not mean that the student is now a complete expert on the topic on which he has been tested. Nor does a mark of 0% mean that he knows absolutely nothing about it. Nor does 50% mean that his state of knowledge and understanding is halfway between that of the person most ignorant and person most expert in the field. It may or may not mean that he has performed acceptably on 50% of the objectives being tested.

Some percentage markers do operate as if they have in mind some performance criteria appropriate to the level a student is working at. Such markers would likely want to maintain that a mark of 50% is one they would give to a student who had appeared to show competence on just half of the relevant criteria. Similarly, the student with a score of

75% would have shown competence on half as many more criteria, the 25% student on only half as many as the 50% student. The student with a score of 0% would have shown no competence on the present criteria (though he may have scored 100% on the criteria appropriate to the previous stage of the work). The scores of 100%, of course, go to those students who perform satisfactorily on all criteria.

Many other percentage markers, however, use the percentage scores simply to rank the students. That is, if they give scores of, say, 20% and 40% and 80%, they are not implying that the 40% student has performed twice as well as the 20% student and half as well as the 80% student. Nor are they implying that any of these students has achieved a certain percentage of some relevant performance criteria. All they wish to maintain is that the higher-scoring students are more proficient than those with lower scores. The ability-gap between the 10% and 20% students may or may not be bigger than that between the 35% and 45% or the 83% and 93% students.

In fact, although percentage markers have one-hundred-and-one marks to choose from, they usually restrict themselves to a narrower range. Where the range lies — say, between 20 and 80 or between 40 and 90 — will vary, like the size of the range itself, from one teacher to another, some spreading out their marks much more widely than others. Such vagaries among assessors, and the consequent lack of reliability, or consistency of marking, has encouraged the use of the letter-grade system: e.g. A, B, C, D, E. The fewer the categories to which a student can be allotted, the fewer disagreements there are likely to be among assessors. For instance, a group of assessors who might have wanted to respond to a particular student's work with ten different marks between 70 and 85 would find themselves no longer in disagreement if all marks between 70 and 85 were, in effect, replaced by a grade of B.

With the A, B, C, D, E system, only five levels of performance need to be distinguished. However, as with percentage marking, a particular grade may or may not mean to report that a student has reached a particular level of performance (e.g. achieved half the objectives). The system may be applied in a criterion-referenced fashion: such-and-such a performance for a C, so much extra for a B, twice as much more for an A, half as much for a D, and so on, though not necessarily with each division on the scale meant to indicate approximately equal increments in observed performance. For instance, Gerald Miller (1974) describes how his students first earn a D by outlining the books required as basic reading for his course, and then progress (as far as they wish) to C, B, and A grades by successfully tackling assignments that demand increasingly independent work. Yet again, allocation of letter grades may be quite norm-referenced (as in GCE) with the distribution decided before the students have 'performed' at all, and no particular levels of performance being implied. Thus A may be reserved for the best 5% of the students, B for the next best 20%, C for the next 50%, D for the next 20%, and E for the lowest 5%. Such a distribution can hardly be based on the assumption that only five levels of performance are distinguishable and that the proportions of students displaying each can be predicted in advance. More likely it implies that, while many levels of performance can be distinguished, for practical purposes they can be divided into five groups with agreed proportions in each. Notice that such a distribution would allow for two students with C to be less similar to each other than two students with D or B and far less similar than two with E or A.

Some such predetermined distribution as that above is often used to convert percentage marks into letter grades. In thus reducing the categories, we lose a good deal of precision. We might for instance expect two students each with a grade of B to be far less equal in performance than two students each with 75%. However, the preciseness of the percentage mark should not lead us to assume it is also accurate. Taking into account the 'unreliability' factor, it would not be unreasonable to read 75% as 75±10%. The two students with a mark of 75% might easily have come out twenty points apart on another test of the same subject matter, or on another day, or had their work been marked by a different assessor. Even in the case of 'rigorous' psychological tests, a psychologist would admit, say, that a student with a measured IQ of 110 might be less intelligent (as defined by the test) than one with a measured IQ of 100.

It is at this point that many assessors have pushed for changes in the system. Some are distressed by the coarseness of the five categories and the presumed loss of information about the students. They will wish to add pluses and minuses, making perhaps a range of fifteen possible categories: A+, A, A—, B+, B, B—, C+, C, C—, D+, D, D—, E+, E, E—. (Double pluses and double minuses would extend the range even further!) At the same time, those other assessors who are more distressed by the wide uncertainty attached to any precise-seeming discriminations between students may recommend operating with fewer categories. They may suggest three (e.g. Distinction, Satisfactory, Unsatisfactory) or just two (e.g. Pass and Fail). A few may even go along with the principle of blanket grading, giving the same grade to all students in the group — perhaps on the grounds that the assessment task has been performed co-operatively or perhaps in the belief that grades cannot distinguish meaningfully between the performances of individual students.

The fewer the grades, the greater the significance of the boundary between one grade and the next. A student who gets 56% will not usually care if another piece of work, which he regards as about equal in merit, gets 57%. But he is likely to care if one piece gets C and the other B. The boundary between passing grades and a failure will be particularly significant. If there is only one failing grade, it will not be recorded whether students given that grade have only just failed or have failed disastrously. With percentage grading, however, there need in principle be no point at which a slightly poorer performance results in a new and derogatory label being attached. In practice, however, a certain percentage is often arbitrarily fixed as the pass-mark and those above it and below it are sorted into sheep and goats. To rank students in order of achievement is an act of assessment. But to distinguish between different levels of achievement, saying that some represent distinction and some failure is a *decision*, often taken for political or administrative reasons. It adds nothing of substance to a student's record and, in the case of 'failures', loses information that might be beneficial to the student. Thus, John Pearce (1972, p. 161) laments as a 'social casualty' the fact that thousands of British students every year emerge from two-year examination courses with 'nothing to show for it' because they have not reached pass-standard. The fact that a student has not done well enough to pass should not relieve us of the obligation to report what he *has* managed to do. Periodically, someone protests that students who've scored, say, 39% have *only just* missed the pass-mark of 40% and shouldn't they be squeezed through? This, of course, would be to reduce the effective pass-mark to 39% and raise the question again but this time in relation to students who've *just* missed with a score of 38%! Jonathan Warren (1971) mentions the practice, observed in the U.S.A., of tactfully (but unjustifiably) setting the boundaries at points where there happen to be gaps in the score distribution; the converse, observed in Britain (Vesselo, 1962, p. 131), is 'the peak of charity' which often shows up in the distribution of examination scores with rather fewer scores than might be expected of say 37, 38, 39 (if the pass score is set at 40) and rather more than might be expected of 40, 41, 42.

Just *what* is reported by a numerical mark or letter grade? Neither carries much of a message. If a student's essay or laboratory practical is given 80% or B+, this does not tell him, or anyone else who may be interested, which aspects of the assessed performance he has done well in or in which he still needs to improve. It may or may not help him to predict what eventual summative grade he would achieve on his present standard of work. All it tells him for certain is that he is deemed to have done better or worse than colleagues (or himself on previous occasions) who have very different scores. How much better or worse is something neither he nor anyone else will know unless they have some kind of information about his colleagues' scores also.

Ranks

Instead of reporting the student's score, his relative position in the group may be given. That is, all scores will be arranged in order and ranked 1, 2, 3, . . . etc., from the highest to the lowest. Where norm-referenced assessment is required, e.g. when selecting the best or poorest X% of the group for some purpose, it will be more important to know how each student ranks than to know what percentage of the available marks he has scored. However, Max Marshall (1968, p. 37) cautions those who would take precise rankings too seriously (bearing in mind the scope for error in the original data): 'The simple fact is that a small group of ten students can be ranked in precisely 3,628,800 ways. A choice of a single one of these seems somewhat precarious. With one more student, 39,916,800 possible arrangements are available. . . . A twelfth student would add nearly half a *billion* new possible arrangements. . . . Everyone knows that statistics are notoriously tricky, but few, especially when faced with neat figures they want to believe, realize how tricky they can be.'

A letter grade conveys a cruder, less challengeable idea of a student's rank, provided we know what other grades have been awarded. Thus, a student with B could be expected to rank below those students in his group who have earned an A. If none have, then this is the highest rank. If his letter grade is reported together with the percentage of his group who gained higher and lower grades, his relative standing will be more evident. Even so, grade C might contain the middle 40% or 50% of students, and we are left to guess whether a particular student with C was nearer the top or nearer the bottom of the C grade, or whether they were all much of a muchness.

One of the weaknesses of ranking is that there appear to be equal intervals between the rank positions. That is, one might assume that the students ranked 1 and 2 are as far apart in quality of performance as are students 2 and 3. However, Student 1 may have scored 100%, while 2 and 3 scored only 50% and 49% respectively. To avoid giving the wrong impression it may sometimes be necessary to report something about the shape of the score distribution as well as the performance of the individual student. This could be done, for example, by drawing a graph of the distribution with the particular student's score indicated. Alternatively, we could give, as well as his score, some reference points in the form of *percentiles* — that is, some of the scores that divide the class into percentage slices. For example, we might record that:

90% of students scored less than 60
75% of students scored less than 48
50% of students scored less than 33
25% of students scored less than 20
10% of students scored less than 9

Bill's score = 57

From this we could see that Bill's score is exceeded by at least 10% of his group, but at least 75% scored less. If the raw scores were not regarded as significant, we might show Bill's standing with a 6-grade report like this:

Grade A   top 10%
      B   next 15%
      C   next 25%
      D   next 25%
      E   next 15%
      F bottom 10%

Bill's grade = B

The other main weakness of ranks, or of norm-referenced reports generally, is that a student's standing relative to his colleagues does not tell us how 'good' he is in relation to any external criteria. The student who is bottom of a good group may be better at his subject than the student who is top of a poor group. While the student's performance can be ranked (against others), it cannot be appreciated (as itself) by the recipient of the report. Not unless he risks a number of assumptions about what such a rank might signify. To be told that a particular restaurant has been voted 'best restaurant in the district' does not help you decide what kind of restaurant it is or whether you and your friends would relish eating there. It is significant that 'consumer guides' on restaurants, and on recorded music for that matter, may suggest some rough rank order by awarding, say, a certain number of stars, but also write about the 'candidates', recognizing that their desirability to consumers may not necessarily be inferred from the ranking. To appreciate the thing (or person) discussed one needs words, prose, narrative — description and criticism.

Words

So the assessor may use words, as well as or instead of, numbers and letters in reporting on the student's work. One minimal use of words is the attachment of labels. Clearly, labels like 'Excellent', 'Good', and 'Poor', or *Optimi, Inferiores (Boni), Pejores* — as at eighteenth-century Yale, are ranking symbols and could be replaced by A, B, and C or 1, 2 and 3 without loss of information. Slightly more sophisticated are labels which appear to classify rather than to rank or grade. 'Hyperactive', 'dyslexic' and 'dim' seem to be such words. Even then, a ranking is often implied, as J. O. Urmson (1950) points out in his searching analysis of the language of grading, e.g. witness the labels 'rash'/'brave'/'cowardly' or 'extravagant'/'liberal'/'mean'. Again, such verbal labels carry no more information than would letters or numbers from some agreed scale of preference. The point is, one cannot know what to make of a label like 'good' or 'brave' or 'dim' unless one knows where it sits in relation to the underlying scale. As Urmson says: 'One obvious trick of sellers of graded wares is to use "good" very nearly at the bottom and a number of superlatives above it.' Hence, if a teacher has it reported to him that a child is 'dim', is he to expect the utmost difficulty in teaching him? Or would such extreme difficulty attach only to those labelled 'thick' or 'stupid'?

No wonder that labels which mean so much to the reporters often mean so little to the recipients. Because the criteria for their application are so obscure, so too are their implications. A teacher may use some such shorthand in his own student records, but in reporting to people who are not so familiar with his frame of reference — employers, administrators, other teachers, parents, and even his own pupils to some extent — more explicit reports are necessary. Education is not the only arena for unhelpful reporting. Michael Balint (1964, p. 98) tells how family physicians are often ill-served by the reports given them on their patients by consulting psychiatrists: 'During my lifetime I have witnessed the change in fashion from neurasthenia to psychasthenia, then to neurotic character, and recently to anxiety or depressive states;

but the help given the general practitioner by describing his patient by any of these names has not changed much.' Similarly with students referred by teachers; e.g. Reed *et al* (1968) reviewed 101 articles and found that no educational implications attached to a diagnosis of 'brain damage'. Assessment labels usually suffer from the same weakness as numbers and letters. They give norm-referenced information to people who really need it criterion-referenced. They tell you whether the student's work is towards this end or that end of some spectrum but leave unstated the kinds of knowledge and understanding that characterize different positions in the spectrum. What gets reported is often the assessor's feelings about the student's work:

A = 95% = Excellent = I like it! *I like it!*! I LIKE IT!!!

The recipient of such a report is given nothing that might enable him to reconstruct an image of the student's work for his own evaluation. He must rely on the assessor's evaluation — without evidence on which to decide whether this is a reasonable thing to do.

Reports that rely on evaluative labels fall into the trap that advisers on rhetoric and creative writing have been warning against ever since Aristotle. That is, decription and the evocation of experience is not accomplished by adjectives but by verbs. Not by describing your reactions to the experience but by re-creating the experience itself and letting the reader have his own reactions. In short, don't tell him . . . show him. Hence the need for a method of reporting not merely that the student has demonstrated more or fewer valued qualities than others, nor even to what extent the student has shown valued qualities, but which valued qualities the student has shown. (Valued by the assessor and / or the student that is; whether they are valued by the recipient of the report he will now be able to decide.) Such a report needs words, but words arranged as statements.

The statements can take the form of a checklist of objectives. List the learning objectives which are aimed at in a particular piece of work or during a certain period of time; and, for each one, say whether or not the student has attained it. Many teachers keep student records in some such form. Figure 7.1 below shows part of the mathematics record card used in Winnetka schools — a list of mathematical abilities which the teacher can tick off for each student as he masters them. Students themselves may keep such records. In areas where objectives are 'infinitely improveable' (e.g. How would the 'tick off for attainment'-method work with objectives like those listed on p.96?), the tick could

Figure 7.1
Part of Mathematics Record Card from Winnetka Schools
(Tyler and Wolf, 1974, p. 80)

Recognizes number groups up to 5 — — — —
Recognizes patterns of objects to 10 — — — —
Can count objects to 100 — — — —
Recognizes numbers to 100 — — — —
Can read and write numerals to 50 — — — —
Recognizes addition and subtraction symbols — — — —
Understands meaning of the equality sign — — — —
Understands meaning of the inequality signs — — — —
Can count objects:
    by 2's to 20 — — — —
    by 5's to 100 — — — —
    by 10's to 100 — — — —
Recognizes geometric figures:
    triangle — — — —
    circle — — — —
    quadrilateral — — — —
Recognizes coins (1¢, 5¢, 10¢, 25¢) — — — —
Knows addition combinations 10 and under using objects — — — —
Knows subtraction combinations 10 and under using objects — — — —
Recognizes addition and subtraction vertically and horizontally — — — —
Shows understanding of numbers and number combinations
    1. Using concrete objects — — — —
    2. Beginning to visualize and abstract — — — —
    3. Makes automatic responses without concrete objects — — — —
Can tell time
    1. Hour — — — —
    2. Half hour — — — —
    3. Quarter hour — — — —
Addition combinations 10 and under (automatic response) — — — —
Subtraction combinations 10 and under (automatic response) — — — —
Can count to 200 — — — —
Can understand zero as a number — — — —
Can understand place value to tens — — — —
Can read and write numerals to 200 — — — —
Can read and write number words to 20 — — — —
Use facts in 2-digit column addition (no carrying) — — — —
Roman numerals to XII — — — —

simply indicate 'satisfactorily performed' (whatever that might mean) and would need to be augmented with further comment.

The assessor would also need to report on qualities that had *not* been anticipated. The more open the assessment, the more such qualities he might find to include. This brings us to what might be called the 'free response' report, in which we describe everything significant we happen to have noticed about the student in a particular piece of work or during a particular period of time, regardless of any pre-specified objectives. The report quoted on p. 208 is rather of that type; so is this example from a primary school-teacher's record sheets (written for the guidance of her colleagues):

> Andrew still cannot write a sentence on his own though he continues to work well from comprehension cards. His hand-writing is very good but he has no grasp of word sequence in sentence construction and is vague about spelling. He has read the sixth Greenbook and the Reading with Rhythm book 'The Little Kettle' and is now reading 'Soup for Dinner' in the same series. In number work, I am still trying to establish number bonds to 10. Andrew is able to do addition and subtraction only by physically partitioning a set. He is easily upset in number work which makes him incapable even of working with aids. Needs very gentle handling and cannot work without an adult's help.

The Conflation Problem

As we go from reporting the student's performance on one piece of work towards reporting his development over several, we are brought to consider a problem that looms larger and larger as the span of assessment increases. This is the problem of combination or conflation. How are we to conflate — to bring together and report in some coherent way — the results of assessments made in a variety of situations or over a considerable period of time?

Consider the Open University student. In each course he takes, a 'report' (grade) is produced on each assignment he writes for his tutor and on each assignment he submits for computer-marking. In many cases, the assignment grade will be conflated from assessments made of his perfor-mance on several separate aspects of the assignment. These assignment grades are conflated to produce a composite grade for his 'continuous assessment' performance. Similarly, with the end-of-course examina-tion, each question he tackles will elicit a grade from the assessor and these will be conflated to produce an examination 'result'. The reported results on continuous assessment and examination will be conflated to produce a 'report' on his performance on the course as a whole. This process will be repeated for each of the courses he takes, eight perhaps, and the separate course assessments are finally conflated to produce an overall 'report' which is, in effect, the 'kind', or more specifically 'class', of degree he is awarded.

Secondary school students are subject to conflation when course work is assessed as well as examinations. American students are constantly aware of the problem in the shape of the 'grade-point-average'. But, actually, some conflation is usually present in what may seem the simplest assessment response. Even within an individual essay, the assessor may, consciously or unconsciously, conflate his responses to several aspects of it in reaching his overall response.

So how is conflation to be performed? How to report on the student's work as a whole? (Or on what sometimes seems to be the *student* as a whole?) One way seems to be based on the assumption that the whole is the sum of the parts. To report on the whole, you add up the parts. If that doesn't produce a sensible result, like five scores adding up to 320%, you divide by the number of separate assessments and average it out at 64%. I have commented earlier on the fact that such a 'sensible' overall report may bear little resemblance to any of the contributory assessments (e.g. 100, 100, 50, 40 and 30).

But fearsome demons are rumoured to lie in wait for those who combine scores and grades without observing the proper rites. Take the question of *weighting*. Suppose students sit two examination papers in chemistry and their performances on the two papers are to be given equal weight in reporting their overall performance in chemistry. That is to say, a student's overall score should be no more like his score on Paper I than like his score on Paper II. It is generally assumed that if both papers are marked out of the same total, say 100%, then papers are weighted equally. Thus, to treble the weight of one paper compared with the other you might expect to mark it out of 300, instead of 100. However, life is more complicated. The papers may turn out to have different weights, to exert different amounts of influence on the student's scores, even if they are both marked out of the same total. What is significant is not the total possible, nor even the average score on each paper, but how much scatter there is among the scores. The paper on which scores are more spread out will exert the greater weight.

As a simple but dramatic example, suppose four students only (A, B, C and D) take two papers meant to have *equal* weight. Here are their scores and ranks on each paper:

Student		A	B	C	D
Paper I	Score	10	21	38	50 (out of 100)
	Rank	4	3	2	1
Paper II	Score	100	95	85	80 (out of 100)
	Rank	1	2	3	4

How might we report each one's overall performance? The 'obvious' method — adding his two scores — give the following totals and rank positions.

Student	A	B	C	D
Total Score	110	116	123	130 (out of 200)
Rank	4	3	2	1

Notice, however, that the overall ranking of the students is exactly the same as on Paper I, and the reverse of that on Paper II. In other words, far from having equal weight, Paper II has had no effect at all on the students' relative positions (although it had pulled the percentage scores closer together). This has happened because the spread of scores on Paper I is twice that on Paper II — the ranges are 40 marks and 20 marks. Consequently, as far as overall ranking is concerned, a student would have done himself most good by scoring highly in the paper with most spread of marks (or least harm by scoring lowly in the paper with least spread).

Various means are suggested for 'correcting' the situation by 'scaling' the marks (e.g. see Lacey, 1960; Vesselo, 1962, p. 133; Thyne, 1974, p. 131; Forrest, 1974). Essentially, the trick is to 'stretch' the least scattered distribution so that its range of scores (or, for greater rigour, its standard deviation) matches that of the other. When several distributions are being combined, they may all be mapped onto a common scale of say 0—100. Many secondary school teachers will have used the 'nomogram' method for scaling, based on the idea of similar triangles as shown in Figure 7.2. The maxima on the two scales are connected by two straight lines, as are the minima. A line drawn through the point of intersection from a score on one scale will lead to the corresponding score on the other scale. Thus, if we make scores of 100 and 80 on Paper II, equivalent to 50 and 10 on Paper I, we find that Paper II scores of 95 and 85 scale out to 40 and 20 when 'stretched', though the rank-position of those scores is not affected. (In fact the nomogram, though quick, is also crude in that it is based entirely on two extreme scores rather than on the scatter near the centre of a distribution, around the mean, where most of the scores are likely to lie. Rigorous scaling is done by standardizing all marks to a common mean and standard deviation — see Mackintosh and Hale [1976, p. 106] for a simple graphical method.)

Figure 7.2
Nomogram for Scaling Marks

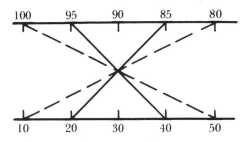

Having been scaled, the two sets of scores now have comparable spread and can be added in the knowledge that both papers carry equal weight. When we do so, we find the ranking quite transformed:

Student	A	B	C	D
Paper I Score	10	21	38	50
Scaled Paper II Score	50	40	20	10
Total	60	61	58	60
Rank	2½=	1	4	2½=

The student previously in third place has come out on top; the student previously second is now fourth; the two students who each came out best on one of the papers now share middle rank. These figures were loaded to emphasize a point. Real-life distributions are not likely to show such large differences in spread of score as well as a perfect negative correlation between high rank on one and low on the other. Figure 7.3 shows a more everyday example of conflating the scores on two questions which are supposed to carry equal weight. By and large, students scoring highly on one question do so on the other also; low scorers tend to score low on both. The spread of scores on Question 2 is about 50% bigger than on Question 1, so the Question 1 scores are scaled to give them equal weight. As shown in the table below, the effect on rankings is undramatic but nevertheless evident: students D and G change places, as do F and K, and H and O. This may or may not matter much to the people involved. But if, for example, only the top three were to be awarded distinctions, O would now get one instead of H.

Figure 7.3

	RAW SCORES				SCALED SCORES		
STUDENTS	X Qu. 1	Y Qu. 2	X + Y Total	Rank	Z Qu. 1	Y + Z Total	Rank
A	86	83	169	1	85	168	1
B	75	85	160	2	69	154	2
C	74	72	146	7	68	140	7
D	70	82	152	5	62	144	6*
E	72	67	139	10	65	132	10
F	66	69	135	12	56	125	13*
G	79	72	151	6	75	147	5*
H	80	75	155	3	77	152	4*
I	71	67	138	11	63	130	11
J	73	72	145	8	64	136	8
K	76	58	134	13	71	129	12*
L	76	64	140	9	71	135	9
M	67	58	125	14	58	116	14
N	65	55	120	15	55	110	15
O	84	70	154	4	83	153	3*

As long as there is *some* difference in spread and *some* students are not ranked similarly in the two separate distributions, then there will be a tendency for *some* students' rank-positions to be different according to whether or not the scores are scaled before being added together.

Thus the teacher who confidently tells students that 'All papers will be given equal weight' or 'Question One will carry three times as much weight as any other question' may unintentionally be breaking his promises. To mark all papers out of the same total if equal weight is required, or to mark a question out of three times the usual total if three-fold weight is required, enables the required weighting to occur but does not guarantee it. For that, the full spread of scores available must actually be *used*. In fact, the relative variability of scores on two or more papers or questions is rarely very apparent, especially if one ignores the range as being a rather undependable indicator of spread. Standard deviations take some while to calculate and more than a little arithmetic is necessary to ensure that the two or more sets of scores are combined with the weightings desired. There are short-cuts, of course, some even quicker (and dirtier) than the nomogram method (e.g. the simplest is to add the ranks instead of the marks) but the fact that they are liable to all give slightly different results would seem to strain 'the principles of allowable witchcraft'.

Besides, it is not entirely self-evident that distributions *should* always be 'corrected' on account of differing spread of scores. If we send Tom and John to the store and they take the following times to go and return

	Going	Returning
Tom	30 min.	5 min.
John	15 min.	10 min.

we don't say they did equally well on the round-trip because each was faster in one direction. We rightly say that John did better because he'd been there and back before Tom had even reached the store. He was faster overall. Similarly, teachers who see their assessment as criterion-referenced may say it makes sense to add the scores on two or more questions or tests and compare students' standings on the raw total. They may argue that if Billy has reached 80% of the organic chemistry objectives and 60% of the inorganic objectives, it means something to say he has reached 70% of the chemistry objectives; he can be compared directly with students who have attained, say, 77% or 64%. The fact that his 80% was almost the poorest achievement in his group because all did very well and at much the same level of performance, while his 60% attainment put him well out in front on 'inorganic' which seemed to spread people out more, is neither here nor there. They can't accept that the 'organic' marks should be stretched to the same spread as the 'inorganic' if this means that Billy ends up with a total suggesting he has mastered less chemistry than colleagues who in fact achieved fewer objectives than he did but were fortunate enough to do better than he in the test where everyone did well. Thus they might argue that addition of the raw scores gives equal weight to the achievement of the two kinds of objectives. If, for some reason, it were desired to give, say, double or treble weight to one or the other, it would be necessary to double or treble the corresponding scores.

What such teachers are objecting to, at base, is the hidden ideology of norm-referenced assessment which is, of course, what inspires the admonitions against careless addition of scores. Norm-referencers do not accept that marks or scores indicate how much a student is judged to have learned nor even how much compared with other students. For them the mark indicates only that he is judged to have learned more or less than others. In other words, the mark functions as a ranking symbol, as Albert Pilliner (1973, p. 9 in Appendix 1) makes clear: 'Raw marks should be used only to place a batch of examination scripts in meaningful rank order. The "raw" marks should then be scrapped. Only after this should "final" marks or percentage bands be assigned in accordance with an agreed convention.'

To someone who assumes that this is how scores are being used, it clearly would not be acceptable that one assessor should use ranking symbols with a big spread of values while another uses a smaller spread. The result of adding scores from the two distributions would seem to him as silly as adding together temperatures expressed in Fahrenheit and Centigrade. It would also seem misleading and unfair as a report on the relative overall standings of the students involved.

Worse, he might regard a narrow range of scores as evidence of inadequate assessment. Thus he might assume that the organic chemistry test was poor because it did not 'spread them out' as the 'inorganic' test did. Here may be some basic expectation that the students *ought* to be as differentiable in one topic as in another, their scores in all areas correlating with one another, indicating in effect some *general factor* of 'scientific ability', or 'literary ability' or just 'academic ability'. Hence the teacher who says all his students have reached much the same standard must have been asking the wrong questions and his students' scores need a little Procrustean stretching to make them as different here as they are elsewhere.

So what do we conclude about conflating scores? A teacher who knows that his scores or grades are criterion-referenced may be able to justify adding them as they are. A teacher who is norm-referencing, and using scores as ranking symbols, however, must consider the need to scale or standardize them. Otherwise the resulting totals may have unintended weightings that unjustly penalize or benefit certain individuals. This might apply from the level of conflating results on several courses right down to the level of the score for an individual exercise if several sub-scores are contributing to it — and with 'impression making' one may not even be aware the conflation is taking place. However, it would not be too unkind to suggest that many teachers would not be sure how they were using marks — whether as indicating achievement of criteria or as ranking devices. It is hard not to believe that considerable unreliability may creep into conflated results thanks to arbitrary, subjective or unremarked weightings being present. The Nuffield group investigating assessment of a new system for three-year science degrees among London colleges found that 'every college . . . uses a different formula for combining individual course results, and in some cases different departments within the same faculty use different techniques for standardizing raw scores; in one case the final calculation proved so complex that it had to be processed by computer' (Nuffield, 1973, p. 9). The opportunities for mystification, of self and of others, are profound.

Towards Richer Reporting

But there is another aspect to the conflation problem. What if everyone *did* agree on a standard way of summarizing in a symbol the results of assessing the student in a variety of different tasks, or times, or situations? What if we all did know whether the '75%' or 'B' or '2nd-class' was generated by a norm- or a criterion-referenced totting-up system? We would still know precious little worth knowing about the student. From such reductive symbols, life escapes. What the assessors perhaps knew of the student is lost. If the symbol is norm-referenced we know that he is 'better-than', but not what he is 'good at'. Even if criterion-referenced, we may know he is good at some of the things involved but not necessarily which. For example, suppose a student takes a Spanish exam consisting of reading, writing, speaking and responding to native speakers, and gets a criterion-referenced 75%; has he failed one of the four aspects but done as well as expected on the others, or is he about three-quarters proficient on all four, or what?

So many different student qualities may be scrambled together under a uni-dimensional grade and the uniqueness of their contributions ignored. We *can* add apples and oranges — e.g. 3 apples and 20 oranges = 23 fruit — but to do so may not be very helpful to the consumer. The consumer may have been taught to expect it, but that is another matter. A *New Yorker* cartoon once showed a teacher saying to a child's parents: 'Well, Johnny's a good student, and always gets A for effort and A for intelligence, but I have to give D for co-operation — except in Math, where he helps me with the slow ones'; but the baffled parents reply, 'So what *grade* does he get?' In fact, to attempt such a summation would be no more helpful than for a doctor to give his patient a 'vitality quotient' conflated from measurements of blood-pressure, pulse-rate and lung-capacity; or to add together his height, weight and chest-expansion as a statement of his overall 'size'. In education, the wider the span of student activity reported in a single grade, the less useful it is. Even as a response to the student's answer to a single question, a grade is rather uninformative. Still more so if grades for several questions or several kinds of assessment, or several courses, or several years are totted up to arrive at a single summative symbol.

Assessment results are recorded so that someone — students, other teachers, parents, employers — can use them to make decisions. Such decisions often cannot rationally be made on aggregated results. For example, '40%' may tell the student he needs to improve but not where or how. Again, a student's overall grade may express his overall performance in areas W, X, Y and Z; but if one employer values W- and Z-type skills while another values X- and Y-type skills, neither can place much confidence in the overall grade as a recommendation, especially if the skills he values are not 'critical elements' in achieving a good grade. Consequently, recent years have seen much interest in playing down conflation and presenting the decision-maker instead with separate assessments on the various components, leaving him to weight them according to their importance to him. Such a reporting response is usually called a *profile*. (See Mansell, 1972; Owens, 1973; Hinton, 1973; Klug, 1974, 1977; Morrison, 1974; Simpson, 1976; etc).

Profiles

The idea of profiles has entered education *via* psychological testing especially of personality and aptitudes. Broadly, a profile is a panoramic representation — alpha-numerical, graphical or verbal — of how the student seems to his assessors across a range of qualities, or on one quality but as seen through a range of assessment methods. The use of profiles carries no stipulations about what should be assessed or how. They can be used in reporting any assessments.

The crudest form of profile is obtained by quoting the student's scores or ranks on all *component* dimensions instead of averaging them out into an overall grade. Thus American students will emerge from college clutching a 'transcript', which defines their degree by listing the titles of courses they have taken and the grade obtained in each. For example:

Mervyn Mynde   Class of '77
Degree of Master of Arts (Education)

ES608	Educational Concepts and Research	A
ES611	Epistemology and Education	A
ES612	Moral and Social Education	B
P641	Ethics and Political Philosophy	A
P653	Philosophy of Science	C
P654	Philosophy of Social Science	B
P672	Phenomenology and Existentialism	C

Open University students get something similar, except that the results may *also* be translated for the reader into a degree classification. In effect, GCE students are now given a profile. Whereas under the previous School Certificate system, several subjects had to be passed in order to qualify for the certificate (as for a degree), the candidate now gets a certificate showing his grade on however many (or few) subjects he has tackled.

A profile could also be issued instead of (or as well as) calculating the student an overall grade in an individual course, e.g.:

Physics — Seroja Shah

Heat:	75%
Light:	40%
Sound:	79%
Electricity:	86%
Mechanics:	50%

Within a course, a profile could be used to show how the student performed on various assessment methods:

Laboratory work:	40%
Personal project:	89%
Homework:	70%
Final examination:	57%

How one interprets such a set of scores (e.g. is 50% for mechanics better than 40% for light?) depends on whether one knows them to have been standardized or not. Rankings can, of course, be shown in a profile by indicating the student's percentile position. Figure 7.4 is an example, illustrating also that profiles can incorporate a graphical element:

Figure 7.4

French — Larry Boyle

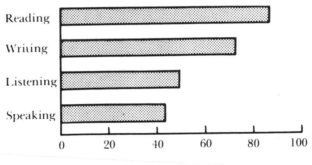

Percentile ranking

Such charts may allow easier comparison of one aspect of a student's work with another. They may also allow easy comparison of one student with another. Figure 7.5, for example, shows graphical profiles for two student-teachers (based on Morrison, 1974). Apart from teaching practice and history of education, their grades in which are reversed, both students have the same set of grades.

Conflation might suggest that both these students were of equal merit — as well they might be to anyone in whose eyes proficiency in history of education and practical teaching were equally and interchangeably valuable. Inspection of the profiles, however, suggests that someone

Figure 7.5

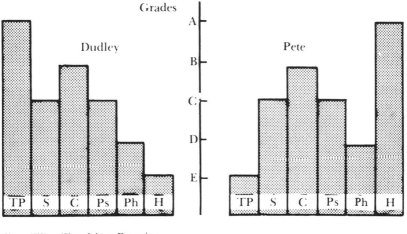

Key: TP = Teaching Practice
     S = Sociology
     C = Comparative Education
     Ps = Psychology
     Ph = Philosophy
     H = History of education

looking for a classroom teacher would prefer Dudley, though Pete might excel him in some other branch of education, e.g. educational journalism.

Being based on grades or ranks, the profiles we've looked at so far have been rather uncommunicative about what the student can actually *do*. Profiles can, however, be used to spell out more specific talents and abilities observed in the student. The honours graduate of Birmingham School of Architecture (see Hinton, 1973) is given not a classified degree but a profile which takes the form of a sheet with various qualities listed and ticks against those on which he has shown 'special interest' or 'above-average ability'. The sheet might thus indicate, for example, that a particular graduate was good but not outstanding in width of knowledge, reasoning skill and aptitude for research; showed a subject bias towards technology and social sciences; displayed outstanding practicality in problem-solving (but no special originality or sensitivity); worked best as leader of a team (rather than as a team member or as an individual); was outstanding on drive and determination (but not on concentration or precision); and communicated particularly well orally and visually (but not in writing).

Michael Simpson (1976) describes a rather more sophisticated profile worked out with medical students of McMaster University in Canada after each major phase or unit within their curriculum. It consists of two sheets. The first (Figure 7.6) enables the tutor to indicate and comment upon the extent of the student's attainment of the general goals of the medical curriculum. The second sheet carries tutor comment on how far he has attained the goals of the particular phase or unit and his own additional personal objectives; his areas of exceptional ability are also remarked upon, as are areas requiring extra attention; finally the sheet carries the overall decision as to whether he is ready for the next phase of the course.

Clearly, the dimensions of a student's work can be laid bare in great detail in a profile. In his profile for a given course, for example, we could indicate the student's performance on each and every objective (as in the checklist shown in Figure 7.1). At present, there is no such information made available about the students who 'pass' CSE, or GCE 'O'- and 'A'-levels. To produce a profile covering several courses, say, a year's schoolwork or a full degree programme, one could simply put together separate profiles for individual courses. Or one could produce a synoptic profile, distinguishing between minor and major objectives (perhaps on the process/content division) and concentrating on those that transcend any particular course. Thus, for example, a profile for the educational philosophy student mentioned on p. 229, might contain, in addition to his separate course performances, an appraisal of his prowess in such general 'philosophical' process-abilities as these (borrowed from Klug, 1974):

1. Ability to discriminate between essentials and inessentials, to spot the key issue in a complex situation.

2. Ability to see structural similarities in arguments, transfer ideas from familiar to unfamiliar situations.

3. Ability to make critical appraisal and analysis of the arguments of others, to review and comment on the usefulness of particular proposals.

4. Ability, when faced with a problem, to develop one's own solution, to synthesize systematically and constructively.

Figure 7.6

Extract from Student Profile Form (Simpson, 1976)

Key to Ratings in Section A

Few or none of these behaviours demonstrated	Some of these behaviours shown, but definitely lacks some	Many of these behaviours, but some minor difficulties	Outstanding ability demonstrated	Not applicable

Please mark where the student was at the beginning and end of the phase in each of the following respects, according to the above key. Give an explanation for your ratings in the spaces provided, as appropriate.

Section A: General Goals of the M.D. Programme	Explanation Comments
1. Problem-Solving Ability: Able to identify and define health problems, search for information, and synthesize information into a conceptual framework. Beginning ___ N A End ___ N A	
2. Understanding of Concepts and Mechanisms: Given a health problem, is able to examine the underlying physical or behavioural mechanisms, including a spectrum of phenomena, from molecular events to those involving the patient's family and community, as appropriate. Beginning ___ N A End ___ N A	
3. Personal Characteristics Recognizes, maintains, and develops personal characteristics and attitudes relevant to professional life. These include: (a) Awareness of personal assets, potential, limitations, and emotional reactions. Shows intellectual honesty insight. Beginning ___ N A End ___ N A	
(b) Responsibility and Dependability, e.g. comes prepared to contribute to the tutorial, fulfills commitments Beginning ___ N A End ___ N A	
4. Clinical Skills (See specific form for this phase or unit)	
5. Self-Directed Learning Is becoming a self-directed learner, recognizing personal educational needs, selecting appropriate learning resources and evaluates progress validly. Beginning ___ N A End ___ N A	
6. Group Interpersonal Skills Is able to function as a productive member of a small group; acknowledges other's contributions; shows awareness of and ability to relate to other's feelings; identifies and copes with group problems. Beginning ___ N A End ___ N A	

5. Ability to put across complex ideas in a coherent and understandable way, to explain, communicate, illuminate.

By 'unravelling' a uni-dimensional overall grade or rank, and showing
rather how the student was evaluated in a number of component
dimensions, the profile offers its recipients far more information on
which to make their *own* overall evaluations. But a profile can go
beyond quoting grades and ranks, even for these component
dimensions. They can do more than rate the student on predetermined
objectives supposedly relevant to all students. The compiler can apply
what Max Marshall (1960, 1968) calls the 'flotation technique' and
describe whatever characteristics and qualities and abilities 'float to the
top' of his mind with respect to each individual student. The result will
be a 'case history' report on the student — a verbal profile. In effect, the
assessors' responses quoted on pages 208 and 220 are little profiles,
laying bare the criteria by which a single essay or a term's work is being
judged. Boris Ford (1969) suggests that university examiners should
jointly produce a profile for each candidate — though one might want
it to reveal more than is feasible in the kind of labelling language he
uses in his examples:

My proposal is that the examiners for each paper which a
candidate writes should render a brief description and evaluation
of his performance. This would in fact include: the character of
the examining exercise (e.g. 'This examination took the form of a
long dissertation of about 10,000 words, which the candidate
wrote over a period of two months'; or 'This examination took the
form of a three-hour unseen paper in which the candidate was
asked to answer three out of a list of fifteen questions', etc.) It
would then briefly evaluate the candidate's performance (e.g.
'Had clearly mastered his material and showed an unusual
capacity to discuss the main problems conceptually. Moreoever,
his dissertation was excellently organized and annotated, and
elegantly written.' Or: 'This was a respectable if somewhat
pedestrian statement of the issues, though the candidate was not
able to discuss them with any imaginative grasp.' Or: 'A very
competent handling of the issues involved, if in the last resort just
lacking the spark of real distinction').

As an example of the kind of entries that might appear in profiles of
wider span, here are extracts from several assessors' comments on a
medical student, quoted in Horowitz (1964), a book rich in such
material:

Preceptor's Report (University Hospital):   Charles has been a
very interesting personality to deal with in the past year. He is

quite intelligent and has an active mind, but lacks background and maturity in knowing where to go. . . . He does not know how to handle the 'hot and cold' personal acceptance he gets and this often antagonizes the people he meets casually for the first time. . . . His work with a family and on physical diagnosis is quite good. If handled properly he would do well.

Project Director's Report: Charles has shown great improvement in attitude and aptitude within the past two months. At the start of the project this year he appeared to be disinterested and was careless and lazy in the laboratory. He over-estimated his technical ability and succeeded in ruining several experiments. We had a frank discussion of this behaviour in the laboratory and, following this discussion, he has really taken hold.

He is a mediocre student who has recently worked at full capacity and has actually done a good job. He is mature and has a very pleasant personality. He should develop into a satisfactory physician.

Family Clinic Report: This student presents certain complex problems. . . . He has been reticent about obtaining histories, performing the physical examination. . . . It has been difficult for us to get the student to do the type of work that is necessary in the clinic. The student frequently tends to make plans, contact consultants, etc., before the basic examination and historical facts have been obtained.

The above extracts are from a 'formative' profile meant to alert fellow-teachers to Charles's needs for guidance. However, a similar level of detail could just as well go into summative profiles (rather than into references and testimonials perhaps) for the information of parents, possible employers, grant-awarding bodies, and so on. But the fact that such a profile would presumably need to be the student's property, and it would be he who decided whether to show it to outsiders, does raise again the question of how far a profile should 'accentuate the positive' even at the expense of 'forgetting' some of the student's less compelling qualities. As Tom Fawthrop (1968, p. 45) bluntly puts it: '. . . we must reserve the right to eliminate any information which might prejudice our prospects of future employment or compromise our lives in any way.'

In writing about the student, one may avoid explicit symbols of grading and ranking but one can scarcely avoid evaluative, comparative language. Consequently, there cannot really be such a thing as a purely 'descriptive' profile that leaves all judgement to the reader. However, such evaluative prose is revealed quite transparently as opinion, especially if different assessors produce different opinions of the student. It can be seen to be describing the student through the assessor's human, perhaps fallible, responses. Hence those responses, and the perhaps debatable criteria on which they are based, are no longer shielded by the objective-seeming grade to which they would otherwise have been reduced.

The nearest approach to 'pure' description would be Anton Powell's suggestion (Powell and Butterworth, 1971, p. 26) that: 'Certificates could inform anybody interested that so-and-so had attended whatever courses and had produced a certain volume of work, and beyond that each person would have to be judged purely on their merits for whatever job they applied for. It would of course be open to students, when applying for any job, to present samples of any relevant work they had done at university, just as, at present, artists use portfolios of their work.'

So, what is the future for profiles? As we've seen they can vary in extent from simply making explicit the sub-scores from which the overall score has been derived to abandoning summative symbols altogether and using free prose to describe whatever it is that strikes the assessor as significant about the student and his work — or even referring the recipient to particularly representative *examples* of that work. They can also span all ranges of the student's work right down from a complete degree programme to, I suppose, a single assignment. In general, the wider the span, the less likely is the 'all-talking, all-singing, all-dancing' unidimensional grade to convey anything like knowledge of the increasingly variegated qualities on which the student was judged. So the greater is the need for profiling.

Whatever the span encompassed, a profile and especially one that includes narrative analysis, helps *humanize* the reporting response. Even the simplest of profiles differentiates the student from other students who share the 'same' total but 'add up differently' from him. The thrust is from the nomothetic to the idiographic, dividing the students out from one another like the opening out of a fan — not with a view to classifying them or ranking them in order of preferability but, ideally, with a view to showing that each is in a class of his own — '*sui generis* and unique'. Thereby, the recipient of the report is being put into a new and more human relationship with the assessors and the assessed. He is no longer encouraged to view the assessors as expert technocrats who will answer the question 'What's this student worth to everybody?' Rather he is being given a relativistic 'It all depends'-

answer, one that throws him back on his own criteria which he can compare with those the assessors have applied, noticing that the student is, for *him*, good, bad or interesting in parts. The weighting of those parts in coming to a decision about the student is not something that should be done for him by the assessors, especially since it is now revealed that the assessor's criteria and judgements are not all equally relevant to his concerns. No doubt his interpretations of a profile will sometimes be mistaken, but they could hardly be more so if all he had to work on was a uni-dimensional grade. But it is certainly no disadvantage that his interpretations will be more personal and subjective — perhaps, as Brian Klug (1974) remarks, 'a cause for celebration rather than alarm' if users with differing purposes are able to get differently satisfying insights out of the reports.

A shift away from conflative grades and towards profiles might also be expected to encourage changes in teaching as well as reporting. A sceptic might insist rather that the shift would depend on such changes and that is why it will be slow to take place. I am interested to see, however, whether the prospect of more humanistic reporting methods now emerging may open teachers' perceptions to new teaching possibilities.

Knowing that they were expected to describe in detail what a student had done and achieved, rather than give an overall score, would create for teachers both problems and opportunities. The problems, for many, would centre around the need to make plain, both to themselves and others, the criteria by which they assess. An unnamed tutor quoted in Miller and Parlett (1973, p. 36) hints at the traumas ahead:

> We all refuse to recognize that we vary in our marking. We all know it doesn't work but it's too difficult to do anything else. . . .

> We all admit to ourselves that the final degree mark is not very accurate and we ought to get down to discussing the criteria on which we mark. Then it becomes personal and subjective and painful to people.

For some teachers — those who have never reflected on their assessment constructs — it may seem 'too difficult' to elucidate criteria. Others may know quite well what constructs they are exercising but would see it as weakening their power over the student, and the 'expert' status accorded them by outsiders, to make them public. Yet others will know what they are appreciating in the student's work but find it difficult to put into words. However, between them, such teachers ought to be able to persuade and/or help one another to 'come clean'. After all, what should we think of the professional competence of a literary critic who said: 'I have my impressions and feelings about this particular novel, but I can't (or won't) translate them into words for you; instead I'm going to give it B+'?

Please note that this is *not* a disguised plea for pre-specified behavioural objectives. Where the student or teacher can sensibly identify such objectives prior to the learning, or where such emerge during the learning, well and good. They can be used as assessment criteria — if they are still considered important at the time of assessment. What I am more concerned with is that assessors make plain the criteria they have actually used in assessing a student — regardless of whether these are previously considered objectives or constructs. To recall the words of Eliot Eisner, not so much 'Did the student learn what (he or I) intended?' as 'What did the student learn?' I am entirely sympathetic to the teacher who declines to spell out all (perhaps even any) of his objectives in advance — provided he does not proceed to reward and punish his students without *ever* making clear the criteria by which he does so.

The innovation of having assessors explain the grades they give — or better still, award the explanations instead of the grades — seems like a reasonable request for students and other interested parties to make. But, as I hinted earlier, its effect might be nothing less than to transform the system of public assessment. Especially if it were accompanied by the further innovation of enabling students to keep a *carbon copy* of their examination scripts and so make it easy for them to seek a 'second opinion' should they believe they have been unfairly treated.

A swing towards profiling should also have deep repercussions on the curriculum. Course structure and content, teaching and learning methods, and assessment systems could all be beneficially influenced by the decision to spell students out rather than sum them up. In curriculum discussions in the Open University, for instance, I am frequently made aware of how our options are restricted by the pre-ordained necessity to sum up the student's educational career with one of four categories of a graded degree. For instance:

1. Much time is spent debating whether or not certain educational experiences our students have enjoyed prior to joining us are to count and, if so, as the equivalent of how many OU credits, in the eventual award of their degrees. (Uncertificated

experience would not count at all for credit purposes, e.g. a student with a one-year diploma in computer engineering, and no experience, would be more likely to get credit than a student with ten years' experience and no credentials.)

2. Similarly, anxiety is common about the 'real' level of courses. Are science courses more difficult than arts courses? Are second-level courses all of approximately equal standard and are they all truly less demanding than all third-level courses? How can we justify giving mathematics' students credit for a 'remedial' course designed to bring them *up to* the level at which most other universities start their students?

3. Comparability of content is also a problem. How can we be sure that two courses don't have some overlap of content, resulting in students who take them both being given double credit for the same learning? Do courses that stress 'creativity' rather than cognitive content really qualify as 'proper' university courses? Do two ½-credit courses or three ⅓-credit courses really demand no more of the student than one full-credit course?

4. And what about teaching methods? How far can we let courses depart from the 'traditional' pattern of weekly correspondence text and broadcasts with evenly spaced assignments? What about projects? Can we let the student, with advice from his tutor, pursue his own objectives, design his own 'course'? How about a 'tutorial credit' for advanced students willing to tutor beginners on lower-level courses they have already been through?

5. Assessment questions really expose the raw curriculum tissue. How can we let different courses have different assessment schemes? How can some be self-, some norm-, and some criterion-referenced? How can some require continuous assessment only, and others terminal examination only, when the standard form is to have both? How can we let different students within a course choose how they wish to be assessed and even decide on their own assessment topics? Can we let some courses assess without grading? How can we, for each student, sensibly conflate the results from very diverse learning experiences?

The assumed need for fair comparison, by means of a small set of grades (1st class, upper 2nd, lower 2nd, and third), encourages standardization. It inhibits flexibility, innovation and experiment in curriculum. Do away with the need to so label the student's educational career and the barrier is lifted. Instead of a graded degree, provide a profile *describing* the courses he has done, their content and the form they took, together with an appraisal of what he has learned and where his strengths and interests lie. Many of the above questions would still need to be asked — but for educational rather than bookkeeping reasons.

Profiling relieves us of the need to pretend that two quite different educational careers can sensibly be summed up by the same labelling. The 'degree' then becomes not a badge of general approbation, guaranteed some mystic equivalence with others of the same grade, but a statement of *what the student has done and of how he seems to his assessors at a particular point in time* — which those who are interested must evaluate how they will. It could, in theory, be made available at any time in the student's career and he would always 'have something to show' if for any reason he needed to interrupt or terminate his programme of studies or wished to move to another educational institution. This might be partly to return to an earlier meaning of 'degree' as defining a *step* — perhaps along the road of *continuing* education?

How Shall We Know Them? Some Modest Proposals

Let me, at last, outline an answer to the question posed in the title of this book. How shall we know the students? To what extent and in what manner? This depends on the 'we' in question. As teachers, 'we' may, through our pedagogic assessments, gain much well-founded knowledge about what our student knows, can do, and is. But when 'we' are the recipient of other assessors' reports, our knowledge cannot be as rich and suggestive as theirs. We cannot know the student as we would had we worked with him ourselves; we cannot even know him as we might know, say, a character in a novel by D. H. Lawrence. Indeed, unless the producer of the report is extraordinarily gifted, both with words and with a grasp of our world-view, the best we can expect are intimations, metaphors, and sporadic insights that might guide us into some form of conversation with the student and so facilitate our getting to know him for ourselves.

So what can be done about assessment to ensure that the 'greatest possible number' of people get maximum benefit and least harm from it? It should be clear by now that I am not an 'abolitionist'. Not only do I insist that, as teachers, we cannot function without assessing (and nor can learners), I also maintain that it is reasonable for students to seek from us reports as to our assessment impressions which they can use in engaging the co-operation of other people. I also believe that it is reasonable for those other people, say employers or other teachers to whom our student might be going, to ask us what we know about our student that might help them in deciding how to respond to him.

Here is what I believe we need to do, both to teach better and to provide reports that are in our students' (and the community's) best interest. Let us:

1.   Articulate as clearly as possible the criteria by which we assess — the aims and objectives we espouse, what qualities we look for in students, in general and in individual cases; let us strive to become more aware of our implicit assessment constructs, and constantly question why we value the qualities we do.

2.   Be more adventurous in our choice of assessment methods, recognizing that different methods will bring out different qualities in our students; choose whichever methods seem most relevant educationally and most likely to elicit qualities of the type being sought.

3.   Anticipate the emergence of unexpected qualities also — give credit for what the student has learned as well as whether he has learned what was intended.

4.   Where possible, assess 'naturalistically', concentrating on processes and products pursued for their own educational sakes rather than devising exercises solely for assessment purposes and not themselves meant to be learning experiences.

5.   Always give the student maximum feedback from our assessments — by relating our subsequent teaching to those assessments or, at least (e.g. in an examination, public or school-based), making clear to him what qualities have been discerned in his work and what we see as his strengths and weaknesses (i.e., let us not be satisfied with giving him a grade or rank).

6.   Where our assessments are evaluative rather than descriptive, make clear whether we are comparing our student's work against standard criteria, against that of other students, or against what we expect, or have seen previously, from him.

7.   Accept that equally perceptive colleagues might firmly hold quite different opinions from us about our student's work; at very least this should prevent us being too dogmatic in our response to the student and in some cases might lead us to encourage him in seeking a 'second

opinion' (don't forget to enable him to keep a carbon copy of his examination scripts if the originals cannot be returned to him); do not strive for unnatural consensus among assessors, especially when complex objectives and profound qualities are being discussed.

8.   Resist, nevertheless, the temptation to concentrate on qualities and abilities that are more routinely measurable and less likely to provoke disagreements among assessors.

9.   Encourage the student to build his own 'portfolio' containing selected samples of his work together with assessment reports from his teachers, comments from his peers, and his own self-assessments.

10.   Except in the case of young children, report assessment results to no one but the student, except with his agreement; and, in any case, report only to people with a legitimate interest in his performance, e.g. to his parents and other teachers, not to his peers or the newspapers.

11.   In summative assessments, concentrate on the student's ultimate achievements, unless we are illustrating how he has improved; emphasize his relative strengths but mention those weaknesses that you know to be of relevance to the recipient of the report.

12.   Avoid conflation of assessments from different subjects, courses, qualities, etc.; don't give portmanteau grades, ranks and labels; e.g. for an examination 'result' or a 'degree', prepare a multi-dimensional profile, preferably with considerable narrative content. (Don't let perfection be the enemy of improvement, in this or any other of these proposals; if examining boards still insist on grading candidates, we can start by urging them to produce descriptive profiles *as well*.)

13.   Except where it is our role to certify a candidate as vocationally or professionally competent according to specified criteria, abandon the concept of 'passing or failing'; however low our opinion of the student's qualities, it is up to the recipient of our report, having had those qualities described to him, to decide whether the student passes or fails with *him*. (This is equally true if the recipient of the report is the student himself.)

14.   Refrain from including comments in confidential 'references' that we would be embarrassed to have the student read; if we feel we must say something derogatory about him we should either tell him what it is or else decline to act as referee.

15.   In writing references, or testimonials, or other reports, make clear

that the assessment relates to specific knowledge and skills, understanding and attitudes recently demonstrated — their permanence is not guaranteed; it cannot be taken as evidence of 'general ability', not even of general ability to learn; do not write a report at all without some understanding of how it will be used by the recipient in decision-making; in the case of references, written for a specific institution or employer, expect him to make clear what qualities *he* is looking for in applicants and why.

16.   When we have made predictions about students' future qualities and their chances of developing, take the trouble, where possible, to check whether those students turned out as expected.

17.   Finally, let us reflect on the well-founded scepticism expressed by Sussex University's Working Party on BA Degree Assessment when it said of classified degrees what might equally well be said of CSEs and GCEs (both 'O'- and 'A'-level) and of a host of other certificates and diplomas also:

> . . . prospective employers should be warned . . . that the usefulness of the result is limited. First, because the predictive value of a particular class of degree cannot be guaranteed; second, because the actual measurement is extremely rough; third, because the classified degree may be measuring qualities which are not necessarily relevant to the purposes an employer may have in mind. (Sussex, 1969)

Hence my suggestion that we should cease to award certificates of a kind that encourage simplistic, prejudiced and literally ill-informed expectations about our students. Perhaps all certificates and profiles should carry a Government 'health warning' to the effect that:

> 'Relying too heavily on
> other people's opinions
> can damage your sense of reality.'

References

Abbs, P. (1975) *Autobiography in Education* London: Heinemann.

Abercrombie, M. L. J. (1969) *The Anatomy of Judgement* London: Hutchinson.

Adorno, T. W., Frenkel-Brunswik, D. J., Levinson, D. J., and Sanford, R. N. (1950) *The Authoritarian Personality* New York: Harper and Row.

Ager, M. and Weltman, J. (1967) 'The present structure of university examinations' in *Universities Quarterly* June 1967, pp. 272-285.

Allport, G. W. (1937) *Personality: A Psychological Interpretation* New York: Henry Holt.

Allport,, G. W. (1942) *The Use of Personal Documents in Psychological Science* New York: Social Science Research Council.

Allport, G. W. (1965) *Letters from Jenny* New York: Harcourt, Brace and World.

Angus, E. L. (1974) 'Evaluating experiential education', pp. 77-84 in *New Directions* No. 6, Summer 1974.

Ayllon, T. and Azrin, N. (1968) *The Token Economy* New York: Appleton Century Crofts.

Bain, P. T., Hales, L. W. and Rand, L. P. (1973) 'An investigation of some assumptions and characteristics of the pass-fail grading system', pp. 134-136 in *Journal of Educational Research* Vol. 67, No. 3, November 1973

Balint, M. (1964) *The Doctor, his Patient and the Illness* London: Pitman (first published 1957).

Ball, C. and M. (1973) *Education for a Change* London: Penguin.

Bandura, A. (1970) *Principles of Behaviour Modification* London: Holt Rinehart and Winston.

Barnes, D. (1976) *From Communication to Curriculum* London: Penguin.

Barnett, V. D. and Lewis, T. (1963) 'A study of the relationship between GCE and degree results', pp. 187-226 in *Journal of the Royal Statistical Society* **126** Series A (General).

Bassey, M. (1971) *The Assessment of Students by Formal Assignments* Wellington, N.Z.: Research Office for the Study of Higher Education.

Baume, A. D. and Jones, B. (1974) *Education by Objectives* London: North East London Polytechnic.

Beard, R. M., Healey, F. G. and Holloway, P. J. (1968) *Objectives in Higher Education* London: Society for Research into Higher Education.

Bebell, C. F. S. (1970) 'The evaluation we have', pp. 1-46 in F. T. Wilhelms *Evaluation as Feedback and Guide* Washington, D.C.: Association for Supervision and Curriculum Development, N.E.A. (First published 1967).

Beck, B. and Becker, H. S. (1969) 'Modest proposals for graduate programs in sociology', pp. 227-234 in *American Sociologist* Vol. 4, August 1969.

Becker, H. S., Geer, B. and Hughes, E. C. (1968) *Making the Grade: The Academic Side of College Life* New York: Wiley.

Bennett, R. (1974) *First-class Answers in History* London: Weidenfeld and Nicolson.

Berg, I. (1973) *Education and Jobs: The Great Training Robbery* (first published 1970) London: Penguin.

Berger, P. L. and Luckmann, T. (1966) *The Social Construction of Reality* London: Penguin.

Bernstein, B. (1971) 'Open schools, open society' in Cosin, B. R. *et al* (eds) *School and Society: A Sociological Reader* London: Routledge and Kegan Paul.

Birney, R. C. (1964) 'The effects of grades on students' in *Journal of Higher Education* February 1964, pp. 96-98.

Bishop, A. (1971) 'Mathematics' in R. Whitfield (1971) (See below).

Black, H. (1963) *They Shall Not Pass* New York: Morrow.

Black, P. J. (1969) 'University examinations', pp. 93-99 in *Physics Education* Vol. 3, No. 2.

Block, J. H. (1971) 'Criterion-referenced measurements: potential', pp. 289-298 in *School Review* **79**.

Block, J. H. (ed) (1974) *Schools, Society and Mastery Learning* New York: Holt, Rinehart and Winston.

Bloom, B. S. (ed) (1956) *Taxonomy of Educational Objectives: Cognitive Domain* New York: McKay.

Bloom, B. S., Hastings, J. T. and Madaus, G. F. (1971) *Handbook on Formative and Summative Evaluation* New York: McGraw-Hill.

Bloom, B. S. (1971) *Individual Differences in School-Achievement: A Vanishing Point?* Bloomington, Indiana: Phi Delta Kappa.

Bloom, T. K. (1974) 'Peer evaluation — a strategy for student involvement', pp. 137-138 in *Man, Society, Technology* Vol. 33, Part 5.

Blount, C. (1973) p. 45 in J. Lauwerys and G. Tayer (eds) *Education at Home and Abroad* London: Routledge and Kegan Paul

Bock, R. D. and Wood, R. (1971) 'Test theory', pp. 193-224 in *Annual Review of Psychology* Vol. 22.

Boocock, S. S. and Schild, E. O. (eds) (1968) *Simulation Games in Learning* Beverley Hills, California: Sage.

Bourdieu, P. and Passeron, J. C. (1970) *La Reproduction* Paris: Editions de Minuit.

Bowley, R. L. (1967) *Teaching Without Tears* London: Centaur.

Brereton, J. L. (1944) *The Case for Examinations* Cambridge: Cambridge University Press.

Briggs, D. (1970) 'The influence of handwriting on assessment', pp. 50-55 in *Educational Research* Vol. 13, Part 1.

Brophy, J. E. and Good, T. L. (1974) *Teacher-Student Relationship* New York: Holt, Rinehart and Winston.

Bruner, J. S. (1964) 'Some theorems on instruction, illustrated with reference to mathematics' in Hilgard, R. (ed) *Theories of Learning and Instruction* (The 63rd Yearbook of the National Society for the Study of Education), University of Chicago Press.

Buhler, C. and Massarik, F. (1968) *The Course of Human Life* New York: Springer.

Burke, R. J. (1969) 'Some preliminary data on the use of self-evaluation and peer-ratings in assigning university course grades', pp. 444-448 in *Journal of Educational Research* Vol. 62, No. 10.

Buros, O. K. (1972) *The Seventh Mental Measurements Yearbook* New York: Gryphon.

Cantor, N. (1972) *Dynamics of Learning* New York: Agathon (First published 1946).

Cashdan, A. (1971) *Learning Styles* Unit 1 of Course E281 (Personality Growth and Learning) Bletchley, Bucks: Open University Press.

Cazden, C. (1970) 'The neglected situation in child language research and education' in F. Williams (ed) *Language and Poverty* Chicago: Markham.

Chanan, C. and Gilchrist, L. (1974) *What School is For* London: Methuen.

Clignet, R. (1974) 'Grades, examinations, and other check-points as mechanisms of social control', Ch. 10 (pp. 327-358) in *Liberty and Equality in the Educational Process* New York: Wiley.

Coard, B. (1971) *How the West Indian Child is Made Educationally Subnormal in the British School System* London: New Beacon.

Coghill, N. (1948) 'Sweeney Agonistes', p. 86 in R. Marsh and Tambimuttu (eds) *T. S. Eliot* London: Editions Poetry.

Cole, H. P. (1972) *Process Education* Englewood Cliffs, New Jersey: Educational Technology Publications.

Cornford, C. (1976) *Our Conversation with Things and Places* Unit 2 in Course TAD292 (Art and Environment) Milton Keynes: Open University Press.

Cowan, J. (1975) 'The ability to appraise one's own work', pp. 127-128 in *Higher Education Bulletin* Vol. 3, No. 2, Spring 1975.

Cowell, B. (1972) 'Who's for exams?' letter in *Times Educational Supplement* 16 June 1972.

Cox, C. B. and Dyson, A. E. (1970) *Black Paper Two: The Crisis in Education* London: Critical Quarterly Society.

Cox, C. B. (1971) 'In praise of examinations', pp. 71-77 in C. B. Cox and A. E. Dyson (eds) *The Black Papers on Education* London: Davis-Poynter.

Cox, G. and Collins, H. (1975) 'Arts assessment: who cheats and who cares?', pp. 13-34 in *Assessment in Higher Education* Vol. 1, No. 1, September 1975.

Cox, R. (1967) 'Examinations, Identity and Diversity' — a talk given at the symposium on Recent Results of Research in Higher Education, organized jointly by South Birmingham Technical College and the Society for Research into Higher Education, Midlands Branch.

Cox, R. (1973) 'Traditional examinations in a changing society', pp. 200-216 in *Universities Quarterly* Spring 1973.

Crichton, M. (1969) *Five Patients* New York: Knopf.

Cureton, L. W. (1971) 'The history of grading practices', pp. 1-8 in *Measurement in Education* Vol. 2, No. 4, 1971.

CVC (1969) *Assessment of Undergraduate Performance* London: Committee of Vice-Chancellors and Principals.

Dailey, C. A. (1971) *Assessment of Lives* San Francisco: Jossey-Bass.

Dave, R. H. and Hill, W. H. (1974) 'Educational and social dynamics of the examination system in India', pp 24-38 in *Comparative Education Review* Vol. 18, No. 1, February 1974.

Davis, J. A. (1964) 'Faculty perceptions of students. III Structure of faculty characterizations' Research Bulletin RB/64/12 Princeton, New Jersey: Educational Testing Service.

Dean, J. (1972) *Recording Children's Progress* London: Macmillan.

Dennis, N. (1955) *Cards of Identity* London: Penguin.

Diederich, P. (1957) *The Improvement of Essay Examinations* Princeton, New Jersey: Educational Testing Service.

Dixon, J. (1972) *Growth Through English* London: Oxford University Press.

Dore, R. (1976) *The Diploma Disease* London: Allen and Unwin.

Douglas, J. W. B. (1964) *The Home and the School* London: MacGibbon and Kee.

Downey, M. E. (1977) *Interpersonal Judgements in Education* London: Harper and Row.

Duchastel, P. (1976) 'TAD292 — "Art and environment" and its challenge to educational technology' in *Programmed Learning and Educational Technology* Vol. 13, No. 4, October 1976.

Ebel, R. (1972) *Essentials of Educational Measurement* Englewood Cliffs, New Jersey: Prentice-Hall.

EDC (1969) *Elementary Science Study*, Newsletter No. 19, Newton, Mass: Educational Development Centre.

Edgeworth, F. Y. (1890) 'The element of chance in competitive examinations', pp. 400-75 and 644-63 in *Journal of the Royal Statistical Society* Vol. LIII, September/December 1890.

Eggleston, J. F. and Kerr, J. F. (eds) (1969) *Studies in Assessment* London: English Universities Press.

Eisner, E. W. (1972) *Educating Artistic Vision* New York: Macmillan.

Elbow, P. H. (1969) 'More accurate evaluation of student performance', pp. 219-230 in *Journal of Higher Education* 40.

Elkan, W. (1974) 'Bringing economics back to earth', p. 13 in *The Times Higher Education Supplement* 13 December 1974.

Ellsworth-Jones, W. (1974) 'How to fail an exam and become a martyr' in *The Sunday Times*, 3 November 1974.

Esland, G. *et al* (1972) *The Social Organization of Teaching and Learning* Units 5-8 in Course E282 Bletchley, England: Open University Press.

Evans, L. D. (1942) *The Essentials of Liberal Education* Boston: Ginn.

Fairbrother, R. (1975) 'The reliability of teachers' judgements of the abilities being tested by multiple-choice items', pp. 202-210 in *Educational Research* Vol. 17, No. 3, 1975.

Farnes, N. C. (1973) *Reading Purposes, Comprehension and the Use of Context* Units 3-4 in Course PE261 Bletchley: Open University Press.

Fawthrop, T. (1968) *Education or Examination* London: Radical Student Alliance.

Flanders, N. (1970) *Analysing Teacher Behaviour* London: Addison-Wesley.

Ford, B. (1969) 'The use of description in assessment' Appendix B in Sussex (1969) below.

Forrest, G. M. (1974) 'The presentation of results', pp. 197-207 in H. G. Macintosh (1974) *Techniques and Problems of Assessment* London: Arnold.

Foster, J. (1971) *Recording Individual Progress* London: Macmillan.

Friedenberg, E. Z. (1970) 'Social consequences of educational measurement', pp. 23-30 in *Proceedings of the 1969 Invitational Conference on Testing Problems* Princeton, New Jersey: Educational Testing Service.

Getzels, J. W. and Jackson, P. W. (1972) *Creativity and Intelligence* New York: Wiley.

Gilmore, J. B. (1973) 'Learning and student self-evaluation', pp. 54-57 in *Journal of College Science Teaching* Vol. 3, Part 1, October 1973.

Glaser, R. (1963) 'Instructional technology and the measurement of learning outcomes: some questions', pp. 519-521 in *American Psychologist* 18.

Glaser, R. and Nitko, K. J. (1970) *Measurement in Learning and Instruction* Pittsburgh: University of Pittsburgh Learning Research and Development Centre.

Glenn, J. A., (1977) *Teaching Primary Mathematics: Strategy and Evaluation* London: Harper and Row.

Goffman, E. (1976) *Interaction Ritual* Chicago: Aldine.

Goodman, P. (1971) *Compulsory Miseducation* London: Penguin (1st published 1962).

Gronlund, N. E. (1971) *Measurement and Evaluation in Teaching* London: Macmillan.

Guilford, J. P. (1965) *Fundamental Statistics in Psychology and Education* London: McGraw-Hill.

Haak, L. A. (1960) 'A method of measuring individual student progress', pp. 252-256 in *Journal of Higher Education* May 1960.

Hamilton, G. V. (1916) 'A study of perseverance reactions in primates and rodents' *Behavioral Monographs* Vol 3, No. 13.

Hargreaves, D. H. (1967) *Social Relations in a Secondary School* London: Routledge and Kegan Paul.

Hargreaves, D. H. (1972) *Interpersonal Relations in Education* London: Routledge and Kegan Paul.

Harrison, B. (1974) 'The teaching-learning relationship in correspondence tuition', pp. 2-8 in *Teaching at a Distance* No. 1, November 1974.

Harrison, R. and Hopkins, R. (1967) 'The design of cross-cultural training: an alternative to the university model', pp. 431-440 in *Journal of Applied Behavioural Science* Vol. 3, No. 4.

Hartog, P. and Rhodes, E. C. (1935) *An Examination of Examinations* London: Macmillan.

Hartog, P. and Rhodes, E. C. (1936) *The Marks of Examiners* London: Macmillan.

Hartshorne, H. and May, M. A. (1928) *Studies in Deceit* New York: Macmillan.

Head, J. J. (1967) 'Flexibility in interpretation of an O-level mark scheme', pp. 118-128 in *Educational Review* Vol. 19.

Henry, J. (1969) 'In suburban classrooms' in Gross, R and B. (eds) *Radical School Reform* New York: Simon and Schuster.

Himmelweit, H. (1967) 'Towards a rationalization of examination procedures', pp. 359-372 in *Universities Quarterly* June 1967.

Hinely, R. T. (1968) 'An equal chance — a fantasy', pp. 72-76 in B. L. Turney (ed) *Catcher in the Wrong: Iconoclasts in Education* Itasca, Ill: Peacock.

Hiner, N. R. (1973) 'Grading as a cultural function', pp. 356-361 in *The Clearing House* XLVII, February 1973.

Hinton, D. (1973) 'A teamwork graduate profile to replace the grading sieve' in *The Times Higher Education Supplement* 20 April 1973.

Hirst, P. H. (1968) 'The contribution of philosophy to the study of the curriculum' in J. F. Kerr *Changing the Curriculum* London: University of London Press.

Hirst, P. H. and Peters, R. S. (1970) *The Logic of Education* London: Routledge and Kegan Paul.

Hoffman, B. (1962) *The Tyranny of Testing* New York: Collier.

Holderness, G. (1972) 'Those anecdotes can be relevant' Letter in Open University newspaper *Sesame* Vol. 2, No. 4, May 1973.

Holland, J. L. (1960) 'The prediction of college grades from personality and aptitude variables', pp. 245-254 in *Journal of Educational Psychology* Vol. 51, No. 5, October 1960.

Holloway, P. J., Hardwick, J. L., Morris, J. and Start, K. B. (1967) 'The validity of essay and viva-voce examining techniques', pp. 227-232 in *British Dental Journal* 123, 5.

Holly, D. (1971) *Society, Schools and Humanity* London: MacGibbon and Kee.

Horowitz, M. J. (1964) *Educating Tomorrow's Doctors* New York: Meredith.

Hoste, R. and Bloomfield, B. (1975) *Continuous Assessment in the CSE* Schools Council Examination Bulletin No. 31, London: Evans / Methuen.

Hoyt, D. P. (1965) *The Relationship Between College Grades and Adult Achievement* Iowa City: American College Testing Program.

Hudson, B. B. (1973) *Assessment Techniques* London: Methuen.

Hudson, L. (1966a) 'Selection and the problem of conformity' in J. E. Meade and A. S. Parkes (1966) *Genetic and Environmental Factors in Human Ability* Edinburgh: Oliver and Boyd.

Hudson, L. (1966b) *Contrary Imaginations* London: Methuen.

Hudson, L. (1970) *Frames of Mind* London: Penguin.

Huff, D. (1961) *Score: The Strategy of Taking Tests* London: Penguin.

Hughes, E. C., Becker, H. S. and Geer, B. (1958) 'Student culture and academic effort', pp. 70-80 in *Harvard Educational Review* Vol. 28, Winter 1958.

Husbands, C. T. (1976) 'Ideological bias in the marking of examinations: a method for testing its presence and its implications' pp. 17-38 in *Research in Education* No. 15.

Hyam, R., (1974) p. 135 in R. Bennett (1974) (See above).

Insel, P. M. and Jacobson, L. F. (1975) *What Do You Expect? An Enquiry into Self-Fulfilling Prophecies* Menlo Park, California: Cummings.

Jackson, B. and Marsden, D. (1962) *Education and the Working Class* London: Routledge and Kegan Paul.

Jackson, P. W. (1968) *Life in Classrooms* New York: Holt, Rinehart and Winston.

James, C. (1968) *Young Lives at Stake* London: Collins.

James, W. (1902) *The Varieties of Religious Experience* New York: Modern Library.

Jenkins, B. (1972) *Teachers' views of particular students and their behavior in the classroom*, unpublished doctoral dissertation. University of Chicago (extensively discussed in Brophy and Good, above, pp. 133-138).

Jones, R. T. (1969) 'Multi-form assessment: a York experiment', pp. 43-47 in *Cambridge Review* 15 November 1969.

Kandel, I. (1936) *Examinations and their Substitutes in the United States* Carnegie Foundation for the Advancement of Teaching, Bulletin 28, New York.

Kapfer, M. B. (ed) (1971) *Behavioral Objectives in Curriculum Development* Englewood Cliffs, New Jersey: Educational Technology Publications.

Kaufman, B. (1964) *Up the Down Staircase* Englewood Cliffs, New Jersey: Prentice-Hall.

Keddie, N. (1971) 'Classroom knowledge' in M. F. D. Young (ed) *Knowledge and Control* London: Collier-Macmillan.

Keith, A. B. (1961) *Speeches and Documents on Indian Policy 1750-1921* Oxford: Oxford University Press.

Kelly, E. (1958) 'A study of consistent discrepancies between instructor grades and term-end examination grades', pp. 328-334 in *Journal of Educational Psychology* Vol. 49.

Kelly, G. A. (1955) *The Psychology of Personal Constructs* New York: Norton.

Kennedy, D. (1974) *Preliminary report on case study project in the Yorkshire Region* Leeds: Open University. Limited internal circulation.

Kilcross, M. C. and Bates, W. T. G. (1975) *Selecting the Younger Trainee* London: HMSO.

Kirchenbaum, H., Napier, R. and Simon, S. (1971) *Wad-ja-get? The Grading Game in American Education* New York: Hart.

Klug, B. (1974) *Pro Profiles.* London: NUS Publications.

Klug, B. (1977) *The Grading Game* London: NUS Publications.

Kohl, H. (1967) *36 Children* London: Penguin.

Krathwohl, D. R., Bloom, B. S. and Masia, B. (1964) *Taxonomy of Educational Objectives: Affective Domain* New York. McKay.

Labov, W. (1972) 'The logic of non-standard English' in P. P. Giglioli (ed) *Language and Social Context* London: Penguin.

Lacey, C. (1970) *Hightown Grammar: The School as a Social System* Manchester University Press.

Lacey, O. L. (1960) 'How fair are your grades?', pp. 281-283 in *Bulletin of American Association of University Professors* Vol. 46.

Laird, S. (1972) 'Tick off for tedium' in *The Guardian* (Education Section) 2 May 1972.

LATE (1965) *Assessing Compositions* London: Blackie.

Leacock, E. (1969) *Teaching and Learning in City Schools* New York: Basic Books.

Learned, W. S. (1935) *Thirtieth Annual Report* New York: Carnegie Foundation for the Advancement of Teaching.

Learned, W. S. and Wood, B. (1938) *The Student and His Knowledge* New York: Carnegie Foundation for the Advancement of Teaching.

Lecky, P. (1945) *Self-Consistency: A Theory of Personality* New York: Island Press.

Lewis, B. N. (1973) 'Educational technology at the Open University: an approach to the problem of quality', pp. 188-204 in *British Journal of Educational Technology* Vol. 4, No. 3, October 1973.

Lewis, D. G. (1974) *Assessment in Education* London: University of London Press.

Lewis, R. and Tomlinson, N. (1977) 'Examples of tutor-student exchanges by correspondence', pp. 39-46 in *Teaching at a Distance* No. 8, March 1977.

Lindquist, R. F. (1966) *Educational Measurement* Washington, D.C.: American Council of Education.

Lindvall, C. M. (1961) *Testing and Evaluation: An Introduction* New York: Harcourt, Brace and World.

Loe, D. C. (1975) 'Informal assessment during clinical teaching', pp. 467-472 in *Academic Therapy* Vol. 10, Pt 4, Summer 1975.

Lopez, F. M. (1966) *Evaluating Executive Decision-Making* New York: American Management Association.

Macdonald, F. J. (1971) 'A model of the decision-making process' in M. D. Glock (ed) *Guiding Learning* New York: Wiley.

MacIntosh, H. G. (ed) (1974) *Techniques and Problems of Assessment* London: Arnold.

MacIntosh, H. G. and Hale, D. E. (1976) *Assessment and the Secondary School Teacher* London: Routledge and Kegan Paul.

MacKenzie, K. (1974) 'Some thoughts on tutoring by written correspondence in the Open University', pp. 45-51 in *Teaching at a Distance* No. 1, November 1974.

MacKenzie, K. (1976) 'Student reactions to tutor comments on the tutor-marked assignment', pp. 53-58 in *Teaching at a Distance* No. 5, March 1976.

Mager, R. F. (1962) *Preparing Instructional Objectives* Palo Alto, California: Fearon.

Mansell, J. (1972) 'Complete picture', pp. 313-314 in *Education and Training* October 1972.

Marcus, D. (1973) *Reports and Reporting* Leicester: Bosworth College.

Markus, R. A. (1974) 'Principles of marking' in *The Times Higher Education Supplement* 1 March 1974.

Marshall, M. S. (1960) 'The flotation technique: teaching without grades', pp. 23-29 in *Improving College and University Teaching* Vol. 8.

Marshall, M. S. (1968) *Teaching Without Grades* Corrallis, Oregon: Oregon State University Press.

Marx, K. (1844) *Economic and Philosophic Manuscripts of 1844* Moscow: Progress, 1967.

McClelland, D. C. (1973) 'Testing for competence rather than for intelligence', pp. 1-14 in *American Psychologist* January 1973.

McFarland. H. S. N. (1973) *Intelligent Teaching* London: Routledge and Kegan Paul.

McIntyre, D. (1970) 'Assessment and teaching' in D. Rubinstein and C. Stoneman, (eds) *Education for Democracy*, second edition, London: Penguin.

Meehl, P. (1954) *Clinical vs. Statistical Prediction* Minneapolis: University of Minnesota Press.

Meux, M. and Smith, B. O. (1964) 'Logical dimensions of teaching behavior' in B. J. Biddle and W. J. Elena (eds) *Contemporary Research on Teacher Effectiveness* London: Holt Rinehart and Winston.

Merton, R. (1948) 'The self-fulfilling prophecy', pp. 193-210 in *Antioch Review* 8.

Miller, C. (1973) *'Intellectual Development, Confidence and Assessment'*, paper from Centre for Research in the Educational Sciences, University of Edinburgh.

Miller, C. and Parlett, M. (1973) *Up to the Mark: a Research Report on Assessment* Occasional Paper 13. University of Edinburgh: Centre for Research in the Educational Sciences.

Miller, G. D. (1974) 'Grades for reinforcing independent thinking', pp. 179-180 in *Improving College and University Teaching* Vol. 22, No. 3, Summer 1974.

Miller, G. E. (1976) 'Continuous assessment', pp. 81-86 in *Medical Education* 1976, Vol. 10.

Miller, R. (1972) *Evaluating Faculty Performance* San Francisco: Jossey-Bass.

Miller, S. (1967) *Measure, Number and Weight: A Polemical Statement of the College Grading Problem* Learning Research Center: University of Tennessee.

Mitchell, P. (1975) Private communication to the author.

Mittler, P. (ed) (1973) *Assessment for Learning in the Mentally Handicapped* Edinburgh: Churchill Livingston.

Miyazaki, I. (1976) *China's Examination Hell* New York: Weatherhill.

Montgomery, R. J. (1965) *School Examinations: An Account of their Evolution as Administrative Devices in England* London: Longman.

Morris, N. (1969) 'An historian's view of examinations' in S. Wiseman (ed) *Examinations and English Education* Manchester University Press (first published 1961).

Morrison, R. B. (1974) 'The application of statistics to assessment' pp. 146-156 in H. G. Macintosh, above.

Murray, H. A. (1938) *Explorations in Personality* New York: Oxford University Press.

Musgrove, F. (1971) 'Curriculum objectives' in R. Hooper (ed) *The Curriculum: Context, Design and Development* Edinburgh: Oliver and Boyd.

Nash, R. (1973) *Classrooms Observed: The teacher's perception and the pupil's performance* London: Routledge and Kegan Paul.

Nash, R. (ed) (1976) *Teacher Expectations and Pupil Learning* London: Routledge and Kegan Paul.

Nicholson, R. J. and Galambos, P. (1960) *Performance in GCE A-Level Exams and University Exams* Occasional papers of the Institute of Education, University of Hull.

Nisbet, J. and Welsh, J. (1966) 'Predicting student performance' in *Universities Quarterly* 20 September 1966.

Nuffield (1973) *Newsletter No. 3* (October 1973) of Nuffield Foundation Group for Research and Innovation in Higher Education, London.

Nursing Times (1972) 'And still they failed', editorial in *Nursing Times* 27 July, 1972.

Open University (1973) *Teaching by Correspondence in the Open University* Milton Keynes, England: Open University Press.

Oppenheim, A. N., Jahoda, M. and James, R. L. (1967) 'Assumptions underlying the use of university examinations', pp. 341-45 in *Universities Quarterly* June 1967.

Owens, G. (1973) *The Individual Profile* mimeographed paper from Trent Polytechnic, Nottingham.

Page, C. F. (1974) *Student Evaluation of Teaching: The American Experience* London: Society for Research into High Education.

Page, E. B. (1958) 'Teacher comments and student performance' pp. 173-181 in *Journal of Educational Psychology* 49, 1958.

Pearce, J. (1972) *School Examinations* London: Collier-Macmillan.

Perry, W. G. (1970) *Forms of Intellectual and Ethical Development in the College Years* New York: Holt, Rinehart and Winston.

Petch, J. A. (1961) *GCE and Degree* Manchester: Joint Matriculation Board.

Phenix, P. H. (1964) *Realms of Meaning* New York: McGraw-Hill.

Pidgeon, D. and Yates, A. (1969) *An Introduction to Educational Measurement* London: Routledge and Kegan Paul.

Pilliner, A. E. (1968) 'Examinations' in H. J. Butcher (ed) *Educational Research in Britain* Vol. 1, London: University of London Press.

Pilliner, A. E. G. (1973) *Assessment — Principles and Practice with Special Reference to Education in Pakistan* University of Edinburgh: Centre for Research in the Educational Sciences.

Pirsig, R. M. (1974) *Zen and the Art of Motorcycle Maintenance* New York: Morrow.

Platt, J. (1972) *Report of Research into the Operation of the New Pattern of BA Finals Assessment* University of Sussex.

Pollard, A. (1970) 'O and A level: Keeping up the standards', pp. 72-79 in C. B. Cox and A. E. Dyson, (above) London: Penguin.

Popham W. J. and Baker, E. L. (1970) *Systematic Instruction* Englewood Cliffs, New Jersey: Prentice-Hall.

Popham, W. J. and Husek, T. R. (1969) 'Implications of criterion-referenced measurement', pp. 1-9 in *Journal of Educational Measurement* Vol. 6, No. 1.

Popham, W. J. (1975) *Educational Evaluation* Englewood Cliffs, New Jersey: Prentice-Hall.

Postman, N. (1970) 'Curriculum change and technology' in S. G. Tickton (ed) *To Improve Learning* New York: Bowker.

Postman, N. and Weingartner, C. (1971) *Teaching as a Subversive Activity* London: Penguin.

Powell, A. and Butterworth, B. (1971) *Marked for Life* London: Institute of Classical Studies.

Pusey, D. F. G. (1974) 'Games without gimmicks' in *The Times Higher Education Supplement* 18 October 1974.

Quann, C. J. (1974) 'Pass/fail grading — an unsuccess story', pp. 230-235 in *College and University* Vol. 49, No. 3.

Reed (1973) *Development of the Reed College Grading System* Portland, Oregon: Reed College.

Reed, N. C., Rabe, E. F. and Mankinen. M. (1968) 'Teaching reading to brain-damaged children: a review', pp. 289-298 in *Reading Research Quarterly* Vol. 1.

Reik, T. (1948) *Listening with the Third Ear* New York: Farrar, Strauss.

Rein, R. K. (1974) 'Educational Testing Service: the examiner examined', pp. 40-46 in *Change* Vol. 6, No. 3.

Rhys, S. M. (1975) 'The process of marking assignments: the tutor in action', pp. 52-56 in *Teaching at a Distance* No. 4, November 1975.

Rippere, V. L. (1974) 'On the "validity" of university examinations: some comments on the language of the debate', pp. 209-218 in *Universities Quarterly* Spring 1974.

Rist, R. (1970) 'Student social class and teacher expectations: the self-fulfilling prophecy in ghetto education', pp. 411-451 in *Harvard Educational Review* 1970, **40**.

Roethlisberger, F. J. and Dickson, W. J. (1939) *Management and the Worker: An Account of a Research Program Conducted by the Western Electric Company, Hawthorne Works, Chicago* Harvard University Press.

Rogers, C. R. (1965) *Client-Centered Therapy*, New York: Houghton Mifflin.

Rosenthal, R. and Jacobson, L., (1968) *Pygmalion in the Classroom* New York: Holt, Rinehart and Winston.

Roth, J. A. (1963) *Timetables* Indianapolis: Bobbs-Merrill.

Rowntree, D. (1974) *Educational Technology in Curriculum Development* London: Harper and Row. (Second edition published 1982).

Rowntree, D. (1975) 'Two styles of communication and their implications for learning', pp. 281-293 in J. Baggaley *et al* (eds) *Aspects of Educational Technology* VIII London: Pitman.

Rowntree, D. and Harden, R. (1976) *Undergraduate Training in the Medical Faculty of Cairo University, Egypt* Geneva: World Health Organization.

Russell, N. H. (1966) 'End of a semester', p. 414 in *American Association of University Professors Bulletin* Winter 1966.

Sanders, N. M. (1966) *Classroom Questions: What Kinds?* New York: Harper and Row.

Sassenrath, J. M. and and Garverick, C. M. (1965) 'Effects of differential feedback from examinations on retention and transfer', pp. 259-263 in *Journal of Educational Psychology* 1965, Vol. 56, No. 5.

Schneider, J., Johnson, J. and Duncan, J. K. (1973) 'Evaluation' in J. R. Frymier (ed) *A School for Tomorrow* Berkeley, California: McCutchan.

Schofield, H. (1972) *Assessment and Testing: an introduction* London: Allen and Unwin.

Schools Council (1963) *The Certificate of Secondary Education*: Examinations Bulletin No. 1 London: H.M.S.O.

Schools Council (1971) *A Common System of Examining at 16+* Examinations Bulletin No. 23 London: Evans/Methuen.

Schram, S. R. (ed) (1974) *Mao Tse-Tung Unrehearsed: Talks and Letters* London: Penguin.

Schwab J. J. (1954) 'Eros and Education', pp. 51-71 in *Journal of General Education* Vol. VIII, October 1954.

Schwab, J. J. (1969) *College Curriculum and Student Protest* Chicago: University of Chicago Press.

Scott, J. P. (1972) *Animal Behaviour* Chicago: University of Chicago Press.

Scriven, M. (1967) 'The methodology of evaluation' in R. W. Tyler *et al* (eds) *Perspectives of Curriculum Evaluation* Chicago: Rand McNally.

Shepherd, E. M. (1929) 'The effect of quality of penmanship on grades', pp. 102-105 in *Journal of Education Review* Vol. XIX, Part 6, 1929.

Shils, E. (1975) 'The confidentiality and anonymity of assessment', editorial in *Minerva* Vol. XIII, No. 2, Summer 1975.

Shneidman, E. (1969) 'Orientations towards death' in R. W. White (ed) *The Study of Lives* New York: Atherton Press.

Shouksmith, G. (1968) *Assessing Through Interviewing* London: Pergamon.

Siann, G. and French, K. (1975) 'Edinburgh students' views on continuous assessment', pp. 1064-1070 in *Durham Research Review* 7, Autumn 1975.

Simon, B. (1971) *Intelligence, Psychology and Education* London: Lawrence and Wishart.

Simon, J. (1963) 'Examinations policy in comprehensive schools', pp. 2-8 in *Forum* Vol. 16, Part 1, Autumn 1973.

Simpson, E. (1967) 'Educational objectives in the psychomotor domain' reprinted in M. B. Kapfer (1971) above.

Simpson, M. A. (1976) 'Medical student evaluation in the absence of examinations', pp. 22-26 in *Medical Education* 1976, Vol. 10.

Small, A. A. (1973) 'Marking practices in historical perspective', pp. 189-197 in *Educational Studies* Vol. 4, No. 4.

Snyder, B. R. (1971) *The Hidden Curriculum* New York: Knopf.

Sperry, L. (ed) (1972) *Learning Performance and Individual Differences* Glenview, Illinois: Scott, Foresman.

Spriggs, J. (1972) 'Doing English Lit.', pp. 221-246 in Pateman, T. (ed) *Counter Course* London: Penguin.

Spurgin, C. G. (1967) 'What earns the marks?', pp. 306-307 in *Physics Education* Vol. 2, 1967.

Stevens, F. (1970) *English and Examinations* London: Hutchinson.

Supreme Court of the U.S. (1971) *Willie S. Griggs et al vs. Duke Power Company* No. 124 October Term 1970 (March 8, 1971) pp. 1-12.

Sussex (1969) *Final Report of BA Degree Assessment Working Party* University of Sussex.

Taba, H. (1962) *Curriculum Development* New York: Harcourt, Brace and World.

Tansey, P. J. and Unwin, D. (1969) *Simulation and Gaming in Education* London: Methuen.

Taylor, C. W., Price, P. B., Richards, J. M. and Jacobsen, T. L. (1965) 'An investigation of the criterion problem for a group of medical general practitioners', pp. 399-406 in *Journal of Applied Psychology* 1965, **49**, 6.

Taylor, J. L. and Walford, R. (1973) *Simulation in the Classroom* London: Penguin.

Taylor, W. (1963) *The Secondary Modern School* London: Faber and Faber.

Terwilliger, J. S. (1971) *Assigning Grades to Students* Glenview, Illinois: Scott, Foresman.

Thomas, R. H. (1976) 'The necessity of examinations — and their reform', pp. 23-29 in *Studies in Higher Education* Vol. 1, No. 1, 1976.

Thompson, E. P. (ed) (1970) *Warwick University Ltd: Management, Industry, and the Universities* London: Penguin.

Thorndike, R. L. (ed) (1972) *Educational Measurement* (2nd edition) Washington, D.C.: American Council on Education.

Thyne, J. M. (1974) *Principles of Examining* London: University of London Press.

Torbett, W. R. and Hackman, J. R. (1969) 'Taking the fun out of out-foxing the system', Chapter 9 (pp. 156-181) in P. Runkel *et al* (eds) *The Changing College Classroom* San Francisco: Jossey-Bass.

Tough, J. (1973) *Focus on Meaning* London: Allen and Unwin.

Tough, J. (1976) *Listening to Children Talking* London: Ward Lock.

Tyler, R. W. (1949) *Basic Principles of Curriculum and Instruction* Reprint 1971 London: University of Chicago Press.

Tyler, R. W. and Wolf, R. M. (eds) (1974) *Crucial Issues in Testing* Berkeley, California: McCutchan.

UCCA (1969) *The Sixth Report: Statistical Supplement 1967-68* Cheltenham: Universities Central Council on Admissions.

Urmson, J. O. (1950) 'On grading', pp. 145-169 in *Mind* LXIX 1950.

Valentine, C. W. (1938) *Examinations and the Examinee* Birmingham: The Birmingham Printers.

Vandome, P. *et al* (1973) *Why assessment?* A paper given limited circulation in the University of Edinburgh.

Veblen, T. (1918) *The Higher Learning in America* New York: B. W. Heubsh.

Vessclo, I. R. (1962) *How to Read Statistics* London: Harrap.

Wankowski, J. A. (1920) *GCEs and Degrees* University of Birmingham.

Warren, J. R. (1971) *College Grading Practices: An Overview* Washington, DC: ERIC Clearing house on Higher Education.

Webb, E. J., Campbell, D. T., Schwartz, R. D. and Sechrest, L. (1969) *Unobtrusive Measures: Non-reactive Research in the Social Sciences* Chicago: Rand McNally.

Webster, E. C. (1964) *Decision-Making in the Employment Interview* Montreal: Industrial Relations Centre, McGill University.

Werthman, C. (1963) 'Delinquents in schools: a test for the legitimacy of authority' reprinted in Cosin, B. R. et al (eds) (1971) *School and Society* London: Routledge and Kegan Paul.

White, R. W. (1964) *The Study of Lives* New York: Atherton.

Whitehand, J. W. R. (1966) 'The selection of research students', pp. 44-47 in *Universities Quarterly* Vol. 21.

Whitfield, R. (ed) (1971) *Disciplines of the Curriculum* Maidenhead: McGraw-Hill.

Wilhems, F. T. (1970) *Evaluation as Feedback and Guide* Washington, DC: Association for Supervision and Curriculum Development NEA.

Wilson, J. (1970) *Moral Thinking* London: Heinemann.

Wilson, J. (1973) *The Assessment of Morality* Slough, Bucks: NFER.

Wiseman, S. (1961) *Examinations and English Education* Manchester University Press.

Wolff, R. P. (1969) *The Ideal of the University* Boston: Beacon.

Wood, B. D. (1921) 'Measurement of college work' in *Educational Administration and Supervision* Vol. VII.

Wood, R. and Napthali, W. A. (1975) 'Assessment in the classroom: what do teachers look for?', pp.151-161 in *Educational Studies* Vol. 1, No. 3, October 1975.

Zoellner, R. (1969) 'Talk-Write: A behavioral pedagogy for composition' *College English* Vol. 30, No. 4, January 1969.

FEEDBACK

The following comments, sent to me by a reader of the first edition of this book, confirm that I am not the only teacher in the world to have encountered assessment practices of the kind I have described. For reasons that will become obvious, my correspondent must remain anonymous. He was writing from a college of higher education where assessments of students' work were 'moderated' (assessed?) by examiners from a neighbouring university.

'I think one thing that will be very valuable is your analysis of the various types of assessment and of the various functions of assessment too. This is crucial since so many of the unintended social effects of assessment schemes seem to occur precisely because assessment items are so ambiguous. Sometimes the ambiguity seems deliberately used — for example, in my present place of work it is not uncommon to "sell" assessment to students on the grounds of it being diagnostic and helpful — and then to use the grades to select those who will proceed to Honours courses, etc.

'What makes this ploy particularly unpleasant is that essays designed with diagnosis in mind are often quite unsuitable for discriminating between students (in that they do not provide a wide enough spread). In such circumstances, the final examination (used *as well*) comes to be all-important (since it *does* spread out students) despite its lesser official weight. My point is that assessment often is not clearly thought out and its function often is switched to a discriminatory one in a crisis (e.g. when "too many" students might qualify). The ambiguous nature of assessment makes it very difficult to spot the switch. (I notice the example you give pp. 183-4.)

'Another issue you discuss concerns the transformation of apparently open-ended, divergent tasks (like projects and simulations) into convergent tests at the point of marking. We use both projects and simulations here and in both cases this transformation occurs. In free-choice projects like dissertations, for example, a whole series of negotiations about titles and themes takes place, and gradually the work is shifted towards what lecturers want and expect. Again, when marking, our external University markers do seem to have a rather narrow "right" project in mind, for marks are added to (or more usually *subtracted* from) our internal College marks according to apparently hard and fast rules of procedure. Naturally, none of this is made public and, as a new member of the Examiners' Panel, I was apparently expected to know what was required without the vulgarity that would arise if they actually had to make their rules explicit.

'I was pleased to find the bit about "maximum marks only for God" (p. 53) for this is our University's attitude too. In their case, this implicit belief that no student could ever get more than 85%, and that there exists in each case some Platonic "perfect" dissertation, has an important consequence. On paper it seems that students have to get an average of 70% over all their assignments to get a first class degree. However, when the "maximum marks only for God" clause is invoked, it becomes impossible to get more than 85% in any one assignment. In effect, then, the student has to get 70 marks out of an *available* 85 (i.e. 82% in real terms). Crafty, no? And again, ambiguous enough to fool people and to allow all kinds of *ad hoc* rules, concepts of "normal numbers of firsts" and so on to be introduced.

'My own modest appeal to these wise men to spell out just what they see and how they respond was seen as awfully embarassing and rather radical (which was the intention, I confess — once out in the open the criteria would not stand up to the slightest criticism and we all knew it). Instead, I was asked to be pragmatic and silent. Indeed the whole affair was rather nasty, and discrepancies between my marks and everyone else's were seen as evidence of incompetence or of subversion and I was hastily removed from the Examiners' Panel (and unpromoted for a year!)

'Your own cool and sensible words on the inevitability of disagreement among markers would be well appreciated in this college. Again, I was in a position to see how inter-marker agreement is *actually* obtained. It is "negotiated" among the individuals who differ. Nothing is explicit, but a wide divergence is seen as embarrassing and one only makes that mistake once. Next time, one takes every precaution to offer for moderation marks that will be within 5% or so of what the University examiners would award. Experience at "pysching out" the examiners works well at our level too! (So does fear of failure!) When in doubt, we play safe and undermark. Again, a kind of semi-secret normal curve system operates — we just don't offer too many papers over the magic 70%, nor do we fail many. No one will say what the curve should look like, no one employs the routine statistical analysis to ensure the curve actually is as expected, no one *designs* assignments to produce a normal curve of results, no one publicly advocates or defends such a practice.

'In any case, the University panel have recently emphasized their own divine right to "adjust" our internally-awarded marks by insisting we mark scripts only *in pencil*. How's that for a new category or status — we college hacks are mere markers in pencil!

Doubtless our own little system is no worse than anyone else's, as your examples seem to show! Interestingly, your point about the trend towards making questions explicit (p. 155) is one I am pursuing myself at the moment. My own questions are usually specific and detailed. As you say, such techniques indicate convergence and reward it — but at least the process is an honest one! Students are awarded marks according to how well they match the "right answer" in my head — so I explain what it is I want as clearly as possible. Lacking political power to change assessment, my own solution is at least to try and show *everyone* how convergent it really is, underneath all the liberal stuff about essays, free choice dissertations, etc.

'Many of my colleagues recoil from the thought of using explicit norm-referenced techniques — but they fail to realize that the same *logic* is used whenever they decide to be "realistic" at examiners' meetings. There is also the desire to be "objective" and "fair" too — but not to the extent of publicly using multi-choice tests, etc. The most paradoxical colleagues for me are the English teachers, who advocate the search for personal (intangible) meanings and who also set and mark exams and grade just as rigidly as everyone else. What interests me is how they manage to explain the contradictions to themselves.

'One final point. Your insistence on the validity and relevance of assessment is excellent. Your advocacy of self-assessment is very welcome too. However, the proposal to assess students using a profile system has one danger, it seems. The danger is that the search for greater validity will lead to the universality, the omni-presence of assessment. Humans are complex — but the attempt to capture that complexity in a fully valid profile might lead to a new totalitarianism with even more activities coming under the assessors' gazes. The alternative I prefer (at the moment) is the one you close the book with — to put a warning on academic grades (and profiles). This, I think, is to make the hidden curriculum explicit; I tell my students about the work of Snyder and Becker, etc., partly so they won't be taken in by the assessment they receive or administer themselves when they become teachers. An A grade then should lead no one to think he is perfect, or more worthy as a person, etc., — nor should an E grade have the reverse effect. Anyway, Becker did find, I recall, that cynical (I'd prefer realistic) students did well in tests *and* tended not to suffer so much psychologically.

'Anyway, I must go now — to mark some essays!'

'Yours from the backwoods, Bwwww.'

Index